LAW, CRIME AND LAW ENFORCEMENT

PERSPECTIVES ON POLICING

SELECTED PAPERS ON POLICY, PERFORMANCE AND CRIME PREVENTION

Law, Crime and Law Enforcement

Additional books in this series can be found on Nova's website under the Series tab.

Additional e-books in this series can be found on Nova's website under the e-book tab.

LAW, CRIME AND LAW ENFORCEMENT

PERSPECTIVES ON POLICING

SELECTED PAPERS ON POLICY, PERFORMANCE AND CRIME PREVENTION

HOLLY WHEELER
EDITOR

nova publishers
New York

Library of Congress Cataloging-in-Publication Data

ISBN: 978-1-63484-555-7

Published by Nova Science Publishers, Inc. † New York

CONTENTS

Preface		**vii**
Chapter 1	Crime and Policing Revisited *Anthony A. Braga*	**1**
Chapter 2	Toward a Profession of Police Leadership *Edward A. Flynn and Victoria Herrington*	**27**
Chapter 3	Rightful Policing *Tracey L. Meares and Peter Neyroud*	**43**
Chapter 4	From Warriors to Guardians: Recommitting American Police Culture to Democratic Ideals *Sue Rahr and Stephen K. Rice*	**57**
Chapter 5	Race and Policing: An Agenda for Action *David H. Bayley, Michael A. Davis and Ronald L. Davis*	**69**
Chapter 6	The Police and Public Discourse on "Black-on-Black" Violence *Anthony A. Braga and Rod K. Brunson*	**81**
Chapter 7	Childhood Trauma and Its Effects: Implications for Police *Richard G. Dudley, Jr.*	**101**
Chapter 8	Measuring Performance in a Modern Police Organization *Malcolm K. Sparrow*	**119**
Index		**151**

PREFACE

Can the police reduce crime? In 1991, when the first Executive Session on Policing concluded, the answer to that question was generally described as being in the eye of the beholder. Based on the scientific and practical knowledge available at the time, some well-respected criminologists and police scholars concluded that the police were not able to reduce crime. Promising evidence, however, suggested that if the police changed their approach to crime control and prevention, then they might be able to reduce crime. This book outlines the changes in the nature of police crime control conversations resulting from an unprecedented growth in rigorous evaluation research on what works in police crime prevention; examines what it means to be a leader within the policing field, and advocates for reframing leadership through the adoption of "learning organizations" to increase the capacity to fight crime; describes "rightful policing," which looks at elements of procedural justice in police encounters with the public as a way to organize police work; advocates for democratic ideals within law enforcement to combat the mindset that law enforcement officers are at war with the people they serve; presents the ideas for what police executives might do to alleviate the problems of race in contemporary policing; examines the term "black-on-black" violence, a simplistic and emotionally charged definition of urban violence that can be problematic when used by political commentators, politicians and police executives; summarizes current understanding of the effects of ongoing trauma on young children, how these effects impair adolescent and young adult functioning, and the possible implications of this for policing; and finally, describes strategies police organizations could employ to more effectively measure their performance.

In: Perspectives on Policing
Editor: Holly Wheeler
ISBN: 978-1-63484-555-7

Chapter 1

CRIME AND POLICING REVISITED*

Anthony A. Braga

Can the police reduce crime? In 1991, when the first Executive Session on Policing concluded, the answer to that question was generally described as being in the eye of the beholder (Sherman, 1992). Based on the scientific and practical knowledge available at the time, some well-respected criminologists and police scholars concluded that the police were not able to reduce crime (Gottfredson and Hirschi, 1990; Bayley, 1994). Promising evidence, however, suggested that if the police changed their approach to crime control and prevention, then they might be able to reduce crime (Goldstein, 1990; Wilson and Kelling, 1982; Sherman, Gartin and Buerger, 1989). In a key Executive Session paper that examined crime and policing, Moore, Trojanowicz and Kelling (1988) highlighted the prospect of improved crime prevention as an explicit goal of community policing by developing problem-solving initiatives to address crime-producing situations and dynamics, stimulating informal social control among residents in high-crime neighborhoods, and apprehending repeat offenders through improved information sharing with the community. Because admittedly little rigorous evidence existed to back their claims,

Moore, Trojanowicz and Kelling's argument was largely regarded as theoretical at the time. As such, the view that tended to dominate most academic and policy discussions at the time was that the police could not reduce crime.

Much has changed since then. A growing body of experiential knowledge and scientific evidence now exists that largely supports many of the key ideas informing innovative crime prevention strategies being discussed in policing circles at the close of the first Executive Session (Skogan and Frydl, 2004; Weisburd and Eck, 2004; Braga, 2008). A review of the available evidence would lead most observers to conclude that the police can reduce crime if they take a focused approach to addressing recurring crime problems, engage the community and a diversity of partners, and implement tactics and strategies appropriately tailored to the conditions that give rise to crime problems. Indeed, when the second Executive Session commenced in 2008, crime control discussions among the participants did not center on the

* This is an edited, reformatted and augmented version of a paper, NCJ 248888, in the New Perspectives in Policing series, issued by the U.S. Department of Justice, National Institute of Justice, September 2015.

issue of whether the police could reduce crime or not. Rather, conversations focused on how the policing profession could continue effective crime prevention practices by strengthening their commitments to community problem solving and by remaining flexible and adaptable when addressing evolving crime problems.

The stark differences in the nature of the police crime control conversations between the first and second Executive Sessions were the result of an unprecedented period of police innovation and concomitant growth in rigorous evaluation research on what works in police crime prevention. This essay begins by providing a brief historical overview of what was known about the police and crime prevention at the time of the first Executive Session and what were proposed then as promising new ways for the police to reduce crime. Between the 1990s and 2000s, researchers explored the efficacy of these new ideas for crime reduction. Challenges to the notion that innovative policing strategies generate crime reduction gains are then reviewed. The essay concludes by offering two central ideas on continuing effective police crime prevention policies and practices suggested by participants of the second Executive Session and supported by existing research evidence.

What Was Known Prior to the First Executive Session on Policing

When the first Executive Session on Policing commenced in 1985, there was a crisis of confidence in American policing and a strong sense that fundamental changes were needed in the way policing services were delivered (Bayley and Nixon, 2010). The "professional" policing model was firmly entrenched as the dominant paradigm. And, as U.S. crime rates steadily increased over the course of the 1970s and into the 1980s, it seemed that the police could do little to control crime. Many citizens, especially minorities living in inner city neighborhoods, were not satisfied with the policing services they received. In some cities, however, there was a "quiet revolution" as police departments became more focused on engaging communities and experimented with new crime prevention ideas (Kelling, 1988). The practical experiences of these progressive police chiefs, many of whom were Executive Session participants, fit well within a growing body of research evidence that both identified the flaws in existing police strategies and suggested new crime prevention ideas. This research is summarized here.

The police developed as a mechanism to administer justice by apprehending offenders and holding them accountable (Wilson and McLaren, 1977). Because their primary practical goal was to reduce crime victimization, police long believed that they were in the business of crime prevention (President's Commission on Law Enforcement and Administration of Justice, 1967a). Police strategists relied upon two ideas to prevent crimes: deterrence and incapacitation. The imminent threat of arrest was their main strategy to deter the general public from contemplating or committing crimes. The police attempted to deter criminals specifically by apprehending them and attempting to discourage them from committing crimes in the future. The police also believed that arrests would prevent crime by incapacitating criminals by removing them from the streets and subsequently placing them in jail or prison. In particular, the police sought to prevent repeat offenders from continuing their careers through specific deterrence, incapacitation and, to some degree, rehabilitation (as part of their subsequent incarceration or community supervision). The police relied on the other parts of the criminal justice system to pursue these goals, but they could at least start the process by arresting offenders and building credible cases against them.

In some policing circles prior to the first Executive Session, the subject of crime prevention also pointed to the work of police units that handle juvenile cases (often referred to as "crime prevention units") or to units of officers who conduct educational outreach programs in the schools. Officers formed crime prevention units to encourage people to lock their doors, identify their property, and engage in other target-hardening activities. These programs were neither departmentwide nor large in size, but they were a significant presence; however, the programs were often seen as segregating and compartmentalizing the "prevention" work of the police.

The professional model of policing represented an important series of reforms of corrupt and ineffective policing practices of the pre-1930s "political era" of policing (Kelling and Moore, 1988). The professional model emphasized military discipline and structure, higher education for police officers, adoption of professional standards by police agencies, separating the police from political influence, and the adoption of technological innovations ranging from strategic management techniques to scientific advances such as two-way radios and fingerprinting. Police departments slowly adopted the professional model over the course of the 1940s and 1950s. During the post-World War II period, the police role as "crime fighter" was solidified (Walker, 1992). Policing focused itself on preventing serious crimes and advanced three operational strategies to achieve this goal: preventive patrol, rapid response and investigation of more serious cases by specialized detective units (Kelling and Moore, 1988).

During the 1970s, researchers sought to determine how effective these policing strategies were in controlling crime. Most police executives thought that preventive patrol in radio cars served as a deterrent to criminal behavior. Contrary to this consensus, an early British experiment concluded that crime increases when police patrol is completely removed from beats; however, the level of patrolling in beats makes little difference in crime rates (Bright, 1969). The Kansas City Preventive Patrol Experiment further examined the effectiveness of varying levels of random preventive patrol in reducing crime. The study revealed that crime rates and citizen satisfaction remained the same, no matter what the level of radio car patrol — whether it was absent, doubled or tripled (Kelling et al., 1974). Replications followed and obtained similar results. In Nashville, Tenn., a level of 30 times the normal amount of patrol for selected districts was successful in reducing crime at night but not during the day (Schnelle et al., 1977). However, permanent, long-term increased preventive patrol of an entire district is not cost-effective, economically feasible or practical for a department's operations. Other studies revealed that preventive patrol's inefficiency might be due to the fact that many serious crimes occur in locations (homes, alleys, businesses) not easily visible from a passing radio car (see Eck and Spelman, 1987; Skogan and Antunes, 1979).

In addition, police departments have placed a great emphasis on reducing response time in the belief that it would increase the probability of arrest. However, several studies found that rapid response has little effect on clearance rates (e.g., Spelman and Brown, 1984; Kansas City Police Department, 1978). Only about 3 percent of crimes are arrests that were influenced by police response time, suggesting that rapid response to most calls does not increase the probability of arrest (Spelman and Brown, 1984). The problem is that police departments have no control over two key elements between the time a crime is committed and the time a police officer arrives on the scene: the interval between the commission of a crime and the time it is discovered, and the interval between discovery and the time the citizen calls the police (Walker, 1992). Most crimes are discovered after the fact, and for most "involvement" crimes — where the victim is present (e.g., assault) — there is some delay between victimization and the subsequent call to the police.

The third component of the professional "crime fighter" model — successful investigations — rests on the reputation of detectives as possessing special skills and crime-solving abilities. However, this image is largely perpetuated and romanticized by the media. Several researchers have described the reality that criminal investigations largely consist of routine, unspecialized work that is often unfruitful (Walker, 1992). Studies by the RAND Corporation (Greenwood, Chaiken and Petersilia, 1977) and the Police Executive Research Forum (Eck, 1983) documented that investigations involve mostly paperwork, phone calls and the interviewing of victims and witnesses. Only 21 percent of all "index crimes" are cleared and patrol officers at the scene of the crime usually make these arrests. In fact, most crimes are solved through the random circumstances of the crime scene (and how this scene is handled by the initial responding officer), such as availability of witnesses or the presence of evidence, such as fingerprints, rather than by any special follow-up investigations by detectives.

This series of studies, conducted in the 1970s and 1980s, challenged the three basic tenets of the professional model and raised many questions about proper crime control methods. An even more powerful harbinger of change was the growing community dissatisfaction with the activities of the police departments that served them. During the 1960s and early 1970s, the police officers were called on to quell many conflicts that revolved around larger social issues, such as the civil rights movement and the Vietnam War. College students, minorities and disenfranchised communities clashed with police departments, which symbolized and enforced the norms of a society that did not represent these groups. The police were viewed as part of the problem and not a solution (Weisburd and Uchida, 1993; National Advisory Commission on Civil Disorders, 1968; President's Commission on Law Enforcement and Administration of Criminal Justice, 1967a, 1967b).

The responding tactics of the police were viewed as draconian and there was public outcry over a force that resembled and acted like "occupying armies" rather than civil servants (Kelling and Moore, 1988).

Other research in the 1970s and 1980s pointed the police in promising directions. Frustrated by the shortcomings of the professional model, police administrators tested different strategies designed both to control crime and to bring the police and the public closer together. The Newark Foot Patrol Experiment revealed that although foot patrol did not affect the rate of serious crime, citizens perceived their environments as safer and their opinions about the police improved (Police Foundation, 1981). In Houston, Texas, a multifaceted fear reduction project was implemented. The components of this project included community stations, citizen contact foot patrol, community organizing teams, and a victim re-contact program. The evaluation of the program found generally positive results. Although serious crime did not decrease, communication between police and citizens increased and fear of crime was reduced (Pate et al., 1986).

Another important finding of these projects was that a large gap existed between the serious crime problems that professional departments attacked and the day-to-day concerns of citizens. Frequently, the police officers who staffed these programs were called upon to deal with less serious complaints, such as abandoned cars, raucous neighborhood youth and barking dogs (Trojanowicz, 1983). Disorder in the community was more of an ongoing concern for the average citizen than the risk of being the victim of a serious crime. Police agencies soon learned that social incivilities (such as unsavory loiterers, loud music, public drinking and public urination) and physical incivilities (such as trash, vacant lots, graffiti and abandoned buildings) had a definite impact on the quality of life in communities (Skogan, 1990).

A police focus on controlling disorder has been hypothesized to be an important way to reduce more serious crimes in neighborhoods. Wilson and Kelling's (1982) "broken windows" thesis suggests the link between disorder and serious crime. Signs of deterioration in a community indicate that no one in authority cares and that rules no longer apply. Disorder signals potential or active criminals that offenses will be tolerated; thus, serious crime rates increase (Wilson and Kelling, 1982). Research suggests that incivilities generate fear (LaGrange, Ferraro and Supancic, 1992; Ferraro, 1995) and are correlated with serious crime (Skogan, 1990).[1] Collectively, this body of research argued that if the police wanted to be more efficient at controlling crime, police departments should redefine their role to become more involved in communities and improve the neighborhood environment.

The general consensus among many academics then, however, was that the police did not matter in crime prevention and control. Respected criminologists Michael Gottfredson and Travis Hirschi (1990: 270) reviewed the research described above and concluded, "No evidence exists that augmentation of patrol forces or equipment, differential patrol strategies, or differential intensities of surveillance have an effect on crime rates." Police scholar David Bayley (1994: 3) more definitively stated:

> The police do not prevent crime. This is one of the best kept secrets of modern life. Experts know it, the police know it, but the public does not know it. Yet the police pretend that they are society's best defense against crime. ... This is a myth.

Beyond academic criticisms, soaring crime rates — especially violent crime rates in cities — suggested to the general public that the police were not effective in controlling crime. Between 1973 and 1990, violent crime rates in U.S. cities doubled (Reiss and Roth, 1993). The late 1980s and early 1990s were further characterized by an epidemic of youth gun violence that had its roots in the introduction of crack cocaine in disadvantaged neighborhoods in many U.S. cities (Blumstein, 1995; Braga, 2003).

What the First Executive Session on Policing Proposed

The first Executive Session on Policing ended in 1991 and produced a series of 17 papers that covered a range of topics. Many of these papers touched on how the police could better address crime and disorder problems by engaging community policing and problem-oriented policing strategies (see, e.g., Kelling, 1988; Moore and Trojanowicz, 1988; Moore and Kleiman, 1989). However, in the second paper of the series, simply titled *Crime and Policing,* Mark Moore, Robert Trojanowicz and George Kelling (1988) closely examined crime control as the core mission of policing.

The first part of their essay explored what constitutes serious crime and argued that the police should be responsible for a broader set of crime and disorder concerns. Moore, Trojanowicz and Kelling (1988) suggested that the usual view of serious crime emphasizes three components: violence, significant losses to victims, and predatory strangers. This conventional view on crime missed that the police should and could do more than simply deal with street crime. They suggested an alternate view. The police should not only acknowledge violence as a key component of serious crime but also attend to issues of safety within relationships, the importance of fear, and the extent to which offenses destroy individual lives and social institutions as well as inflicting individual losses. Police should be called upon to deal with recurring problems such as the ongoing terror felt by abused spouses and molested children, the flight of neighborhood businesses driven out by flourishing street drug markets, and the paralyzing fear caused by urban blight and disorderly groups of youth.

The second part of Moore and his colleagues' essay turned to the question of *how* the police should be oriented toward controlling and preventing serious crime. Moore, Trojanowicz and Kelling (1988) suggested the police needed to focus on identifying and addressing the precipitating causes of crime. These were not the so-called "root causes" of crime (e.g., social injustice, unequal economic opportunity, poor schooling, weak family structures, or mental illness). Although police officers are important entry points to social services for many people, Moore, Trojanowicz and Kelling (1988) argued that the police are best positioned to prevent crimes by focusing on situational opportunities for offending, toxic relationships, vulnerable victims and high-rate offenders involved in recurring crimes. Community policing and problem-solving approaches were recommended as potentially powerful enhancements to traditional police crime reduction strategies. Their proposition was framed as a practical theory (1988: 8) grounded in a handful of promising experiences and very limited research evidence, yet to be tested:

> The theory is that the effectiveness of existing tactics can be enhanced if the police increase the quantity and quality of their contacts with citizens (both individuals and neighborhood groups), and include in their responses to crime problems thoughtful analyses of the precipitating causes of the offenses. The expectation is that this will both enhance the direct effectiveness of the police department and also enable the police department to leverage the resources of citizen groups and other public agencies to control crime.

It is important to note here that Moore, Trojanowicz and Kelling (1988) were not the only scholars who drew upon developing practical police experiences and new research findings to make an argument for alternative police crime prevention strategies (e.g., see Skolnick and Bayley, 1986; Goldstein, 1979, 1990; Greene and Mastrofski, 1988; Skogan, 1990). The papers from the first Executive Session, however, were widely disseminated and read by police executives, public officials and others throughout the United States (Bammer, 2006). As the papers were published, the National Institute of Justice (NIJ) mailed them to some 30,000 organizations and individuals. A survey administered to a representative sample of U.S. police organizations serving jurisdictions with 50,000 or more residents found that 84 percent of responding police chiefs (or their designees) were familiar with the *Perspectives on Policing* series (Hartmann, Michaelson and Chen, 1994). For those respondents who were familiar with the series, 82 percent rated the papers as excellent or very good, 65 percent reported using the papers in discussions with community members and city officials, and 52 percent used the papers for training and promotional materials.

WHAT HAS BEEN LEARNED SINCE THE COMPLETION OF THE FIRST EXECUTIVE SESSION ON POLICING

As the first Executive Session ended its formal meetings, community policing was increasingly heralded as a revolutionary alternative to the professional model. Community policing programs became immensely popular in the United States (as well as in the United Kingdom, Australia, Canada and other countries) over the course of the 1990s. The creation of the Office of Community Oriented Policing Services, and the availability of funding to hire additional police officers to implement community policing programs, greatly assisted in the spread of community policing in the United States. By 1999, over 90 percent of police departments in large urban areas reported that they employed fully trained community-oriented policing officers (Hickman and Reaves, 2001). More generally, the 1990s became known as an unprecedented period of police innovation as police departments experimented with and adopted a wide range of complementary crime prevention strategies, such as problem-oriented policing, focused deterrence, disorder policing and hot spots policing (Weisburd and Braga, 2006).

Police Innovation and the 1990s Crime Drop

After decades of increasing crime rates, the United States experienced a surprising crime drop during the 1990s. According to Uniform Crime Report data, violent crime decreased about 33 percent between 1991 (the decade high point) and 2000, and property crime declined about 29 percent in the same time period.[2] Policymakers, academics and journalists attempted to sort out the various explanations for the puzzling crime decrease, such as a strong economy, improved policing, high imprisonment rates, stabilizing crack markets, immigration, new gun policies and demographic shifts (e.g., see Blumstein and Wallman, 2006; Levitt, 2004; Zimring, 2007). A careful read of the available scientific evidence suggests that no single factor can be invoked as the cause of the 1990s crime decline; rather, the explanation appears to lie with a number of mutually supportive, reinforcing factors (Wallman and Blumstein, 2006).

Even though it is difficult to specify their exact contributions, innovative police strategies are commonly credited as plausibly being among the influential factors in the 1990s crime drop (Skogan and Frydl, 2004; Blumstein and Wallman, 2006; Weisburd and Braga, 2006; Zimring, 2012). However, this view on the role of innovative police strategies in reducing crime has been challenged in two ways. First, there are those observers who suggest that police innovations did not contribute much to the unexpected crime reduction of the 1990s.[3] For instance, a recent review concluded that the many and diverse changes in policing strategies and tactics in the United States during the 1990s probably contributed little to the national crime drop (Eck and Maguire, 2006). However, their conclusion seemed to reflect the thinness and quality of the underlying research on the effectiveness of the policing innovations at the time of their review (Rosenfeld, Fornango and Baumer, 2005). As will be discussed later, a number of rigorous evaluations of innovative policing strategies completed during this time period (e.g., Sherman and Weisburd, 1995; Sherman and Rogan, 1995; Braga et al., 1999, 2001) suggest that, at the very least, new police crime control strategies could be associated with crime declines in specific U.S. cities (see also Blumstein and Wallman, 2006; Behn, 2014).

Second, some crime policy scholars suggested that it was an increase in the number of police rather than new police crime control strategies that explained the police role in the 1990s crime decline. Increased staffing is argued to support police departments in reducing crime through an augmented presence to deter crime and enhance the capacity to apprehend offenders. University of Chicago economist Steven Levitt (2004) found that innovative policing was not related to the crime decline; the increase in the number of police in the 1990s contributed between 10 and 20 percent of the crime drop. In his analysis of crime trends in U.S. cities between 1980 and 2004, Florida State University criminologist Eric Baumer (2006) reported inconsistent findings for policing variables. His measure of innovative policing strategies, arrests for public order and weapons offenses, was unrelated to crime rates, but increases in police force size and the certainty of arrest (the ratio of arrests for serious crimes to the number of serious crimes known to the police) were associated with crime reductions.

In general, however, there is little evidence that simply increasing police numbers leads to reductions in crime. The National Research Council's Committee to Review Research on Police Policy and Practices (hereafter, NRC Panel on Police) concluded that the research in this area is ambiguous and, as such, it is difficult to reach a conclusion on the matter (Skogan and Frydl, 2004). More recently, methodologically rigorous analyses of the relationship between numbers of police and crime rates have not shown evidence that more police reduce crime (Evans and Owens, 2007; Kleck and Barnes, 2014). Continued crime declines after recent decreases in the number of police, especially after the deep recession beginning in 2008, further challenged the purported direct relationship between police numbers and crime reductions. Some observers proposed that we may now be in an era of police "doing more with less" in their crime prevention and control efforts (Weisburd, Telep and Lawton, 2014); this suggests that what the police do to prevent crime may be more salient than how many police officers are available. Of course, police departments face the persistent dilemma of having enough police officers to handle basic functions while staffing innovative crime prevention programs. However, there seems to be little support for the idea that increasing the size of police departments alone translates into decreased crime rates.

Current Evaluation Evidence on the Impact of Innovative Policing on Crime

The number of rigorous evaluation studies examining the impact of police strategies on crime increased dramatically since the end of the first Executive Session. This growth was especially pronounced in the 1990s and 2000s, which included the completion of some 54 randomized experiments in policing (Braga et al., 2014). A much stronger knowledge base now exists to appraise whether innovative police strategies do indeed prevent and control crime. The NRC Panel on Police reviewed this growing body of research evidence (Skogan and Frydl, 2004: 5) and concluded:

> There is strong evidence that the more focused and specific the strategies of the police, the more they are tailored to the problems they seek to address, [and] the more effective the police will be in controlling crime and disorder.

Police seem to be effective in controlling crime when their strategies focus on identifiable risks and, in addition to increased law enforcement attention, engage a wider spectrum of partners to develop appropriate strategies that address recurring crime and disorder problems.

The available empirical and theoretical evidence suggests that crime is concentrated at a small number of high-risk places during high-risk times and generated by a small number of very risky people (Sherman, 1992; Braga, 2012). The existing research also points to important place-level dynamics and situational factors, and the daily activities and behaviors of people in the offender and victim populations, to understand the concentration of crime at specific small places during specific months of the year, days of the week, and hours of the day (Eck and Weisburd, 1995; Clarke, 1997; Clarke and Felson, 1993; Felson and Poulsen, 2003). Similarly, for high-crime offenders, research documents the salience of co-offending patterns and the central role of group-based dynamics and norms in persistent violent crime problems in urban settings (Papachristos, Braga and Hureau, 2012; Papachristos, Hureau and Braga, 2013). Although these patterns are very concerning, they also represent important opportunities for more effective police crime prevention and control. If police departments could organize themselves to control the small number of risky places, risky times and risky people that generate the bulk of their crime problems, they could more effectively manage citywide crime trends.

The remainder of this section briefly reviews the available evidence evaluating the effectiveness of four major innovations in police strategy for crime prevention: community policing, problem-oriented policing, hot spots policing and focused deterrence strategies. These innovations have generated a great deal of attention in public policy, practice and academic circles. And, as will be discussed further, these strategic innovations overlap and complement each other in important ways. Readers interested in a more comprehensive assessment of a wider range of innovative police strategies should consult the Evidence-Based Policing Matrix,[4] maintained by George Mason University's Center for Evidence-Based Crime Policy (Lum, Koper and Telep, 2011).

Much of the evaluation evidence summarized here was gleaned from systematic reviews of policing programs managed by the Campbell Collaboration. Formed in 2000, the Campbell Collaboration Crime and Justice Group aims to prepare and maintain systematic reviews of criminological interventions and to make them electronically accessible to scholars, practitioners, policymakers and the general public (www. campbellcollaboration.org). In systematic reviews, researchers attempt to gather relevant evaluative studies in a specific area, critically appraise them, and make judgments about what works, "using explicit, transparent, state-of-the-art methods" (Petrosino et al., 2001: 21). Rigorous methods are used to summarize, analyze and combine study findings.

Community Policing

Community policing has been described as both a philosophy of policing and an organizational strategy (Skogan and Frydl, 2004; Greene, 2000). Community policing departments tend to embrace a larger vision of the police function (Skogan and Hartnett, 1997). As Kelling and Moore argue, "During the 1950s and 1960s, police thought they were law enforcement agencies primarily fighting crime" (1988: 4). In departments adopting a community policing philosophy, the police function broadens and includes "order maintenance, conflict resolution, provision of services through problem solving, as well as other activities" (Kelling and Moore, 1988: 2). The justification for this expanded view of police responsibilities was drawn either from the fact that, historically, the police had indeed carried such functions or that the community from which the police gained legitimacy saw these as important functions of the police (Weisburd and Braga, 2006).

Community policing is not a specific set of programs. Rather, communities have different problems and bring to bear a variety of resources against them, so police will implement different strategies. However, as an organizational strategy, the community policing process leaves setting priorities and the means of achieving them largely to residents and the police that serve in their neighborhoods. The three core, and densely interrelated, elements of community policing are citizen involvement in identifying and addressing public safety concerns, the decentralization of decision-making down the police organizational hierarchy to encourage development of local responses to locally defined problems, and *problem solving* to respond to community crime and disorder concerns (Skogan, 2006). The iterative problem-oriented policing process described here is commonly used as an important framework when dealing with local community concerns proactively.

The NRC Panel on Police concluded that broad-based community policing programs generally do not produce crime reduction gains but do seem to improve other important outcomes such as citizen views of the police (Skogan and Frydl, 2004; Weisburd and Eck, 2004). Any observed crime prevention impacts were more directly associated with specific strategies — such as distinct problem-oriented policing initiatives — implemented within community policing programs. More recently, a Campbell systematic review, sponsored by the United Kingdom's National Policing Improvement Agency, identified 25 evaluation reports containing 65 controlled tests of community policing programs (Gill et al., 2014). Their meta-analysis of 37 tests suggested that these programs generated positive effects on citizen satisfaction, perceptions of disorder and police legitimacy, but the programs had limited effects on crime and fear of crime.

Problem-Oriented Policing

In 1979, Herman Goldstein, a respected University of Wisconsin law professor and former aide to Chicago police superintendent O.W. Wilson, made a simple and straightforward proposition that challenged police officers to address problems rather than simply respond to incidents. According to Goldstein (1979, 1990), behind every recurring problem there are underlying conditions that create it. Incident-driven policing never addresses these conditions; therefore, incidents are likely to recur. Answering calls for service is an important task and still must be done, but police officers should respond systematically to recurring calls for the same problem. In order for the police to be more efficient and effective, they must gather information about incidents and design an appropriate response based on the nature of the underlying conditions that caused the problem(s) (Goldstein, 1990).

Problem-oriented policing seeks to identify the underlying causes of crime problems and to frame appropriate responses tailored to problems based on the results of analysis (Goldstein, 1979). Using a basic iterative approach of problem identification, analysis, response, assessment, and adjustment of the response, this adaptable and dynamic analytic approach provides an appropriate framework to uncover the complex mechanisms at play in crime problems and to develop tailor-made interventions that engage a wider range of community, social service and criminal justice partners to address criminogenic situations, dynamics and characteristics that cause crime problems to recur (Eck and Spelman, 1987; Goldstein, 1990; Braga, 2008). Several published volumes on problem-oriented policing case studies provide a good sense for the work being done as well as the strengths and weaknesses of some of the better problem-oriented efforts (see, e.g., Eck and Spelman, 1987; O'Connor and Grant, 1998; Sole Brito and Allan, 1999; Sole Brito and Gratto, 2000; Scott, 2000). Indeed, the widespread use of problem-oriented policing as a central crime prevention and control strategy in police agencies around the world is a strong indicator of the practical value of the approach.

There is a growing body of evaluation evidence that problem-oriented policing generates noteworthy crime control gains. The NRC Panel on Police concluded that problem-oriented policing is a promising approach to deal with crime, disorder and fear. The panel recommended that additional research be conducted to understand the organizational arrangements that foster effective problem solving (Skogan and Frydl, 2004; Weisburd and Eck, 2004). This conclusion contrasts with an earlier review by Sherman (1991) that suggested there was little rigorous evaluation evidence in support of Herman Goldstein's (1990) contention that problem-oriented policing was privileged over traditional policing methods in preventing crime. More recently, David Weisburd and his colleagues (2010) completed a Campbell Collaboration systematic review of the crime prevention effects of problem-oriented policing on crime and disorder. Their meta-analysis of 10 controlled evaluations revealed that problem-oriented policing programs generated a modest but statistically significant impact on crime and disorder outcomes. The Campbell problem-oriented policing review also reported the crime prevention effects of 45 simple pre- and post-comparison evaluation studies. Although these studies did not include a comparison group and were less methodologically rigorous, Weisburd and colleagues (2010) found that 43 of the 45 evaluations reported that the problem-oriented policing approach generated beneficial crime prevention effects.

Hot Spots Policing

Over the past 30 years, research has demonstrated that crime is not evenly distributed across urban areas; rather, it is concentrated in very small places, or hot spots, that generate half of all criminal events (Pierce, Spaar and Briggs, 1988; Sherman, Gartin and Buerger, 1989). Hot spots policing is not simply the application of police strategies to units of geography (Weisburd, 2008; Braga and Weisburd, 2010). Traditional policing in this sense can be seen as place-based. Police have routinely defined their units of operation in terms of large areas, such as police precincts and beats. In hot spots policing, place refers to a very different level of geographic aggregation than has traditionally interested police executives and planners. Places in this context are very small micro-units of analysis, such as buildings or addresses, block faces or street segments, or clusters of addresses, block faces and street segments (Eck and Weisburd, 1995). When crime is concentrated in such places, they are commonly referred to as hot spots. A majority of U.S. police departments currently use hot spots policing strategies to reduce crime (Police Executive Research Forum, 2008; Weisburd et al., 2003).

The crime control effectiveness of hot spots policing is supported by two complementary theoretical perspectives: general deterrence and criminal opportunity reduction (Nagin, 2013). Evaluation evidence has found support for both theoretical perspectives. For instance, in the Minneapolis hot spots patrol experiment, Sherman and Weisburd (1995) claimed evidence of place-specific general deterrence associated with increased police presence in hot spot areas. Moreover, in Lowell, Mass., Braga and Bond (2008) suggested that the crime reduction impacts observed in their randomized experiment were primarily generated by problem-oriented policing strategies that modified criminal opportunity structures at crime hot spots. Indeed, as suggested by early experiences in Newport News, Va. (Eck and Spelman, 1987), problem-oriented policing, with its emphasis on using analysis to understand recurring crime problems, is a natural complement to hot spots policing programs in framing strategies to control persistently problematic places.

Drawing on studies from an ongoing Campbell review of hot spots policing evaluations (Braga, 2001), the NRC Panel on Police concluded that "a strong body of evidence suggests that taking a focused geographic approach to crime problems can increase policing effectiveness in reducing crime and disorder" (Skogan and Frydl, 2004: 247). The most recent iteration of the Campbell hot spots policing review identified 19 rigorous evaluations involving 25 tests of hot spots policing programs (Braga, Papachristos and Hureau, 2014). Meta-analyses of these controlled evaluations found that these programs produced significant crime reductions in the targeted hot spots areas and tended to generate "spillover" crime prevention effects in surrounding areas that did not receive focused police attention. Moreover, the meta-analyses suggested that problem-oriented policing strategies, designed to change underlying conditions at crime hot spots, generated stronger crime control gains relative to programs that simply increased traditional police activities, such as patrol, in crime hot spots (Braga, Papachristos and Hureau, 2014).

Disorder Policing

Dealing with physical and social disorder, or "fixing broken windows," has become a central element of crime prevention strategies adopted by many American police departments (Sousa and Kelling, 2006; Kelling and Coles, 1996). The general idea of dealing with disorderly conditions to prevent crime is present in myriad police strategies. These range from "order maintenance" and "zero-tolerance" policing, where the police attempt to impose order through strict enforcement, to community and problem-oriented policing, where police attempt to produce order and reduce crime through cooperation with community members and by addressing specific recurring problems (Cordner, 1998; Eck and Maguire, 2006; Skogan, 2006). Although its application can vary within and across police departments, disorder policing is now a common crime control strategy.

More than 30 years of evaluation research on the impact of disorder policing strategies on crime has produced a large body of studies characterized by an array of positive, null and negative effects (Braga, Welsh and Schnell, 2015). Until recently, scholars and policy analysts have not attempted to synthesize the findings of these empirical studies in a systematic way. Prior narrative reviews of this body of research privileged the findings of particular studies over others and, as a result, produced divergent conclusions on the crime control efficacy of disorder policing. For instance, in a published debate, University of Chicago law professor Bernard Harcourt concluded that there was “no good evidence that broken windows policing reduces serious crime,” whereas University of Michigan public policy professor David Thacher suggested that there were some indications that disorder policing may positively impact crime rates (Harcourt and Thacher, 2005: 15).

The preliminary results of an ongoing Campbell systematic review and meta-analysis suggest that disorder policing strategies do generate crime control gains (Braga, Welsh and Schnell, 2015). Importantly, these strategies yielded consistent crime reduction effects across a variety of violence, property, drug and disorder outcome measures. These findings provide support for police paying attention to social and physical disorder when seeking to reduce more serious crimes in neighborhoods. Indeed, beyond disorder policing, these general ideas support key strategies and tactics employed by a wide range of recent police innovations, such as community policing, problem-oriented policing and hot spots policing (see Weisburd and Braga, 2006). Police departments should continue to engage policing disorder tactics as part of their portfolio of strategies to reduce crime.

Perhaps of greatest interest, to police leaders and policymakers alike, was the preliminary Campbell review finding that the types of strategies used by police departments to control disorder seemed to matter the most (Braga, Welsh and Schnell, 2015). Aggressive order maintenance strategies that targeted individual disorderly behaviors did not generate significant crime reductions. In contrast, community problem-solving approaches designed to change social and physical disorder conditions at particular places, such as crime hot spots, produced significant crime reductions.

Focused Deterrence

A recent innovation in policing that capitalizes on the growing evidence of the effectiveness of police crime prevention strategies is the “focused deterrence” framework, which is often referred to as “pulling-levers policing” (Kennedy, 1997, 2008). Pioneered in Boston as a problem-oriented policing project to halt serious gang violence during the 1990s (Braga et al., 2001), the focused deterrence framework has been applied in many U.S. cities through federally sponsored violence prevention programs such as the Strategic Alternatives to Community Safety Initiative and Project Safe Neighborhoods (PSN) (Dalton, 2002). Focused deterrence strategies honor core deterrence ideas, such as increasing risks faced by offenders, while finding new and creative ways of deploying traditional and nontraditional law enforcement tools to do so, such as communicating incentives and disincentives directly to targeted offenders (Kennedy, 2008).

In its simplest form, the focused deterrence approach consists of selecting a particular crime problem, such as gang homicide; convening an interagency working group of law enforcement, social service and community-based practitioners; conducting research to identify key offenders, groups and behavior patterns; framing a response to offenders and groups of offenders that uses a varied menu of sanctions (“pulling levers”) to stop them from continuing their violent behavior; focusing social services and community resources on targeted offenders and groups to match law enforcement prevention efforts; and directly and repeatedly communicating with offenders to make them understand why they are receiving this special attention (Kennedy, 1997, 2008). These new strategic approaches have been applied to a range of crime problems, such as overt drug markets and individual repeat offenders. The ultimate targets of focused deterrence strategies are the pro-violence norms and dynamics that drive offending and victimization for high-risk individuals.

In response to conflicting reports on the crime control efficacy of these new prevention strategies (see, e.g., Braga et al., 2001; Rosenfeld, Fornango and Baumer, 2005; Wellford, Pepper and Petrie, 2005), the United Kingdom's National Policing Improvement Agency provided funds to support a Campbell Collaboration systematic review of the available evaluation evidence on the crime control efficacy of focused deterrence strategies. The Campbell review found that focused deterrence strategies were associated with significant reductions in targeted crime problems, particularly gang homicide (Braga and Weisburd, 2012). More recent research suggests that focused deterrence strategies not only reduce serious violence by targeted gangs but also deter serious violence by socially connected gangs not directly subjected to the program (Braga, Hureau and Papachristos, 2014; Braga, Apel and Welsh, 2013).

The Work of the Second Executive Session on Policing and Public Safety

The second Executive Session on Policing and Public Safety commenced in 2008 and ended in 2014. During this second series of meetings, the author believes there was a consensus among the academic and police executive participants that the police were performing well in controlling crime. Crime had decreased steadily over the previous 18 years and there were many success stories. Although dealing with crime remained an important topic, it certainly was not the main topic of conversation. The participants considered a variety of new challenges to the policing profession, including dealing with terrorist threats and homeland security in a post-9/11 world (Bayley and Nixon, 2010), making policing more affordable in light of the 2008 recession (Gascón and Foglesong, 2010), addressing wrongful convictions (Batts, deLone and Stephens, 2014), promoting better relationships between the police and minority communities (Meares, 2015; Bayley, Davis and Davis, 2015), managing the boundaries between private and public policing (Sparrow, 2014), and other pressing concerns.

The broader scope of challenges to the policing industry considered during the second Executive Session does not suggest that the participants thought crime wasn't an ongoing concern to police executives throughout the world. Indeed, conversations were dedicated to considering the persistent problem of serious gun violence in disadvantaged minority communities (Braga and Brunson, 2015), the burgeoning problem of prisoner reentry in an era of mass incarceration (Travis, Davis and Lawrence, 2012), and how to get detectives more focused on crime prevention work (Braga et al., 2011). However, there was a sense among participants that a general crime control "game plan" existed and it needed to be protected by advancing two broad ideas: (1) strengthening existing commitments to community problem-solving efforts, and (2) remaining flexible and adaptable in the crime control task environment.

Strengthening Existing Commitments to Community Problem-Solving Efforts

Even though community problem-solving policing concepts are now ubiquitous in the policing profession, the experiences of the police executives in the session, coupled with the available literature on implementation, suggest that many police departments are not embracing these approaches with fidelity to the original ideas.

For instance, the available research suggests that community policing has been unevenly implemented within police departments, with responsibility for community-based initiatives sometimes relegated to specialized units composed of a small number of officers rather than spread across police departments (Skogan and Frydl, 2004; Skogan, 2006). Police officers also often find it difficult to implement problem-oriented policing properly with deficiencies in all stages of the process, resulting in an overreliance on traditional policing tactics (Braga and Weisburd, 2006; Cordner and Biebel, 2005). Too many police departments seem to rely on oversimplistic tactics, such as "putting cops on dots" or launching indiscriminate zero-tolerance initiatives rather than engaging a coherent crime prevention strategy.

Community policing should be the foundation of any general crime prevention approach. Simply engaging the community doesn't seem to translate directly into crime reduction gains. However, community engagement can provide important inputs to help focus crime reduction strategies such as problem-oriented policing, hot spots policing and focused deterrence approaches, which do seem to reduce crime. Developing close relationships with community members helps the police gather information about crime and disorder problems, understand the nature of these problems, and solve specific crimes. Community members can also help with key components of strategies tailored to specific problems by making improvements to the physical environment and through informal social control of high-risk people. Indeed, a central idea in community policing is to engage residents so they can exert more control over situations and dynamics that contribute to their own potential for victimization and, by doing so, influence neighborhood levels of crime. Police departments should also strive to develop similar working relationships with local businesses, social service agencies and other criminal justice organizations.

Problem-oriented policing seems well-positioned to be a central crime prevention strategy implemented within a broader community policing approach. Eck (2006: 118– 119) summarized problem-oriented policing as having three core principles:

1. The *empirical principle* is that the public demands that police handle a wide range of problems.
2. The *normative principle* is that police are supposed to reduce problems rather than simply responding to incidents and applying the relevant criminal law.
3. The *scientific principle* asserts that police should take a scientific approach to crime problems and apply analytical approaches and interventions based on sound theory and evaluation evidence.

Although knowledge and practice will continue to evolve, the core principles of the approach that drive its popularity seem likely to remain constant. There seems to be consensus among police leaders, scholars and the public that police agencies should be focused on problem reduction — that is, ensuring fewer, less serious and less harmful crime and disorder problems (Eck, 2006).

Hot spots policing, disorder policing and focused deterrence strategies are evidence-based crime prevention strategies that fit well within a community problem-solving framework. Community members will undoubtedly expect police departments to address high-crime locations, disorderly conditions and repeat offenders within their neighborhoods. Relative to increased traditional policing actions, problem-oriented policing seems to generate stronger crime reduction impacts when applied to control crime hot spot locations (Braga and Weisburd, 2010; Braga, Papachristos and Hureau, 2014). Community problem-solving efforts have long been recommended as desirable ways to control social and physical disorder associated with more serious crime problems (Wilson and Kelling, 1989; Kelling and Coles, 1996). Focused deterrence strategies developed from a problem-oriented approach to gang violence (Kennedy, Piehl and Braga, 1996) and involve community engagement in changing pro-violence norms and behaviors by criminally active groups and high-rate offenders.

Other Executive Session papers address the issue of police legitimacy, especially in minority communities (Meares, 2015; Braga and Brunson, 2015; Bayley, Davis and Davis, 2015). Throughout these papers, the authors acknowledge in varying ways that it is extremely important to balance the implementation of effective crime prevention strategies with maintaining positive community perceptions of the quality and appropriateness of police services. Certainly, much has been learned about enhancing police legitimacy. Community policing has been found to improve police-community relationships and enhance police legitimacy in white and non-white communities (Skogan, 2006). Handling police-citizen encounters in a respectful, procedurally just manner also seems to enhance police legitimacy (Tyler, 2006; Mazerolle et al., 2013). It is also important to note here that the composition of police departments has changed notably over the past 30 years (Sklansky, 2005; Batts, Smoot and Scrivner, 2012). Today's police departments have better educated officers and more closely resemble the communities they police — with larger shares of female and minority officers.

Engaging a focused and analytical approach to crime control and prevention also seems well-positioned to improve police legitimacy with the public they serve. First, communities expect the police to control crime. Ineffective strategies that lead to unnecessarily high crime rates will undoubtedly undermine police legitimacy. Second, community engagement in developing appropriately focused strategies helps to safeguard against indiscriminate and overly aggressive enforcement tactics and other inappropriate policing activities, which in turn erode the community's trust and confidence in the police and inhibit cooperation. Third, preventing crimes from happening by addressing underlying crime-producing situations and dynamics reduces harm to potential victims as well as harm to would-be offenders by not relying solely on arrest and prosecution actions.

Remaining Flexible and Adaptable in the Crime Control Task Environment

The police crime control research summarized in the previous section carried out the important task of determining whether specific innovative policing programs had an impact on crime reduction. Rigorous evaluation research generally attempts to isolate causal relationships between programs and outcomes through the use of comparison groups and statistical controls (Shadish, Cook and Campbell, 2002). Clearly, conducting isolated tests of specific interventions is critically important in developing a body of knowledge on what works in police crime reduction (Weisburd and Neyroud, 2011). However, in practice, research findings should be used to inform a general approach to crime reduction that includes a diverse set of proven practices but can also be flexible enough to understand new crime problems and develop appropriate interventions to address the risky situations, dynamics and people that cause problems to recur (Sparrow, 2009, 2011). Police departments should be developing a strategic orientation to crime reduction rather than simply adopting specific programs and tactics that may stifle innovation. The existing research evidence suggests a police crime prevention approach that focuses on identifying and addressing "precipitating" causes of specific crime problems, engages the community and a broad range of governmental and nongovernmental partners, and uses a diversity of tools and strategies including, but certainly not limited to, law enforcement actions.

Developing and maintaining a strong analytical capacity within police departments is clearly essential to strategic crime prevention in a community problem-solving framework. A focused approach to crime reduction requires identifying high-risk situations, people and places. It also requires developing an understanding of the underlying conditions that cause these identifiable risks to persist. Measuring whether implemented crime prevention strategies are generating the desired impact on crime reduction is also important; ineffective police strategies can be discontinued and more appropriate interventions developed. This orientation obviously puts a premium on data collection and analysis systems, and on developing the human capital within police departments to carry out such analytic work. By virtue of their representation as patterns within commonly available criminal justice databases (such as data on arrests, crime incidents, and calls for service), these risks are easily identifiable through simple analysis. Through the collection of other data (such as offender and victim interviews) and more sophisticated analysis (such as social network analysis and geo-temporal analytics), the underlying conditions and dynamics associated with the genesis and continuation of these recurring problems can be understood. Training police officers in crime analysis, hiring civilian crime analysts, and developing strategic partnerships with external researchers will better position police departments to carry out problem identification, analysis and assessment.

Compstat, a key element of the NYPD's attack on crime during the 1990s (Silverman, 1999), has become a popular management accountability system used by most major police departments in the United States (Weisburd et al., 2003). Compstat can be viewed as an important administrative innovation that holds mid-level managers accountable for understanding and addressing crime trends and problems in the geographic areas (precincts, districts) they command. These administrative systems can be used to help drive the community problem-solving efforts described throughout this essay. However, police departments engaging Compstat processes must be careful to ensure that the process does not undermine the creativity and flexibility needed to launch more powerful responses to crime problems (Weisburd et al., 2003; Sparrow, 2015). Performance accountability systems, like Compstat, can be effective if leadership teams apply them creatively, analytically and persistently (Behn, 2014). Police managers should be held responsible for developing responses that go beyond simply increasing arrests and summons in problem areas.

Conclusion

In his fictional case study on addressing crime in Heron City, Sparrow (2009) examines the relationships among a range of current policing strategies, and the nature of analytic support that modern operational policing requires. Sparrow (2009) advances the idea that police departments engaging multiple crime control strategies need to safeguard against rigid adherence to any particular approach that could result in a diminished capacity to respond to new and evolving crime and disorder problems. Police departments need to be creative and versatile rather than stagnant and inflexible. Crime problems need to be deconstructed through analysis, and responses need to be tailored to underlying conditions and local community needs. Whereas Moore, Trojanowicz and Kelling (1988) focused more on how the community can be integrated into police crime prevention efforts, they similarly advocated for a flexible approach rooted in thoughtful analyses of crime problems and the development of responses tailored to proximate causes (see also Goldstein, 1979, 1990; Clarke, 1997).

This essay reviewed the available research on specific police crime prevention programs. Most of the available scientific evidence was conducted in the years between the first and second Executive Sessions on Policing. In the first paper of the second Executive Session, Sparrow (2009) drew some much-needed attention to these ideas. The available research suggests that the ideas that flowered after the first Executive Session were invaluable in advancing the police response to crime and disorder problems. And, although the evaluation evidence tended to cluster within specific types of police crime prevention programs, the study findings are actually quite complementary when aggregated into common themes. In essence, the police should adopt a flexible "community problem-solving" approach to dealing with crime and disorder problems and draw upon specific kinds of programs when they fit local community needs. This approach should be rooted in community engagement, the analysis of crime problems, and the development of appropriate prevention responses.

References

Bammer, G. (2006). "Harvard's Executive Sessions — An Interim Overview and Commentary." Working paper. Cambridge, MA: Harvard Kennedy School, Hauser Center for Nonprofit Organizations.

Batts, A.W., M. deLone and D. Stephens. (2014). Policing and Wrongful Convictions. New Perspectives in Policing Bulletin. Washington, DC: U.S. Department of Justice, National Institute of Justice.

Batts, A.W., S. Smoot and E. Scrivner. (2012). Police Leadership Challenges in a Changing World. New Perspectives in Policing Bulletin. Washington, DC: U.S. Department of Justice, National Institute of Justice.

Baumer, E. (2006). "An Empirical Assessment of the Contemporary Crime Trends Puzzle: A Modest Step Toward a More Comprehensive Research Agenda." In A. Goldberger and R. Rosenfeld (eds.), Understanding Crime Trends: Workshop Report. Committee on Understanding Crime Trends, Committee on Law and Justice, Division of Behavioral and Social Sciences and Education. Washington, DC: National Academies Press.

Bayley, D. (1994). Police for the Future. New York: Oxford University Press.

Bayley, D., M. Davis and R. Davis (2015). Race and Policing: An Agenda for Action. New Perspectives in Policing Bulletin. Washington, DC: U.S. Department of Justice, National Institute of Justice.

Bayley, D. and C. Nixon (2010). The Changing Environment for Policing, 1985–2008. New Perspectives in Policing Bulletin. Washington, DC: U.S. Department of Justice, National Institute of Justice.

Behn, R. (2014). The PerformanceStat Potential. Washington, DC: Brookings Institution Press.

Blumstein, A. (1995). "Youth Violence, Guns, and the Illicit Drug Industry." *Journal of Criminal Law and Criminology* 86: 10–36.

Blumstein, A. and J. Wallman. (2006). "The Recent Rise and Fall of American Violence." In A. Blumstein and J. Wallman (eds.), *The Crime Drop in America* (rev. ed.). New York: Cambridge University Press.

Braga, A.A. (2001). "The Effects of Hot Spots Policing on Crime." *Annals of the American Academy of Political and Social Science* 455: 104–125.

Braga, A.A. (2003). "Serious Youth Gun Offenders and the Epidemic of Youth Violence in Boston." *Journal of Quantitative Criminology* 19: 33–54.

Braga, A.A. (2008). Problem-Oriented Policing and Crime Prevention (2nd ed.). Monsey, NY: Criminal Justice Press.

Braga, A.A. (2012). "High Crime Places, Times, and Offenders." In B.C. Welsh and D.P. Farrington (eds.), *The Oxford Handbook on Crime Prevention*. New York: Oxford University Press.

Braga, A.A., R. Apel and B.C. Welsh. (2013). "The Spillover Effects of Focused Deterrence on Gang Violence." *Evaluation Review* 37: 314–342.

Braga, A.A. and B.J. Bond. (2008). "Policing Crime and Disorder Hot Spots: A Randomized Controlled Trial." *Criminology* 46: 577–608.

Braga, A.A. and R.K. Brunson. (2015). The Police and Public Discourse on "Black-on-Black" Violence. New Perspectives in Policing Bulletin. Washington, DC: U.S. Department of Justice, National Institute of Justice.

Braga, A.A., E.A. Flynn, G.L. Kelling and C.M. Cole. (2011). Moving the Work of Criminal Investigators Towards Crime Control. New Perspectives in Policing Bulletin. Washington, DC: U.S. Department of Justice, National Institute of Justice.

Braga, A.A., D.M. Hureau and A.V. Papachristos. (2014). "Deterring Gang-Involved Gun Violence: Measuring the Impact of Boston's Operation Ceasefire on Street Gang Behavior." *Journal of Quantitative Criminology* 30: 113–139.

Braga, A.A., D.M. Kennedy, E.J. Waring and A.M. Piehl (2001). "Problem-Oriented Policing, Deterrence, and Youth Violence: An Evaluation of Boston's Operation Ceasefire." *Journal of Research in Crime and Delinquency* 38: 195–225.

Braga, A.A., A.V. Papachristos and D.M. Hureau. (2014). "The Effects of Hot Spots Policing on Crime: An Updated Systematic Review and Meta-Analysis." *Justice Quarterly* 31: 633–663.

Braga, A.A. and D.L. Weisburd. (2006). "Problem-Oriented Policing: The Disconnect Between Principles and Practice." In D.L. Weisburd and A.A. Braga (eds.), Police Innovation: Contrasting Perspectives. New York: Cambridge University Press.

Braga, A.A. and D.L. Weisburd. (2010). Policing Problem Places: Crime Hot Spots and Effective Prevention. New York: Oxford University Press.

Braga, A.A. and D.L. Weisburd. (2012). "The Effects of Focused Deterrence Strategies on Crime: A Systematic Review and Meta-Analysis of the Empirical Evidence." *Journal of Research in Crime and Delinquency* 49: 323–358.

Braga, A.A., D.L. Weisburd, E.J. Waring, L. Green Mazerolle, W. Spelman and F. Gajewski. (1999). "Problem-Oriented Policing in Violent Crime Places: A Randomized Controlled Experiment." *Criminology* 37: 541–580.

Braga, A.A., B.C. Welsh, A.V. Papachristos, C. Schnell and L. Grossman. (2014). "The Growth of Randomized Experiments in Policing: The Vital Few and the Salience of Mentoring." *Journal of Experimental Criminology* 10: 1–28.

Braga, A.A., B.C. Welsh and C. Schnell. (2015). "Can Policing Disorder Reduce Crime? A Systematic Review and Meta-Analysis." *Journal of Research in Crime and Delinquency* 52: 567–588.

Bright, J.A. (1969). The Beat Patrol Experiment. Unpublished paper. London, England: Home Office Police Research and Development Branch .

Cerda, M., M. Tracy, S. Messner, D. Vlahov, K. Tardiff and S. Galea. (2009). "Misdemeanor Policing, Physical Disorder and Homicide: A Spatial Analytic Test of 'Broken Windows' Theory." *Epidemiology* 20: 533–541.

Chauhan, P., M. Cerda, S. Messner, M. Tracy, K. Tardiff and S. Galea. (2011). "Race/Ethnic-Specific Homicide Rates in New York City: Evaluating the Impact of Broken Windows Policing and Crack Cocaine Markets." *Homicide Studies* 15: 268–290.

Clarke, R.V. (ed.). (1997). Situational Crime Prevention: Successful Case Studies (2nd ed.). Albany, NY: Harrow and Heston.

Clarke, R.V. and M. Felson (1993). "Introduction: Criminology, Routine Activity, and Rational Choice." In R.V. Clarke and M. Felson (eds.), Routine Activity and Rational Choice. *Advances in Criminological Theory* (Vol. 5). New Brunswick, NJ: Transaction Press.

Cordner, G. (1998). "Problem-Oriented Policing vs. Zero Tolerance." In S.T. O'Connor and A.C. Grant (eds.), Problem-Oriented Policing: Crime-Specific Problems, Critical Issues, and Making POP Work. Washington, DC: Police Executive Research Forum.

Cordner, G. and E.P. Biebel. (2005). "Problem-Oriented Policing in Practice." *Criminology and Public Policy* 4: 155–180.

Corman, H. and N. Mocan (2005). "Carrots, Sticks, and Broken Windows." *Journal of Law and Economics* 48: 235–262.

Dalton, E. (2002). "Targeted Crime Reduction Efforts in Ten Communities: Lessons for the Project Safe Neighborhoods Initiative." U.S. Attorney's Bulletin 50: 16–25.

Eck, J.E. (1983). Solving Crimes: The Investigation of Burglary and Robbery. Washington, DC: Police Executive Research Forum.

Eck, J.E. (2006). "Science, Values, and Problem-Oriented Policing: Why Problem-Oriented Policing?" In D.L. Weisburd and A.A. Braga (eds.), Police Innovation: Contrasting Perspectives. New York: Cambridge University Press.

Eck, J.E. and E. Maguire. (2006). "Have Changes in Policing Reduced Violent Crime? An Assessment of the Evidence. In A. Blumstein and J. Wallman (eds.), The Crime Drop in America (rev. ed.). New York: Cambridge University Press.

Eck, J.E. and W. Spelman. (1987). Problem-Solving: Problem-Oriented Policing in Newport News. Washington, DC: U.S. Department of Justice, National Institute of Justice.

Eck, J.E. and D. Weisburd. (1995). "Crime Places in Crime Theory." In J. Eck and D. Weisburd (eds.), Crime and Place. Crime Prevention Studies (Vol. 4). Monsey, NY: Criminal Justice Press.

Evans, W. and E. Owens. (2007). "COPS and Crime." *Journal of Public Economics* 91: 181-201.

Felson, M. and E. Poulsen. (2003). "Simple Indicators of Crime by Time of Day." *International Journal of Forecasting* 19: 595–601.

Ferraro, K. (1995). Fear of Crime: Interpreting Victimization Risk. Albany, NY: State University of New York Press.

Gascón, G. and T. Foglesong. (2010). Making Policing More Affordable: Managing Costs and Measuring Value in Policing. New Perspectives in Policing Bulletin. Washington, DC: U.S. Department of Justice, National Institute of Justice.

Gill, C., D.L. Weisburd, C. Telep, Z. Vitter and T. Bennett. (2014). "Community-Oriented Policing to Reduce Crime, Disorder and Fear and Increase Satisfaction and Legitimacy Among Citizens: A Systematic Review." *Journal of Experimental Criminology* 10: 399–428.

Goldstein, H. (1979). "Improving Policing: A Problem-Oriented Approach." *Crime & Delinquency* 25: 236–258.

Goldstein, H. (1990). Problem-Oriented Policing. Philadelphia: Temple University Press.

Gottfredson, M. and T. Hirschi. (1990). A General Theory of Crime. Stanford, CA: Stanford University Press.

Greenberg, D. (2014). "Studying New York City's Crime Decline: Methodological Issues." *Justice Quarterly* 31: 154–188.

Greene, J.R. (2000). "Community Policing in America: Changing the Nature, Structure and Function of the Police." In J. Horney, R. Peterson, D. MacKenzie, J. Martin and D. Rosenbaum (eds.), Policies, Processes and Decisions of the Criminal Justice System. Criminal Justice 2000 Series (Vol. 3). Washington, DC: U.S. Department of Justice, National Institute of Justice.

Greene, J.R. and S. Mastrofski (eds.). (1988). Community Policing: Rhetoric or Reality? New York: Praeger.

Greenwood, P., J. Chaiken and J. Petersilia. (1977). The Investigation Process. Lexington, MA: Lexington Books.

Harcourt, B. and J. Ludwig. (2006). "Broken Windows: New Evidence from New York City and a Five-City Experiment." University of Chicago Law Review 73: 271–320.

Harcourt, B. and D. Thacher. (2005). "Is Broken Windows Policing Broken?" Legal Affairs October 17–21: 1–18. http://www.legalaffairs.org/ webexclusive/debateclub_broken windows1005. msp (accessed December 4, 2014).

Hartmann, F., S. Michaelson and G. Chen. (1994). Perspectives on Policing: A Survey of Its Readership. Cambridge, MA: Harvard Kennedy School, Program in Criminal Justice Policy and Management.

Hickman, M. and B. Reaves. (2001). Community Policing in Local Police Departments, 1997 and 1999. Washington, DC: U.S. Department of Justice.

Kansas City Police Department. (1978). Response Time Analysis: Executive Summary. Washington, DC: U.S. Department of Justice.

Keitzer, K., S. Lindenberg and L. Steg. (2008). "The Spreading of Disorder." *Science* 322: 1681–1685.

Kelling, G. (1988). "Police and Communities: The Quiet Revolution." Perspectives on Policing (No. 1). Washington, DC: U.S. Department of Justice, National Institute of Justice.

Kelling, G. and C. Coles (1996). Fixing Broken Windows: Restoring Order and Reducing Crime in Our Communities. New York: Free Press.

Kelling, G. and M.H. Moore. (1988). The Evolving Strategy of Policing. Perspectives on Policing Bulletin (No. 4). Washington, DC: U.S. Department of Justice, National Institute of Justice.

Kelling, G., T. Pate, D. Dieckman and C. Brown. (1974). The Kansas City Preventive Patrol Experiment: A Technical Report. Washington, DC: Police Foundation.

Kelling, G. and W. Sousa. (2001). Do Police Matter? An Analysis of the Impact of New York City's Police Reforms (Civic Report No. 22). New York: Manhattan Institute.

Kennedy, D.M. (1997). "Pulling Levers: Chronic Offenders, High-Crime Settings, and a Theory of Prevention." Valparaiso University Law Review 31: 449–484.

Kennedy, D. M. (2008). Deterrence and Crime Prevention. New York: Routledge.

Kennedy, D. M., A.M. Piehl and A.A. Braga. (1996). "Youth Violence in Boston: Gun Markets, Serious Youth Offenders, and a Use-Reduction Strategy." Law and Contemporary Problems 59: 147–197.

Kleck, G. and J. Barnes. (2014). "Do More Police Lead to More Crime Deterrence?" *Crime & Delinquency* 60: 716–738.

LaGrange, R., K. Ferraro and M. Supancic. (1992). "Perceived Risk and Fear of Crime: Role of Social and Physical Incivilities." *Journal of Research in Crime and Delinquency* 29: 311–334.

Levitt, S. (2004). "Understanding Why Crime Fell in the 1990s: Four Factors that Explain the Decline and Six That Do Not." *Journal of Economic Perspectives* 18: 163–190.

Lum, C., C. Koper and C. Telep. (2011). "The Evidence-Based Policing Matrix." Journal of Experimental Criminology 7: 3–26.

Mazerolle, L., E. Antrobus, S. Bennett and T. Tyler. (2013). "Shaping Citizen Perceptions of Police Legitimacy: A Randomized Field Trial of Procedural Justice." *Criminology* 51: 33–63.

Meares, T.L. (2015). Rightful Policing. New Perspectives in Policing Bulletin. Washington, DC: U.S. Department of Justice, National Institute of Justice.

Messner, S., S. Galea, K. Tardiff, M. Tracy, A. Bucciarelli, T. Markhan Piper, V. Frye and D. Vlahov (2007). "Policing, Drugs, and the Homicide Decline in New York City in the 1990s." *Criminology* 45: 385–414.

Moore, M.H. and M.A.R. Kleiman. (1989). The Police and Drugs. Perspectives on Policing Bulletin (No. 11). Washington, DC: U.S. Department of Justice, National Institute of Justice.

Moore, M.H. and R. Trojanowicz. (1988). Policing and the Fear of Crime. Perspectives on Policing Bulletin (No. 3). Washington, DC: U.S. Department of Justice, National Institute of Justice.

Moore, M.H., R. Trojanowicz and G. Kelling. (1988). Crime and Policing. Perspectives on Policing Bulletin (No. 2). Washington, DC: U.S. Department of Justice, National Institute of Justice.

Nagin, D. (2013). "Deterrence in the Twenty-First Century." In M. Tonry (ed.), Crime and Justice: A Review of Research (Vol. 42). Chicago: University of Chicago Press.

National Advisory Commission on Civil Disorders. (1968). Report of the National Advisory Commission on Civil Disorders. Washington, DC: U.S. Government Printing Office.

O'Connor, S. T. and A. Grant (eds.). (1998). Problem-Oriented Policing: Crime-Specific Problems, Critical Issues, and Making POP Work. Washington, DC: Police Executive Research Forum.

Papachristos, A.V., A.A. Braga and D.M. Hureau. (2012). "Social Networks and the Risk of Gunshot Injury." *Journal of Urban Health* 89: 992–1003.

Papachristos, A.V., D.M. Hureau and A.A. Braga. (2013). "The Corner and the Crew: The Influence of Geography and Social Networks on Gang Violence." *American Sociological Review* 78: 417–447.

Pate, A., W. Skogan, M.A. Wycoff and L. Sherman. (1986). Reducing Fear of Crime in Houston and Newark: A Summary Report. Washington, DC: Police Foundation.

Petrosino, A., R. Boruch, H. Soydan, L. Duggan and J. Sanchez-Meca. (2001). "Meeting the Challenge of Evidence-Based Policy: The Campbell Collaboration. *Annals of the American Academy of Political and Social Science* 578: 14–34.

Pierce, G.L., S. Spaar and L. Briggs. (1988). The Character of Police Work: Strategic and Tactical Implications. Boston: Center for Applied Social Research.

Police Executive Research Forum. (2008). Violent Crime in America: What We Know About Hot Spots Enforcement. Washington, DC: Police Executive Research Forum.

Police Foundation. (1981). The Newark Foot Patrol Experiment. Washington, DC: Police Foundation.

President's Commission on Law Enforcement and Administration of Criminal Justice (1967a). The Challenge of Crime in a Free Society. Washington, DC: U.S. Government Printing Office.

President's Commission on Law Enforcement and Administration of Criminal Justice (1967b). Task Force Report: The Police. Washington, DC: U.S. Government Printing Office.

Reiss, A. and J. Roth (eds.). (1993). *Understanding and Preventing Violence*. Washington, DC: National Academies Press.

Rosenfeld, R., R. Fornango and E. Baumer. (2005). "Did Ceasefire, Compstat, and Exile Reduce Homicide?" *Criminology & Public Policy* 4: 419–450.

Scott, M. (2000). Problem-Oriented Policing: Reflections on the First 20 Years. Washington, DC: U.S. Department of Justice, Office of Community Oriented Policing Services.

Shadish, W., T. Cook and D. Campbell. (2002). Experimental and Quasi-Experimental Designs for Generalized Causal Inference. Belmont, CA: Wadsworth.

Sherman, L. (1991). "Herman Goldstein: Problem-Oriented Policing." Book review. *Journal of Criminal Law and Criminology* 82: 693–702.

Sherman, L. (1992). "Attacking Crime: Police and Crime Control." In M. Tonry and N. Morris (eds.), Modern Policing. *Crime and Justice Series* (Vol. 15). Chicago: University of Chicago Press.

Sherman, L., P. Gartin and M. Buerger. (1989). "Hot Spots of Predatory Crime: Routine Activities and the Criminology of Place." *Criminology* 27: 27–56.

Sherman, L. and D. Rogan. (1995). "Effects of Gun Seizures on Gun Violence: 'Hot Spots' Patrol in Kansas City." *Justice Quarterly* 12: 673–694.

Sherman, L. and D. Weisburd. (1995). "General Deterrent Effects of Police Patrol in Crime Hot Spots: A Randomized Controlled Trial." *Justice Quarterly* 12: 625–648.

Silverman, E.B. (1999). NYPD Battles Crime: Innovative Strategies in Policing. Boston: Northeastern University Press.

Sklansky, D. (2005). "Not Your Father's Police Department: Making Sense of the New Demographics of Law Enforcement." *Journal of Criminal Law and Criminology* 96: 1209–1244.

Skogan, W. (1990). Disorder and Decline: Crime and the Spiral of Decay in American Neighborhoods. New York: Free Press.

Skogan, W. (2006). Police and Community in Chicago: *A Tale of Three Cities*. New York: Oxford University Press.

Skogan, W. and G. Antunes. (1979). "Information, Apprehension, and Deterrence: Exploring the Limits of Police Productivity." *Journal of Criminal Justice* 7: 217–242.

Skogan, W. and K. Frydl (eds.). (2004). Fairness and Effectiveness in Policing: The Evidence. Committee to Review Research on Police Policy and Practices. Committee on Law and Justice, Division of Behavioral and Social Sciences and Education. Washington, DC: National Academies Press.

Skogan, W. and S. Hartnett. (1997). Community Policing, Chicago Style. New York: Oxford University Press.

Skolnick, J.H. and D. Bayley. (1986). The New Blue Line: Police Innovations in American Cities. New York: Free Press.

Sole Brito, C. and T. Allan (eds.). (1999). Problem-Oriented Policing: Crime-Specific Problems, Critical Issues, and Making POP Work (Vol. 2). Washington, DC: Police Executive Research Forum.

Sole Brito, C. and E. Gratto (eds.). (2000). Problem-Oriented Policing: Crime-Specific Problems, Critical Issues, and Making POP Work (Vol. 3). Washington, DC: Police Executive Research Forum.

Sousa, W. and G.L. Kelling. (2006). "Of 'Broken Windows,' Criminology, and Criminal Justice." In D.L. Weisburd and A.A. Braga (eds.), Police Innovation: Contrasting Perspectives. New York: Cambridge University Press.

Sparrow, M. (2009). One Week in Heron City (Parts A and B). New Perspectives in Policing Bulletin. Washington, DC: U.S. Department of Justice, National Institute of Justice.

Sparrow, M. (2011). Governing Science. New Perspectives in Policing Bulletin. Washington, DC: U.S. Department of Justice, National Institute of Justice.

Sparrow, M. (2014). Managing the Boundary Between Public and Private Policing. New Perspectives in Policing Bulletin. Washington, DC: U.S. Department of Justice, National Institute of Justice.

Sparrow, M. (2015). Measuring Performance in a Modern Police Organization. New Perspectives in Policing Bulletin. Washington, DC: U.S. Department of Justice, National Institute of Justice.

Spelman, W. and D. Brown. (1984). Calling the Police: Citizen Reporting of Serious Crime. Research Report. Washington, DC: U.S. Department of Justice, National Institute of Justice.

Travis, J., R. Davis and S. Lawrence. (2012). Exploring the Role of the Police in Prisoner Reentry. New Perspectives in Policing Bulletin. Washington, DC: U.S. Department of Justice, National Institute of Justice.

Trojanowicz, R. (1983). "An Evaluation of a Neighborhood Foot Patrol Program." *Journal of Police Science and Administration* 11: 410–419.

Tyler, T.R. (2006). Why People Obey the Law: Procedural Justice, Legitimacy, and Compliance (rev. ed.). Princeton, NJ: Princeton University Press.

Walker, S. (1992). The Police in America (2nd ed.). New York: McGraw-Hill.

Wallman, J. and A. Blumstein. (2006). "After the Crime Drop." In A. Blumstein and J. Wallman (eds.), The Crime Drop in America (rev. ed.). New York: Cambridge University Press.

Weisburd, D.L. (2008). Place Based Policing. Ideas in American Policing Series (No. 9). Washington, DC: Police Foundation.

Weisburd, D.L. and A.A. Braga. (eds.). (2006). Police Innovation: Contrasting Perspectives. New York: Cambridge University Press.

Weisburd, D.L. and J. Eck. (2004). "What Can Police Do to Reduce Crime, Disorder, and Fear?" *Annals of the American Academy of Political and Social Science* 593: 42–65.

Weisburd, D.L., S. Mastrofski, A.M. McNally, R. Greenspan and J. Willis. (2003). "Reforming to Preserve: Compstat and Strategic Problem Solving in American Policing." *Criminology & Public Policy* 2: 421–457.

Weisburd, D.L. and P. Neyroud. (2011). Police Science: Toward a New Paradigm. New Perspectives in Policing Bulletin. Washington, DC: U.S. Department of Justice, National Institute of Justice.

Weisburd, D., C. Telep, J. Hinkle and J. Eck. (2010). "Is Problem Oriented Policing Effective in Reducing Crime and Disorder?" *Criminology & Public Policy* 9: 139–172.

Weisburd, D.L., C. Telep and B. Lawton. (2014). "Could Innovations in Policing Have Contributed to the New York City Crime Drop Even in a Period of Declining Police Strength?: The Case of Stop, Question and Frisk as a Hot Spots Policing Strategy." *Justice Quarterly* 31: 129–153.

Weisburd, D.L. and C. Uchida. (1993). "Raising Questions of Law and Order." In D. Weisburd and C. Uchida (eds.), Police Innovation and Control of the Police: Problems of Law, Order, and Community. New York: Springer-Verlag.

Wellford, C., J. Pepper and C. Petrie (eds.). (2005). Firearms and Violence: A Critical Review. Committee to Improve Research Information and Data on Firearms. Committee on Law and Justice, Division of Behavioral and Social Sciences and Education. Washington, DC: National Academies Press.

Wilson, J.Q. and G. Kelling. (1982). "Broken Windows: The Police and Neighborhood Safety." *Atlantic Monthly* (March): 29–38.

Wilson, J.Q. and G. Kelling. (1989). "Making Neighborhoods Safe." *Atlantic Monthly* (February): 46–52.

Wilson, O.W. and R. McLaren. (1977). Police Administration (4th ed.). New York: McGraw-Hill.

Zimring, F.E. (2007). *The Great American Crime Decline*. New York: Oxford University Press.

Zimring, F.E. (2012). *The City That Became Safe: New York's Lessons for Urban Crime and Its Control*. New York: Oxford University Press.

AUTHOR NOTE

Anthony A. Braga, Ph.D., is the Don M. Gottfredson Professor of Evidence-Based Criminology at Rutgers University and a Senior Research Fellow in the Program in Criminal Justice Policy and Management at Harvard University.

End Notes

[1] Although correlations between disorder and crime have been consistently observed, the available research evidence on the causal connections between disorder and more serious crime is mixed. For instance, using systematic social observation data to capture social and physical incivilities on the streets of Chicago, Sampson and Raudenbush (1999) found that, with the exception of robbery, public disorder did not lead to more serious crime when neighborhood characteristics such as poverty, stability, race and collective efficacy were considered. However, in the Netherlands, Keitzer, Lindenberg and Steg (2008) conducted six field experiments examining the links between disorder and more serious crime. They concluded that dealing with disorderly conditions was an important intervention to halt the spread of further crime and disorder.

[2] Uniform Crime Report (UCR) data were gathered from the annual Crime in the United States report and from the FBI's UCR website at http://www.fbi.gov/about-us/cjis/ucr/ucr.

[3] Much of this debate has centered on whether the New York City Police Department (NYPD) can claim any credit for reductions in violent crime in New York City. Many nonexperimental analyses have found statistically significant associations between the NYPD policing disorder strategy and decreased violent crime, with effects ranging from modest (Rosenfeld, Fornango and Rengifo, 2007; Messner et al., 2007; Cerda et al., 2009; Chauhan et al., 2011) to large (Kelling and Sousa, 2001; Corman and Mocan, 2002). However, Harcourt and Ludwig (2006) and Greenberg (2014) report no statistically significant violence reduction impacts associated with the NYPD strategy. Even though this body of evidence seems to suggest that the NYPD policing disorder strategy may have impacted violence reduction, the magnitude of effects remains unclear. Given the uncertainties associated with determining causal effects in nonexperimental research designs that use proxy measures (such as the number of misdemeanor arrests) to examine innovative police strategies, it is doubtful that a definitive conclusion will ever be reached by social scientists on the New York crime-drop puzzle (Braga and Bond, 2008; Braga, Welsh and Schnell, 2015).

[4] http://cebcp.org/evidence-based-policing/the-matrix.

In: Perspectives on Policing
Editor: Holly Wheeler
ISBN: 978-1-63484-555-7

Chapter 2

TOWARD A PROFESSION OF POLICE LEADERSHIP*

Edward A. Flynn and Victoria Herrington

INTRODUCTION

Policing has changed in recent years and continues to evolve. Police agencies must contend with new threats, new technologies, new crimes and new communities, all of which create new challenges and opportunities for policing. The public's expectations have changed, and the public safety arena now includes more stakeholders with whom police must work to tackle some of the endemic and complex issues facing communities. As a result, leading police organizations has changed, too. Police leaders are increasingly expected to run efficient businesses that effectively prevent as well as investigate crime. Thus, the skill sets required of police leaders in shaping their organizations today differ greatly from those required 20 years ago.

Although pockets of good practice in police leader development are seen across the nation, the ability of the policing profession to translate these isolated successes into more effective leadership in general is debatable. Most departments continue to view leadership as a "property" of the individual rather than the organization and, therefore, attempts to develop better functioning organizations rest heavily on "improving" individuals. Little attention is given to the system in which the leader operates or to how individuals can create and distribute a climate of leadership throughout a police organization. This — we argue in this paper — limits the innovation that is possible in a police organization, as it reinforces the role of the leader as the individual with all the answers. There are missed opportunities in this, given the complexity of the policing environment as it has evolved, and only by addressing these opportunities can law enforcement organizations hope to meet the challenges they face. Articulating what we hope to achieve through leadership, and how we might better develop and support the qualities that will allow police organizations to reach these goals, allows us to move farther toward a profession of police leadership.

---

* This is an edited, reformatted and augmented version of a paper, NCJ 248573, in the New Perspectives in Policing series, issued by the U.S. Department of Justice, National Institute of Justice, June 2015.

What Is Leadership?

It is a truism that there are as many definitions of leadership as there are people asked to define it, and it is apparent that leadership — and good leadership in particular — means different things to different people (Northouse, 2013). Many theories guide the understanding of leadership, and thinking has evolved from the "great man" theories of classical leadership (e.g., Sun Tzu circa 400-320 B.C.) to a greater appreciation that leadership requires collaboration between groups of individuals operating in systems. We now talk about leaders as being transformative or servant in their approaches and their relationships with (and influence over) their followers as paramount. However, the focus on the individual characteristics of leaders remains strong (Grint, 2011). An understanding of the environment in which leaders operate is lacking.

The Changed Environment of Policing

Policing is both complicated and complex. A complicated environment has many moving parts that operate systematically and require a high level of coordination. This characterizes many of the day-to-day activities of police work, from responding to immediate threats to public order to the investigation and prosecution of cases. Complicated environments have known — if complicated — solutions and respond to well-thought-out standard operating procedures. A complex environment, on the other hand, involves multiple interacting and diverse elements, which create a setting that is not clearly defined (Uhl-Bien, Marion and McKelvey, 2007) and may lead to unintended consequences (Sargut and McGrath, 2011). Responding to complex environments requires new learning, innovation and different ways of doing things. Standard operating procedures have little relevance because the environment calls for exploration, new discoveries and adjustments (Uhl-Bien, Marion and McKelvey, 2007). The organization needs to learn its way out of its problems (Day, 2000).

Much of what occupies police time can be regarded as complex. It is often said that the police are the first responders to a whole range of social issues (Bittner, 1990/2005). Although police may not be statutorily responsible for fixing those problems, there is incentive for them to do so when those problems lead to a rise in crime and a reduction in actual or perceived public safety, the metrics against which police performance is generally measured (Millie and Herrington, 2014). Such social problems involve a range of factors that are more appropriately dealt with upstream, and to prevent crime, police need to engage with other agents to collectively solve complex social ills. We argue that complicated problems (e.g., public (dis)order, crowd control, and investigating crime) require something more akin to management and ensuring that established processes are followed. Complex problems, however, call for true leadership, which might be defined as using one's ability to influence groups and systems to address complex needs.

Although leadership models and development approaches generated to support organizational activity that was grounded in physical production may have been helpful during the last century, they are not well-suited to a complex modern policing environment (Uhl-Bien, Marion and McKelvey, 2007). Modern policing organizations need to recognize the importance of the leader as an enabler of the learning, innovation and adaptation required rather than the top-down bureaucratic administrator of technical fixes to well-known problems (Uhl-Bien, Marion, and McKelvey, 2007). Heifetz, Grashow and Linsky (2009b) note that leaders most commonly fail by treating leadership problems with management solutions. This is particularly tempting, as management problems — even complicated ones — have a known solution or set of solutions. A leader can rely on using his or her authoritative expertise to get the job done: The answer is known, and the leader's role in this is to encourage others to apply the "fix" effectively. Where issues are complex and only a group that has learned new ways of operating can tackle them, leaders need to experiment and engage with stakeholders rather than simply apply technical and authoritative expertise. Because complex problems do not have straightforward answers, leaders do not necessarily have the answer, and they achieve nothing by using their authority to dictate what should be done. "Faking expertise" in complex environments can be counterproductive. In Schafer's (2009) review of the FBI's National Academy development program for midcareer police supervisors, he noted that participants expressed the belief that leaders "[f]eeling like [they] have the answers and are always right" inhibited effective leadership (Schafer, 2009: 249). Our own experience working with police leaders across the world tells us that leaders feel pressure to use their technical expertise to try to solve complex problems. Members of police organizations continue to expect that the person with the most pips, crowns, bars or stars on his or her shoulder will be in a position to tell the rest of the group what to do (Heifetz, Grashow and Linsky, 2009a). Police leaders find this expectation hard to resist because authoritative expertise has most often been rewarded by promotion through the ranks of the organization. As such, even if leaders accept that they do not always have the answers, they arguably feel an immense pressure to proceed as if they do.

The Consequences of Using Authoritative Expertise Instead of Leadership

Evidence shows that giving in to the temptation to treat authoritative expertise as a substitute for leadership is counterproductive for police organizations and for public safety in general. A study from the U.K. compared one force's strategic plans between 1997 and 2009 to identify whether its strategic priorities had changed during that time (Marnoch, Topping and Boyd, 2014). The authors concluded that, instead of dealing with new problems, the strategic plans repackaged unsolved problems and recycled solutions across the years. Another, as yet unpublished, analysis of the minutes from the Australia and New Zealand Police Commissioners' Forum from 1920 to the present demonstrated remarkable similarity in issues across the years (G. Ashton, personal communication, March 12, 2014). That problems have not been "solved" suggests that, instead of using leadership and learning new ways of doing things, police organizations have continued to administer the same authoritative and technical (and ineffectual) fixes to complex problems. Marnoch, Topping and Boyd (2014) concluded that this reflected a constrained form of decision-making that did not consider all options. To say the same thing another way, for the leaders in this force (and perhaps many others), when all you have is a hammer, everything looks like a nail.

Reframing Leadership and Its Development

If the solutions to complex problems lie in galvanizing stakeholders to think about and deal with things differently rather than exercising authoritative expertise, then we can perhaps best characterize true leadership as an emergent, interactive dynamic between individuals working in networks to produce new patterns of behavior or new modes of operating (Uhl-Bien, Marion and McKelvey, 2007). Leadership is not simply the work of an individual but a process that individuals within an organization engage in. Leaders are those who act to influence this dynamic (Uhl-Bien, Marion and McKelvey, 2007; Day, 2011; Iles and Preace, 2006). This has significant implications for our approach to leader and leadership development. Instead of treating leadership as the property of the leader, with individual enhancements resulting in hoped-for benefits to the organization, developing leadership must focus on creating social capital within an organization (Edmonstone, 2011). Instead of sending individuals to courses to make them better leaders, we must improve leadership as an activity in the organizational system (Bolden and Kirk, 2006; Edmonstone, 2011; Ylitalo et al., 2006). This requires a move away from investing only in those at the top of the organization who have authority roles to recognizing the importance of (informal) leaders dispersed throughout the police force. It necessitates a very different approach to developing police leaders from that currently available across much of the U.S. In essence, we are talking about supporting the development of learning organizations.

LEADERSHIP AND THE LEARNING ORGANIZATION

In learning organizations, "people continually expand their capacity to create the results they truly desire, where new and expansive patterns of thinking are nurtured, collective aspiration is set free, and people are continually learning how to learn together" (Senge, 1990: 3; Davie and Nutley, 2000). The development of learning organizations is facilitated by a recognition that learning is an investment that improves actions and performance, that learning is appreciated (and measured) by customers and client groups, and that being focused on staff engagement and wellbeing benefits this end (Shipton, Zhou and Mooi, 2013). Challenging existing ways of doing things is key, and fostering the learning of staff members is a central strategic goal (Shipton, Zhou and Mooi, 2013; Yeo, 2005), even though this collective learning may be slower to achieve (Campbell and Armstrong, 2013). Stone and Travis (2011), in an earlier paper in this series, saw learning new ways of doing things (innovation as experimentation) as one of the four planks of a new professionalism (the other three are accountability, legitimacy and national coherence). Although this might be difficult for police departments to achieve, this learning is how policing can elevate itself from a trade to a profession. However, such innovation can be dangerous. Mitzberg, Ahlstrand and Lempel (1998) argue that an organization that values innovation must also be tolerant of mistakes and willing to celebrate and learn from errors as well as successes. We do not believe that this characterizes most police departments, although there is evidence from overseas that policing and learning organizations need not be mutually exclusive (Filstad and Gottschalk, 2011).

There is something of a chicken-and-egg dilemma about creating learning organizations. Organizational cultures that facilitate collective learning are supported by formal leaders who value a distributed leadership approach, but such leaders can only be developed within a culture that values organizational learning and shared leadership. The role for the formal leader is in setting a climate in which employees can continuously expand their capacity to learn, understand complexity and set the vision for the organization (Dalakoura, 2010). For this to happen within existing leader development paradigms, organizations need to equip formal leaders with an understanding of leadership, as reliant on more than their individual roles, and create a climate conducive to such an understanding. The question is: how much of a refocus of existing leader development programs and organizational culture would this involve?

Developing Leaders, Leadership and Learning Organizations

Moving from Training to Developing Police Leaders

We make a deliberate distinction between development and training. Training suggests that there are certain knowns that a leader must have, and that there are proven solutions to identified problems. Development, on the other hand, embraces the goal of building capacity to respond to a range of unknown and unforeseen problems (Day, 2011). Given our previous discussions around the complexity of the police leadership environment, it stands to reason that we endorse a development rather than a training approach. The leadership-learning literature is evolving, but we actually know very little about what works in police leadership and its development. Much of what we know about police leadership is based on limited observations, small case studies, "and anecdotal accounts of 'celebrity' chiefs" (Schafer, 2009: 239; Pearson-Goff and Herrington, 2014; Neyroud, 2010; Kodz and Campbell, 2010; Campbell and Kodz, 2011), all of which invariably focus on the individual leader rather than leadership. As we attempt to articulate an approach to leadership development, we must be careful not to unconsciously revert to type and simply construct a technical-skills-based system. What we know is that, in moving toward being learning organizations, police departments need to consciously capture and develop the collective thinking of organizational competency programs for leaders.

The process used to develop police leaders across the U.S. tends to be ad hoc. U.S. policing invests heavily in tactical and operational training and uses the U.S. Constitution as a text for governing activities. The police profession then provides and prioritizes training throughout the police officer's career to respond to high-liability issues such as use of force or response to domestic violence, with more tailored training in operational excellence in specialty units such as organized crime, narcotics, gangs or violent crime investigation. Although this training is generally regarded as good quality and important for successful police work, it is technical and does not focus on developing leaders or supporting leadership.

Leader development emerges at the more senior (largely captain or lieutenant) ranks as officers move into management positions and, through those, into executive leadership roles. Police agencies offer or sponsor some leadership development opportunities, but individual officers committed to their own advancement and growth seek other opportunities.

Leadership in Police Organizations

With funding from the Office of Community Oriented Policing Services, the International Association of Chiefs of Police adapted a leadership course taught at the United States Military Academy at West Point (N.Y.) for use in law enforcement agencies, now entitled "Leadership in Police Organizations." In 2001, the Arlington County (Va.) Police Department operated as a pilot site for LPO. At the time, the chief reasoned that traditional chain-ofcommand formulations had relegated police officers to the role of "privates," not "officers." This drove entry-level training and supervisory practices and belied that first-line officers operate in a leadership role in every sense of the word. Officers routinely exercise decisional authority in complex, ambiguous circumstances, under pressure, with insufficient information. And they must do so in a way that is fair, impartial, and perceived to be so. This requires leadership ability. The formal leaders of the organization must also have a firm grasp of management and leadership principles if they are to credibly guide the organization. The future of the organization and the profession depends on the caliber of leaders developed within police agencies, as the great majority of formal leaders come from the ranks.

At the Arlington pilot site, leadership was defined as the process of influencing human behavior to achieve organizational goals that serve the public while developing individuals, groups and the organization for future service. The three-week course focused on behavioral science, leadership theories, understanding group formation, human motivation, concepts of followership, and the practical application of these concepts to the workplace. LPO was taught primarily to classes of officers from several agencies who would return to their own departments with enhanced skills and new networks.

Milwaukee is another police department that has embraced the LPO program as part of a wider range of operational and technological changes designed to improve the department's performance. This agency had been managed in a traditional, risk-averse manner; however, a generational shift in the junior- and middle-management ranks indicated receptiveness to positive change. LPO slotted neatly into this.

In Milwaukee, rather than providing training to improve individuals' skills and then sending learners back to a perhaps unwelcoming status quo, a vertical slice approach is used to generate a mixed group of ranks. Group discussions elicit different viewpoints and perspectives about the same topic. The stated goals of LPO in Milwaukee are that every department member (sworn and nonsworn) should have a shared understanding of organizational development, group behavior and human motivation; enhanced leadership skills and a common vocabulary to help solve conflict in the workplace; and a network of similarly minded colleagues. LPO's mixed-rank structure gives class members the opportunity to forge connections with officers of different ranks, with whom they can form mentoring relationships and from whom they can seek advice outside the formal chain of command. In this way, leadership, formal and informal, is truly dispersed throughout the organization, and the approach develops not just individuals but networks of individuals who can operate better within the organization. Excellent leadership cannot flourish in a dysfunctional culture but, if dispersed widely enough, it can create a new one.

Either way, the executive-in-training often has to aggressively seek out such opportunities rather than wait to be prepared for advancement by the profession or the police agency.

Highly regarded programs and schools that provide leader development opportunities for mid- and senior-level managers include the University of Louisville's Southern Police Institute, Northwestern University's Center for Public Safety, and Johns Hopkins University's Division of Public Safety Leadership. In addition, the FBI National Academy, the Police Executive Research Forum, and individual organizations utilizing the International Association of Chiefs of Police's Leadership in Police Organizations (LPO) course (see sidebar, "Leadership in Police Organizations") offer opportunities specifically for police leadership development. The wide availability of programs hints at a wide variety of views about what such programs should contain. Academic literature can provide some sense of what police leaders need, although the quality of the research on which such findings are based is often questionable, being largely based on perceptions rather than objective measures. There remains no objective assessment of what is needed from senior police executives (Pearson-Goff and Herrington, 2013; Schafer, 2009). This content becomes even more difficult to agree on when we consider the demands of the complex environment and what is needed to develop leadership, not just better technical leaders. Policing tends to rely on developing individual competencies to address organizational problems (McGurk, 2010), but there is an important, although subtle, distinction between training for competencies and developing for capability. Competence involves telling people what knowledge and skills they need, whereas capability involves equipping individuals to adapt, generate new knowledge and continually learn (Fraser and Greenhalgh, 2001). Clearly, developing capability lends itself more readily to supporting leadership and learning organizations, although much leader development remains preoccupied with the technical knowledge and skills required of those at particular ranks. Although it is certainly important for effective management practices, this training does not develop leaders.

Of course, even those programs of study more closely aligned with developing leader capability are only part of the story in developing distributed leadership and organizational capability to deal with complexity. Yet, in law enforcement in the United States and worldwide, the leader, rather than the system, is the focus of development, and little is made of the organizations to which transformed leaders return (Day, 2011; Bolden and Kirk, 2006; Edmonstone, 2011). Developing individuals is important, but if it is the exclusive focus of an organization's attempts to generate leadership, it neglects the bulk of leadership capacity that resides in the rest of the organization as well as the importance of situation and context in achieving goals (Bolden and Kirk, 2006).

Moving from Developing Police Leaders to Developing Learning Organizations

Some development opportunities, such as LPO, promote leadership at all levels of the police organization by bringing multiple ranks of officers together (in Milwaukee, the ranks of captain, lieutenant, sergeant, detective and officer are routinely found in LPO classes). Although these programs still focus on the individual leader, they acknowledge that leadership happens as part of a larger system which is explored in the classroom (see sidebar,

"Leadership in Police Organizations," on page 7). This contrasts with most other leader development opportunities, which group individuals of similar ranks together to develop their skills away from the workplace. Although there are good reasons for this in hierarchical organizations (where dissent in front of the boss may end a career), this compounds the already individual focus of the development and limits the availability of a realistic, multiranked context in which to practice one's skills (Bolden and Kirk, 2006; Edmonstone, 2011). To the best of our knowledge, LPO has not been formally evaluated, although it is well-regarded by senior officers across a range of jurisdictions (Rosser, 2013). It would be interesting to see if such multilevel programs result in better leadership outcomes than programs that focus only on a small group of rank-peers drawn from across agencies.

Leader development — even that which recognizes leadership in a system — does not automatically give rise to the development of learning organizations. Formal leaders have a role to play here through embracing and valuing organizational learning, but development must target the organization, too (Yeo, 2005). Yang, Watkins and Marsick 2004 provide a three-level structure for a development approach that targets:

- Individual learning through engaging in continuous learning, dialogue and inquiry.
- Group-level learning through teams learning together and collaborating.
- Organizational learning, developing learning-supportive systems, empowering staff, and providing leadership around learning.

Leadership and the development of learning organizations clearly rely on more than traditional classroom learning and require multiple well-coordinated activities to develop employees and the system in which they operate (Dalakoura, 2010). Dixon (1993) provides further insights into what such a development program might look like, describing it as:

- Located in the realities of day-to-day work, not away from them.
- Focused less on experts telling leaders what they should do.
- Allowing longer time frames for "learning."
- Focused on community and organizational learning rather than individual outcomes.

Development needs to be embedded in the workplace, grounded in an environment where individuals share their knowledge with coworkers, and based on an organizational structure that supports collaborative learning (Ortenblad, 2004). These underlying principles require a longitudinal, rather than a snapshot, approach to individual development; place those in the system (rather than the experts at the front of a classroom) in the central role; and support individuals in transforming their learning into workplace action. The term "action learning sets" has been used to describe such an approach and can be used to galvanize learning around a particular issue. For example, a vertical slice of formal and informal leaders in an organization, including those from external agencies, might be brought together (such as in the case of the LPO program) to collectively think about and address a specific problem. Such action learning sets allow for stretching conversations to identify and explore systemic tensions and dilemmas intrinsic to the problem, emphasizing reflection and review. This approach helps build social capital by encouraging people to understand how to relate to others, coordinate their efforts, build commitments and develop extended social networks

(Edmonstone, 2011). The key features of this approach are less about organizational structure and more about how people within the organization think about the relationships between the outside world, their organization, their colleagues and themselves (Davie and Nutley, 2000). Structures become more fluid, and a greater breadth and depth of resources (inside and outside of the organization) are available to deal with concerns. This is the real work for formal police leaders: encouraging their organization to change its values, its established hierarchical practices, and its culture to better prepare itself to meet the challenges ahead — which cannot be achieved by using authority alone (Heifetz and Laurie, 1997). The net result of this work is the development of organizational leadership and, in turn, learning organizations.

The 70:20:10 Framework for Leadership Development

Some workplaces are seeking to support leadership development through the 70:20:10 framework. Although it is still focused on the individual, this framework contextualizes individual learning in the workplace environment and, in doing so, facilitates an organizational shift in thinking about leadership - from regarding it as an individual attribute to viewing it as an organizational commodity. The 70:20:10 approach — based on the work of McCall, Eichineger and Lombardo at the Center for Creative Leadership (Kajewski and Madsen, 2012; Jennings, 2013) — posits that 70 percent of the learning an individual does occurs at work, through stretch assignments, projects and day-to-day experiences; 20 percent occurs through networks and, in particular, through being coached and mentored by peers and more senior staff; and 10 percent occurs through formal schooling opportunities outside the office. Of course, it is the 10 percent that has characterized much of what we know as leader development, and few approaches hold the organization to account for nurturing the 90 percent of development that occurs outside the classroom. That 70 percent of learning occurs through daily work means that if an organization does not create an environment in which individuals can reflect, experiment and adapt, a significant opportunity is lost. This 70 percent does not necessarily need to be structured, although the individual is undoubtedly aided by a better understanding of his or her own learning objectives and actively seeking out opportunities to meet these. Instead, the 70 percent relies heavily on the latent culture of the organization, and the nurturing of learning in line with the characteristics of a learning organization. There are undoubtedly challenges here for policing, with a fast-paced operational life leaving little opportunity for such significant cultural shifts, unless these are undertaken consciously. For an example of the 70:20:10 framework, see the sidebar, "The Australia and New Zealand Police Leadership Strategy."

CHALLENGES TO DEVELOPING LEARNING ORGANIZATIONS

We have already said that, whereas the right organization will support the right sort of leader development approach, the right sort of leader (and leadership) development is also required to give the organization a fighting chance of developing into a learning organization. This is where formal leaders — chiefs and their senior staff — have to lead by example and clear the cultural obstacles that stifle the values inherent in organizational learning. Some of these obstacles are personal and ego-related. It is challenging for a chief to acknowledge that he or she does not have a monopoly on the good ideas that will take the organization forward. But acknowledging that they do not have all the answers and leading from the front in this way is — paradoxically — the sort of authority-laden action required of formal leaders to signal a shift in approach and provide the space required to encourage collective and shared leadership (Jones, 2014). Of course, chiefs tend to become chiefs precisely because they have good ideas, and they are held to account by their political masters to enact these good ideas. It is therefore risky to one's career to admit that others may have better ideas, lest one be replaced. Importantly, also, such culture change is a long-term project, the fruits of which may only be realized after a chief's tenure ends. Buy-in to such an approach across the profession is needed to ensure that when one chief leaves, his or her replacement is more likely to be aware of (and sympathetic toward) the leadership work in progress and to continue to support this work rather than reverting to a traditional technocratic, bureaucratic and authoritarian approach. This is why agreement on what we mean by a profession of police leadership is so important: to protect an organization from lurching back and forth between the ideologies of individual chiefs. When that happens, the opportunity for the longer term development of organizational leadership and a culture of learning may be lost.

Other values inherent to learning organizations can be challenging for police departments to reconcile (Mintzberg, Ahlstrand and Lampel, 1998). We have noted the difficulties police organizations face in tolerating and learning from mistakes. Typically, mistakes lead the pendulum of risk appetite to swing to the extreme, and internal and external calls for bureaucratic safeguards are heeded and applied. Individuals are found at fault, and a culture of blame overtakes any deep and meaningful learning that might be found. Arguably, police departments face a similar problem when learning from their successes. Police culture values individual modesty and concentrating on getting the job done. Focusing heavily on a win is not always rewarded by one's peers, and valuable lessons tend not to be exploited for organizational good. Paradoxically, those seeking to make the most of successes for personal gain, through the promotion system, are rewarded for articulating their individual roles in the success rather than exploring the organizational dynamic that worked. As a result, experimentation and innovation — when they do occur, and even when they succeed — tend to remain parochial.

Police departments tend also to be inward-looking. Many promotions are made from within a department, and with this insularity comes the baggage of individual and departmental history — the good and bad — and a stifling of the diversity of ideas and experience needed to tackle problems in new and innovative ways. Mobility of staff between departments is not common, and neither is lateral entry into the management and leadership of organizations from nonpolice roles. This is starting to emerge overseas, and the U.K. is experimenting with lateral entry of nonpolice into superintendent-level positions (the U.S. rank equivalent would be commander in California, major in many state police agencies, and inspector in most northeastern police forces other than Boston's) (Winsor, 2012; Home Office, 2013). The hope is that this will bring much needed diversity to policing and, with this, diversity in how entrenched and complex policing problems are tackled.

The ledger is not entirely in the negative, however, and one factor in favor of police departments moving toward becoming learning organizations is the policing structure.

The Australia and New Zealand Police Leadership Strategy

The Australia and New Zealand Police Leadership Strategy (PLS) uses the 70:20:10 approach to blend individually focused classroom learning with action and development in the workplace. Instead of employing a traditional didactic approach to leadership development, wherein a more knowledgeable person imparts this knowledge to others, PLS focuses on sharing tacit knowledge about leadership and experimenting with new ways of operating in practice. There is no training in running meetings, setting budgets or dealing with labor contracts, although this may be added into the mix through the selection of technically focused courses to make up the 10 percent. Rather, the focus of the strategy is on exercising and building leadership in the workplace and on reflecting deeply on what true leadership means.

PLS lasts 18 months and includes five three-day workshops held at the Australian Institute of Police Management (AIPM). These workshops account for the 20 percent component and are set up as learning circles. The 10 percent of formal classroom learning and the 70 percent of workplace learning are structured through individual development plans. Individual participants develop these plans and identify what formal courses they feel they need to increase their individual technical skills as well as what workplace experiences and opportunities they require to enhance their leadership practice. There is no standard blend of activities, and participants must identify their own development goals. For some, this includes a commitment to experiment with different approaches to their leadership in the workplace, to test out new ways of doing things and monitor the results. For others, this includes seeking out opportunities to shadow the commissioner at national meetings or identifying and addressing complex organizational issues.

The learning circles (20 percent) provide a sounding board for leadership challenges for the group and an opportunity for individuals to learn and benefit from the collective wisdom of their peers. The organization assists in the development and execution of the individual development plans that structure the remaining 80 percent. If a participant requires an opportunity to experiment with leadership through a stretch project, the organization needs to support this. Similarly, the organizational hierarchy must encourage and sanction opportunities for participants to act in more senior roles (with greater duties). And, of course, applications for external classroom-based learning must be funded.

PLS is designed for aspiring commissioners, deputy commissioners and assistant commissioners from across Australasian policing and law enforcement, and the first cohort completed its 18-month involvement in mid-2014. An initial process evaluation was undertaken by the AIPM. Among other findings, this evaluation identified that the real success of the program is hard to pin down. Should retention, promotion or portability be regarded as an accurate measure of success? Or is the strategy's success better measured through qualitative and personalized means? Certainly all participants perceived a benefit from their involvement, and several have moved on to more senior roles. But it is perhaps too soon to assess whether the strategy has had its desired impact on an organization's learning culture, such that leadership is viewed as owned and nurtured by the organization as well as the individual.

This novel approach to development is not without its challenges. A key aim of the strategy was to move leader development away from a focus on classroom-based learning and empower organizations to take ownership of leadership in the workplace through the 70 percent. This departure from traditional development approaches (where individuals are sent on programs and courses and their development becomes the responsibility of the educators) can be overlooked, with aspects such as the formal workshops and learning circles becoming the strategy instead of being viewed as complementing a broader — workplace-based — approach. To say the same thing another way, organizations must not underestimate their role in building leadership and a culture of learning under a 70:20:10 framework, and a strategy such as PLS must guard against being seen as little more than another formal learning opportunity (i.e., externally provided via the 10 percent and 20 percent components). As such, it is important that, as we experiment with novel ways to develop leaders and organizational leadership, we do not inadvertently rebottle traditional approaches and undermine the bulk of development that must occur in — and be nurtured by — the organization.

Rank and discretion in most police departments are inversely related; the further one progresses through one's organization, the less freedom one has to exercise discretion. By dint of the (relatively) low level of supervisory visibility and high level of discretion experienced by most front-line police during their day-to-day work, they are encouraged to use their judgment and their tacit knowledge rather than rely entirely on the directions of others. The trick for police leaders is to permit the same freedom in decision-making and problem solving when front-line police are in the company of those of higher rank, instead of reinforcing the more natural tendency to default to authority. If we can hold on to this, we can better develop distributed organizational leadership and the learning organizations that we need.

CONCLUSION

The development of learning organizations rests on a shared approach to leadership and a commitment to ongoing organizational learning. Supporting this starts with developing leaders and their individual skill sets, but it does not end there; consideration needs to be taken of the organizational settings required for leadership to flourish and organizations to thrive. If we want true leadership in policing, then we need to support it within police organizations. And that means we need to better understand that leadership is about creating a climate in which innovation, experimentation and collaboration can flourish, valuing this, and accepting that this may be challenging. This new type of leadership requires, perhaps, a new type of chief, a new type of leadership accountability and a new type of leadership development. Rather than simply equipping individual leaders with a given set of competencies and skills to enable them to make the right decisions and do the right thing, development must encourage the creation of an environment that allows for collective learning and feeling one's way through situations. Such leadership development is part of a broader push to develop learning organizations, although we need to understand more about what it is that works here, and how police organizations and public safety can benefit.

With this in mind, we conclude this paper with two calls. First, we advocate a two-pronged approach to developing a profession of police leadership, incorporating both police leader development and leadership development to generate learning organizations. Leaders require a blend of management skills (e.g., planning, organizing, budgeting, staffing and directing), personal skills (e.g., the ability to communicate, motivate and inspire others), leadership skills (e.g., strategic focus, analytical competency and cognitive flexibility), and, in policing, a healthy dose of operational experience (still seen as the sine qua non of credibility). Leadership requires the organization to support the use of these skills to create a learning environment. No one course of study will achieve this, and it requires an individual and organizational commitment to learning. The particular challenge for U.S. law enforcement is developing both highly skilled leaders and organizational leadership coherently across the U.S. Perhaps it needs to start as a pocket of activity in one or two of the larger agencies, with flow-on benefits emanating from there. It would certainly make sense that police departments of sufficient size (e.g., the 5 percent with 100 or more staff; Reaves, 2011) think about their organizational strategy for dealing with complex problems, and how their leader and leadership development approaches contribute to this.

Our second call is for systematic research on leadership and leader development, their impact on developing learning organizations, and the net benefits of this. The established literature on police leadership is noticeably lacking in outcome-focused studies, with most research concentrating on perceptions of "good" leadership rather than objective measures (Pearson-Goff and Herrington, 2013; Schafer, 2009; Neyroud, 2010; Campbell and Kodz, 2011).

Little research has conceptualized or measured the impact of leader or leadership development on an organization, and it remains difficult to articulate the measurable outcomes that one hopes for. Are crime rates a good measure of police leadership? Is community satisfaction?

What about an assessment of the strategic position that a police organization adopts and its engagement with complex social problems? We would argue that if we are looking to identify real leadership in action, then effort and evidence of innovation throughout the organization might be better indicators than outcome success, as they indicate a willingness to experiment rather than maintain the status quo. In any case, the debate needs to continue and we need to identify ways of more meaningfully measuring leadership so that this — rather than short-term gains — is encouraged within our police organizations.

REFERENCES

Bittner, E. 1990/2005. Florence Nightingale in pursuit of Willie Sutton: A theory of the police. In Policing: Key Readings, edited by T. Newburn. Cullompton, England: Willan Publishing, pp. 150–172. (Original work published in 1990).

Bolden, R., and Kirk, P. 2006. From "leaders" to "leadership." Effective Executive, October.

Campbell, T.T., and Armstrong, S.J. 2013. A longitudinal study of individual and organizational learning. *The Learning Organization*, 20(3): 240-256.

Campbell, I., and Kodz, J. 2011. What Makes Great Police Leadership? What Research Can Tell Us About the Effectiveness of Different Leadership Styles, Competencies and Behaviours: A Rapid Evidence Review. London: National Police Improvement Agency.

Dalakoura, A. 2010. Differentiating leader and leadership development: A collective framework for leadership development. *Journal of Management Development* 29(5): 432-441.

Davie, H., and Nutley, S. 2000. Developing learning organisations in the new NHS. *British Medical Journal* 320: 998-1001.

Day, D. 2000. Leadership development: A review in context. The Leadership Quarterly 11(4): 581-613.

Day, D. 2011. Leadership development. In The Sage Handbook of Leadership, by A. Bryman, D. Collinson, K. Grint, B. Jackson, and M. Uhl-Bien. London: Sage.

Dixon, N. 1993. Developing managers for the learning organisation. *Human Resource Management Review* 3(3): 243-254.

Edmonstone, J. 2011. Developing leaders and leadership in health care: A case for rebalancing? *Leadership in Health Services* 24(1): 8-18.

Filstad, C., and Gottschalk, P. 2011. Becoming a learning organization: The espoused values of police managers from two Norwegian districts. *The Learning Organization* 18(6): 486-500.

Fraser, S., and Greenhalgh, T. 2001. Coping with complexity: educating for capability. *British Medical Journal* 323: 799-803.

Grint, K. 2011. A history of leadership. In The Sage Handbook of Leadership, by A. Bryman, D. Collinson, K. Grint, B. Jackson, and M. Uhl-Bien. London: Sage.

Heifetz, R., Grashow, A., and Linsky, M. 2009a. Leadership in a permanent crisis. *Harvard Business Review* 87(7-8): 62-69.

Heifetz, R., Grashow, A., and Linsky, M. 2009b. The theory behind the practice. In The Practice of Adaptive Leadership: Tools and Tactics for Changing Your Organisation and the World. Boston: Harvard Business Press.

Heifetz, R., and Laurie, D. 1997. The work of leadership. *Harvard Business Review* 75(1): 124-134.

Home Office. 2013. Direct Entry in the Police: Government Response. London: Home Office. Available at https://www.gov.uk/ government/uploads/system/uploads/ attachment_ data/ file/249824/Direct_entry_consultation_-_governement_response.pdf. Accessed April 11, 2014.

Iles, P., and Preace, D. 2006. Developing leaders or developing leadership? The Academy of Chief Executives' programmes in the North East of England. *Leadership* 2(3): 317–340.

Jennings, C. 2013. 70:20:10 Framework Explained. 70:20:10 Forum Pty Ltd. Available at https://www.702010forum.com/about-702010- framework. Accessed May 8, 2015.

Jones, S. 2014. Distributed leadership: A critical analysis. *Leadership* 10(2): 129-141.

Kajewski, K., and Madsen, V. 2012. Demystifying 70:20:10. Melbourne, Australia: Deakin University.

Kodz, J., and Campbell, I. 2010. What Works in Leadership Development? A Rapid Evidence Review. London: National Policing Improvement Agency.

Marnoch, G. Topping, J., and Boyd, G. 2014. Explaining the pattern of growth in strategic actions taken by police services during the New Labour years: An exploratory study of an

English police service. Policing and Society: *An International Journal of Research and Policy* 24(3): 302-317.

McGurk, P. 2010. Outcomes of management and leadership development. *Journal of Management Development* 29(5): 457-470.

Millie, A., and Herrington, V. 2014. The great debate: How wide or narrow should the police's remit be? *AIPM Public Safety Leadership Research Focus* 2(4): 1-10.

Mintzberg, H., Ahlstrand, B., and Lampel, J. 1998. Strategy Safari. London: Pearson Education Limited.

Neyroud, P. 2010. Review of Police Leadership and Training. London: Home Office.

Northouse, P. 2013. Introduction. In Leadership: *Theory and Practice* (6th ed.). Thousand Oaks, California: Sage.

Ortenblad, A. 2004. The learning organization: Towards an integrated model. *The Learning Organization* 11(2): 129-144.

Pearson-Goff, M., and Herrington, V. 2013. Police Leaders and Leadership Development: A Systematic Literature Review. Sydney: Australian Institute of Police Management. http://www. aipm.gov.au/wp-content/uploads/2012/09/ Police-leaders-and-leadership-development-Asystematic-review.pdf.

Pearson-Goff, M., and Herrington, V. 2014. Police leadership: A systematic review of the literature. Policing: *A Journal of Policy and Practice* 8(1): 14-26.

Reaves, B. 2011. Census of State and Local Law Enforcement Agencies, 2008. Washington, D.C.: U.S. Department of Justice, Bureau of Justice Statistics.

Rosser, C. 2013. Developing leaders through leadership in police organizations. The Police Chief 77(5): 38-44.

Sargut, G., and McGrath, R. 2011. Learning to live with complexity. Harvard Business Review 89(9): 68-76.

Schafer, J. 2009. Developing effective leadership in policing: Perils, pitfalls and paths forward. Policing: *An International Journal of Police Strategies and Management* 32(2): 238-260.

Senge, P.M. 1990. The Fifth Discipline: The Art and Practice of the Learning Organization. New York: Currency Doubleday.

Shipton, H., Zhou, Q., and Mooi, E. 2013. Is there a global model of learning organizations? An empirical, cross-nation study. *The International Journal of Human Resource Management* 24(12): 2278-2298.

Stone, C., and Travis, J. 2011. Toward a New Professionalism in Policing. New Perspectives in Policing Bulletin. Washington, D.C.: U.S. Department of Justice, National Institute of Justice.

Uhl-Bien, M., Marion, R., and McKelvey, B. 2007. Complexity leadership theory: Shifting leadership from the industrial age to the knowledge era. *The Leadership Quarterly* 18(4): 298-318.

Winsor, T. 2012. Independent Review of Police Officer and Staff Remuneration and Conditions. Final report, Volume 1. London: Her Majesty's Stationery Office.

Yang, B., Watkins, K., and Marsick, V. 2004. The construct of the learning organization: Dimensions, measurement, and validation. *Human Resource Development Quarterly* 15(1): 31-55.

Yeo, R. 2005. Revisiting the roots of learning organization: A synthesis of the learning organization literature. The Learning Organization 12(4): 368-382.

Ylitalo, J., Horelli, J., Ahonen, J., and Heikurainen, P. 2006. Leader and leadership development: Dialogic and reflective approaches. Kehittyvä johtajuus: dialogiset ja reflektiiviset lähestymistavat-Tykes hankkeen loppuraportti. Available at http://scholar.googleusercontent. com/scholar?q=cache:M6-S5_D1UPoJ:scholar. google. com/+ylitalo+2006+leadership+%27di alogic+and+reflective+approaches%27&hl=en & as_sdt=0,5. Accessed September 13, 2013.

AUTHOR NOTE

Edward A. Flynn is Chief of the Milwaukee Police Department. He is the former Massachusetts Secretary of Public Safety and has led the Springfield, Mass., and Arlington, Va., police departments.

Dr. Victoria Herrington is the Director of Research and Learning at the Australian Institute of Police Management (AIPM). She has almost 20 years' experience as an applied policing scholar, working in a number of industry and university roles in the United Kingdom and Australia.

In: Perspectives on Policing
Editor: Holly Wheeler
ISBN: 978-1-63484-555-7

Chapter 3

RIGHTFUL POLICING*

Tracey L. Meares and Peter Neyroud

INTRODUCTION

During the summer of 2009, the nation and the world trained their attention on Cambridge, Massachusetts, a small northeastern city of about 100,000 people abutting Boston and home to Harvard University. That summer, a Cambridge police officer arrested renowned Harvard University African American Studies scholar Henry Louis Gates, Jr., who was attempting to enter his home following a long trip abroad. The media were flooded with stories and accounts of "racial profiling," the nature of the problem and the necessity for a national response. Even President Obama famously commented on the incident.[1]

To understand the controversy following Professor Gates's arrest, it is useful to have a factual context: Sergeant James Crowley, the officer who arrested Professor Gates, radioed that he would go to the Gates residence after receiving a dispatch at 12:46 p.m. on July 16, 2009, that a possible breaking and entering was in progress. Crowley arrived to find Gates in his home, and from there the stories diverge. Crowley's version of the events is that Gates was yelling and behaving in a "tumultuous" manner as Crowley attempted to ascertain enough facts to ensure that a crime was not occurring. Gates's view, on the other hand, is that Crowley disrespected him by failing to respond when Gates asked Crowley for his name and badge number. Gates was also upset that Crowley suspected him — a slight, elderly man with a cane — to be a burglar. It is important to emphasize that Sergeant Crowley arrived at Gates's home in response to a 911 call as opposed to an exercise of his own discretion. This point is critical because the typical conception of racial profiling focuses on its legality, and the legality of police action is primarily framed around placing constraints on when police decide to engage people as opposed to how police engage people. Even though his experience fit somewhat uneasily into the typical legal framework of racial profiling, Professor Gates has described his experience in exactly those terms.

---

* This is an edited, reformatted and augmented version of a paper, NCJ 248411, in the New Perspectives in Policing series, issued by the U.S. Department of Justice, National Institute of Justice, February 2015.

How, then, are we to understand the disjuncture between Sergeant Crowley's insistence — as well as the conclusion of many — that he conducted himself lawfully and Professor Gates's insistence that he was unfairly treated and, therefore, racially profiled?

To find an answer, it is necessary to see how two dominant ways of evaluating police leave little room for considering how ordinary people tend to assess their treatment by state authorities. Experts, whether they are police officials or scholars of policing, tend to assess police action eit her w ith respect to its law fulness or w it h respect to its effectiveness at reducing crime and increasing public safety. Police fidelit y to law, especially constitutional law, has long been used as a criterion to distinguish good from bad policing. In addition to the Fourth, Fifth, and Sixth Amendments, other bodies of law — such as police agency administrative regulations, civil lawsuits, or the very law that authorizes police to act in the first place, substantive criminal law — provide standards by which legal authorities measure and assess whether or not policing is carried out properly.[2]

Effectiveness at crime fighting has become the other primary police evaluation metric. Promoted initially by scholars, this yardstick is newer than lawfulness, because for decades many, including police, believed that law enforcement had little impact on crime rates.[3] David Bayley, in his 1994 book, *Police for the Future,* summed up this view nicely:

> The police do not prevent crime. That is one of the best kept secrets of modern life. Experts know it. The police know it, but the public does not know it. Yet, the police pretend that they are society's best defense against crime and continually argue that if they are given more resources, especially personnel, they will be able to protect communities against crime. This is myth.[4]

This is no longer true. Police executives are expected — and expect themselves — to reduce crime rates in their jurisdictions. Policing scholars devote themselves to finding causal connections between various police practices and crime statistics, typically by relying on a theoretical model that assumes offenders are rational actors who are persuaded to desist from criminal behavior when the prospect of formal punishment out weighs the benefits of that behavior. In arresting Professor Gates that day, Sergeant Crowley pursued these two aims of policing simultaneously. He was an assiduous crime fighter, and he acted in a way that was legal. Does that mean that Sergeant Crowley's conduct was unambiguously rightful?

No, it does not. It does not because there is a third way, in addition to lawfulness and effectiveness, to evaluate policing — "rightful policing." Rightful policing attempts to account for what people say that they care about when they assess indiv idual officer behavior as well as agency conduct generally. It differs from lawful policing and effective policing in at least two ways. First, rightful policing does not depend on the lawfulness of police conduct. Rather, it depends primarily on the procedural justice or fairness of that conduct. Second, rightful policing does not depend on an assessment of police as ever more effective crime fighters (although it turns out that rightful policing often leads to more compliance with the law and therefore lower crime rates). This third way may well help us move toward police governance that is substantively, as opposed to rhetorically, democratic. Finally, rightful policing is better for cops on the street. Its precepts not only encourage the people whom police deal with on a daily basis to comply with the law and police directives, they also encourage behaviors in encounters that tend to keep police safe.

TWO VIEWS: MORE LAW? OR LESS CRIME?

Before this paper delves into greater detail about "rightful policing," it is useful to understand what rightful policing is not. Rightful policing is not confined simply to constitutional policing, nor is it subsumed entirely by policing aimed at crime reduction. Rather, it is about how to achieve both by promoting fairness and engendering trust in police among the public.

This discussion began with a widely publicized example of what many, including the person who was arrested, Professor Henry Louis Gates, believed to be racial profiling by police. New York City, like Cambridge, has been embroiled in its own racial profiling controversy for more than a decade. In New York, the controversy is centered not on one high-profile incident, but, rather, on hundreds of thousands of stops and frisks of nameless, primarily young, African American men. The criticism of "stop and frisk" leveled against the police in New York is not limited to that city or this country. Philadelphia, for example, has been involved in a similar controversy, and London police have come under fire for implementing what critics believe to be a too-aggressive "stop and search" strategy. In each of these cities, there have been vocal complaints about what critics claim is the overbroad exercise of state power in the form of searches and seizures. These criticisms usually are asserted in legal terms and framed around precepts of constitutional law. The critics' preferred remedies in turn are usually described using the same set of tools — the architecture of law and rights.

Thinking about police law fulness in terms of a tradeoff between the risk of arbitrary or oppressive enforcement and an individual's right to privacy and autonomy is a dominant approach in the literature.[5] Those who measure good policing with reference to its lawfulness do not usually focus on police effectiveness at reducing crime. Rather, the lawfulness metric almost always casts police power as a necessary evil as opposed to a welcome utility or a potentially critical mechanism for empowering communities to pursue their own democratically chosen goals and projects. According to the "more lawfulness" view, police adherence to strict dictates that constrain their discretion generally results in less policing and more liberty for individuals. The higher level of crime that might result from less policing is simply a price citizens pay for more freedom in society.[6]

Police executives who are committed to lowering crime rates in their communities do not agree that less policing is an ideal they should seek to achieve. In pursuit of accountability, one of the four cornerstones of the new professionalism advocated by Stone and Travis[7] — the primary components of which include reducing crime and making communities safer, controlling costs, and conducting themselves with respect toward the public whom they serve[8] — police have become much more concerned with effectiveness, considering commitment to crime reduction a prime aspect of accountability.[9] The question is no longer whether or not police can make a difference. Police executives instead ask, "How much of a difference in crime rates can police make?" The new literature on the relationship between crime rates and policing is voluminous. Criminological research over the last couple of decades has shown that deploying police forces in geographically focused ways — "hot spot policing " — can significantly reduce crime without displacing it to other areas.[10] Other scholars have demonstrated that strategies such as problem-oriented policing and community policing can be useful to address crime and/or the fear of crime.[11] The advances in statistical approaches are striking and useful, but a weakness of the scholarship on police effectiveness is that lawfulness is largely irrelevant to it.

Those who promote success at crime fighting as the best way to assess police effectiveness too often fail to understand that police failure to adhere to law is a proper lens through which to view public perception of overbroad policing — in the form of too-prevalent stop and frisk, widespread public surveillance, or other every day policies and practices. Comments by both former Mayor Bloomberg and former Police Commissioner Ray Kelly in reaction to the federal court order striking down New York City's prominent stop, question and frisk practice illustrate this attitude on the part of police agencies and public officials. Following District Judge Shira Sheindlin's order declaring the practice in violation of both the Fourth and Fourteenth Amendments as it operated at the time the order was issued, Bloomberg and Kelly claimed that the judge had imperiled the city's safety by limiting liberal use of the practice.[12] On the other hand, those who promote lawfulness as the best metric to assess good policing too often ignore the fact that crime and predation among individuals result in significantly less freedom for residents of high-crime communities, even though private actors impose that constraint on freedom. Residents of high-crime communities often see higher levels of policing as a way to achieve freedom as opposed to its constraint.[13]

Rightful policing is attentive to both lawfulness and effectiveness, and it captures important dimensions that neither one of the prevalent modes of evaluation does. The notion of rightful policing also includes a critique of a "get-tough" approach to law enforcement, which uses as its principal touchstone instrumental theories of deterrence. Deterrence, without the balance of a focus on legitimacy, can be effective, but its effects often are short-lived and expensive to implement. Moreover, commit ment to some methods of achieving deterrence, such as stop and frisk, can predictably backfire in communities that need crime reduction most. There is also strong reason to believe that many heavy deterrence strategies are not particularly effective in encouraging offenders to desist from crime.

Rightful Policing: It's About Legitimacy

Police actions such as stops and frisks can be costly even when they are lawful, constitutional and short. People do not automatically approve of a stop just because an offcer is legally entitled to make one. This reality crystallizes a basic problem with focusing on lawfulness as the single yards tick for rightful police conduct. Indeed, research I have conducted with Tom Tyler suggests that the public does not recognize lawful police conduct when they see it.[14]

If people do not focus on the lawfulness of police conduct, what do they care about? Although it seems counterintuitive, decades of research show that people typically care much more about how law enforcement agents treat them than about the outcome of the contact. Even when people receive a negative outcome in an encounter, such as a speeding ticket, they feel better about that incident than about an incident in which they do not receive a ticket but are treated poorly.[15]

In addition to being treated with dignity and respect, research demonstrates that people look for behavioral signals that allow them to assess whether a police officer's decision to stop or arrest them was made fairly — that is, accurately and without bias. These two factors — quality of treatment and indications of high-quality decision-making — matter much more to people than the outcome of the encounter.

Two additional factors matter as well. People report higher levels of satisfaction in encounters with authorities if they feel that they have an opportunity to explain their situation and their perspective on it — i.e., to tell their story.[16]

Finally, in their interactions with police, people want to believe that authorities are acting out of a sense of benevolence toward them. They want to believe that the authorities' motives are sincere and well-intentioned and that the authorities are trying to respond to people's concerns.[17]

All four of these factors — quality of treatment, decision-making fairness, voice and expectation of benevolent treatment — make up what psychologists call "procedural justice."

Procedural justice matters a great deal in civil society. One important consequence of people's perceptions of procedural fairness according to these terms is that they lead to popular beliefs of legitimacy. When social psychologists use the term "legitimacy," they are referring to a "property that a rule or an authority has when others feel obligated to voluntarily defer to that rule or authority. A legitimate authority is one that is regarded by people as entitled to have its rules and decisions accepted and followed by others."[18]

This conception of legitimacy is not normative. When psychologists discuss legitimacy, they are not exploring in some philosophical sense whether people ought to defer to legal authorities; rather, they are seeking to determine whether, in fact, people do defer. Their approach is positive and empirical. Thus, when researchers have sought to determine why people obey the law, the legitimacy-based explanation is distinct from an explanation grounded in fearing the consequences of failing to do so and from one grounded in morality. When people voluntarily comply with rules and laws because they believe authorities have the right to dictate proper behavior, their compliance is legitimacy-based. Rightful policing leverages these ideas.

A robust body of social science evidence from around the world shows that people are likelier to obey the law when they believe that authorities have the right to tell them what to do.[19] Research shows that people are motivated more to comply with the law by the belief that they are being treated with dignity and fairness than by fear of punishment. In fact, being treated fairly is a more important determinant of compliance than formal deterrence.[20] When police generate good feelings in their everyday contacts, people are motivated to help them fight crime. All of this encourages desistance from offending, law- abiding and assistance to the police, contributing to lower crime rates.

Although police are conceived and constituted by and through law, focusing on the lawfulness of police conduct can obscure one's ability to identify and remedy policing behavior that the public may well view as problematic. It is important to see that although procedural justice can be related to the lawfulness or legality of police conduct, these two valences do not proceed in lockstep. One way of thinking how these valences relate to one another is to imagine points on a compass (see figure). If we array lawfulness from west to east, with lawfulness to the east and unlawfulness to the west, then we would expect police to be as far east as possible. Now, imagine procedural justice or legitimacy as running north and south on the compass. When police are respectful and procedurally just, they are headed north. When they are not, that behavior is categorized as "running south." Putting the two parts together, one sees that the best place for law enforcement to be is in the northeast.[21] That is where one finds rightful policing.

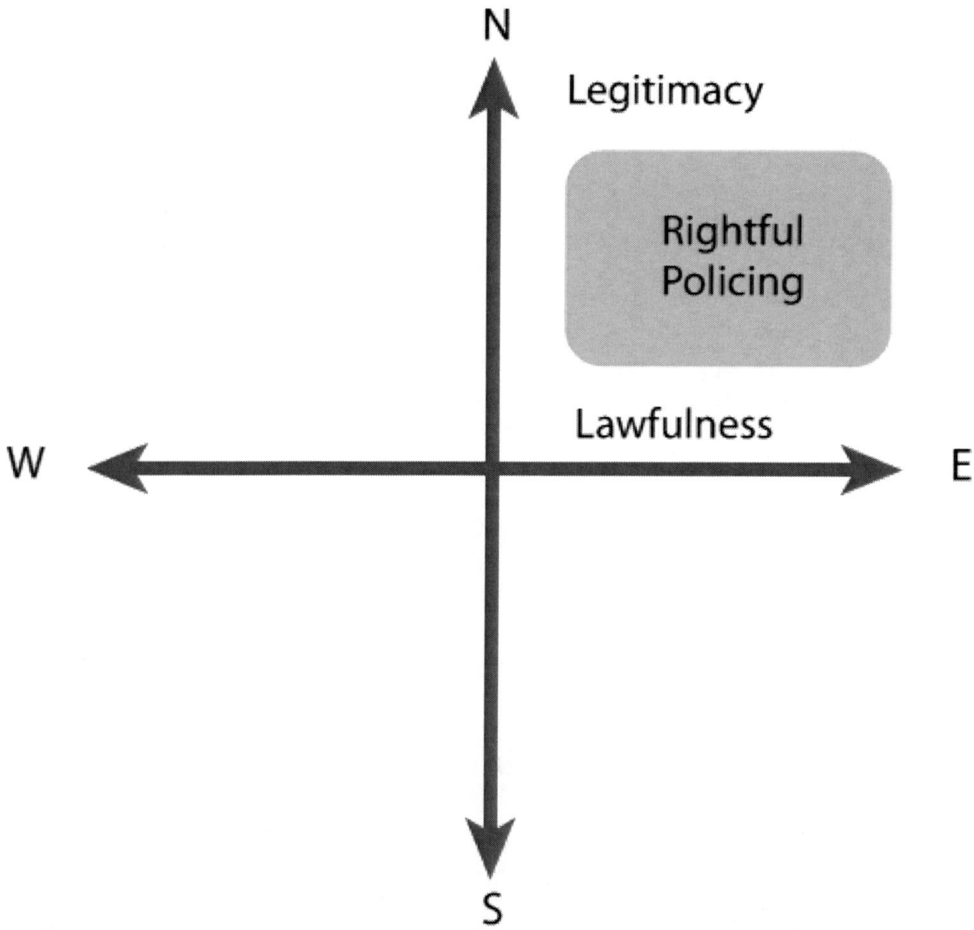

Source: Tracey L. Meares, The Good Cop: Knowing the Difference between Lawful or Effective Policing and Rightful Policing — And Why It Matters, 54 Wm. & mary L. rev. 1865, 1879 (2012).

Figure. Rightful Policing as the Convergence of Lawfulness and Legitimacy.

This image, however, also reveals the southeast and the northwest. A primary problem with street policing in urban cities such as New York and Chicago, and in many communities across the globe, is that too often such policing comprises behavior I would locate in the southeast: police conduct that is very likely lawful, but that citizens in many encounters perceive as deeply illegitimate, using the term as defined here.

In the figure, for example, if one asks a lawyer what constitutes racial profiling, that person typically will answer, "It is police behavior solely or perhaps partially motivated by race"; however, the review earlier in this essay of the events connected to Professor Gates's arrest in the summer of 2009 should make clear that many who believe themselves to have been profiled care little about the legal determinants of their encounters with police.

The bottom line is clear: regardless of the lawfulness of police behavior, lack of procedural justice in encounters can change public perceptions of policing agencies, leading to lack of trust, ill-will and ultimately less law-abiding.[22]

Considering both the law fulness and the legitimacy of police conduct allows both the police officer and the citizen stopped to be right in a way that is not possible when one operates in the single dimension of lawfulness. The possibility of both sides being right can lead to fruitful conversation about the rightfulness of policing.

PUTTING LEGITIMACY TO WORK

This argument raises the question for police of how they can put these ideas into practice. A focus on the procedural justice of encounters can help policing agencies identify behavior, tactics and strategies that many members of minority communities find problematic and that lead to disaffection, even though they may be lawful and, considered in isolation, appear effective.

Second, a focus on the psychological aspects of legitimacy in individual encounters may have important crime control benef its when incorporated into tactics and strategies. Two case studies illustrate this. The first is a strateg y for violence reduction in Chicago, Illinois, which has been running since 2002.[23] The second is an experiment conducted in Queensland, Australia, on road traffc enforcement.[24]

I have deliberately chosen two very different examples to show that legitimacy-based approaches have a wide application across different aspects of the police mission. These two initiatives, however, are not unique. Lorraine Mazerolle and her colleagues recently completed a meta-analysis of legitimacy policing interventions and concluded that "police can achieve positive changes in citizen attitudes to police through adopting procedural justice dialogue as a component part of any type of police intervention."[25]

When the Chicago initiative started, the city's homicide rate hovered near 22 per 100,000. Crime is often concentrated by geography, and in Chicago the neighborhoods on the city's west and south sides drove the city's homicide rate. The highest crime area on the west had a homicide rate of 72 per 100,000. Using funds provided by a billion-dollar nationwide federal initiative to combat gun crime called Project Safe Neighborhoods (PSN),[26] United States Attorney Patrick Fitzgerald proposed a strategy modeled after Project Exile in Richmond, Virginia, targeting ex-offenders in the high-crime areas with federal penalties for gun possession and other gun offenses. Fizgerald believed, from crime analysis, that ex-offenders were primarily responsible for the gun violence in Chicago. This approach is entirely consistent with the typical "get-tough" deterrence-based thinking around crime control — a crackdown on potentially high- harm offenders.[27]

In devising the particulars of the strategy, the program's architects suggested to the task force that the proposed strategy should be wrapped in the theory of legitimacy. The resultant strategy would still target the group the U.S. Attorney thought most vulnerable to gun offending, but the communication strategy to this group would emphasize aspects that research indicated clearly most people care about when determining that law enforcement is fair. Although offenders would be brought in and alerted to the consequences that would follow should they pick up a gun, they would also receive information about services to help them turn away from a life of crime.

Modeled after Operation Ceasefire in Boston,[28] hour-long, roundtable-style meetings were the centerpiece of the new strategy. Each of these forums gathered no more than 20 offenders, who sat around a table with representatives from state and local law enforcement and the community. Instead of simply confronting the offenders with the punitive consequences of their behavior, emphasis was placed on the quality of the interaction — less a tribunal and more a dialogue between citizens — and the potential rewards of law-abiding, which is consistent with attempting to achieve legitimacy-based compliance.

Legitimacy-based law enforcement focuses more on persuasion than punishment. To persuade, authorities must create the necessary social capital that engenders trust between governors and the governed. Simply emphasizing rewards and punishments does not automatically lead to trust, because such an approach assumes that all individuals care about is the bottom line — an assumption that is contrary to the theory of procedural justice and much empirical evidence. The notion that compliance is typically created only by threats of coercion backed up with punishment is fundamentally inconsistent with trust, for such a stance assumes that individuals cannot be counted on to defer to and comply with the law voluntarily.

Statistical assessments of the impact of the Chicago program are striking. Papachristos, Meares and Fagan assessed the impact of Chicago's forums on neighborhood-level crime rates and gun violence, compared with the impact of three other components of PSN — increased federal prosecutions for convicted felons carrying or using guns, the imposition of longer sentences associated with federal prosecutions, and the removal of guns from the street.[29] Their analysis demonst rates that although all tested PSN initiatives were associated with a decrease in the homicide rate, the forums had the largest effect. Comparing the relative effects of the forums and federal gun prosecutions shows that a unit increase in forum participation (or approximately 45 new offenders) among those eligible is roughly 8.5 times more powerful than a unit increase in federal prosecutions in reducing homicide rates.[30]

Further research suggests that the forums make a difference at an individual level as well. Those who attended were significantly more likely to stay out of prison than those who did not, all other things being equal.[31]

In the second example, I shift from tackling serious inner-city violence to the reduction of road deaths by traffic enforcement. The Queensland Community Engagement Trial (QCET)[32] used a randomized field trial to test the application of legitimacy in how Queensland police enforced the drink driving laws.

Police officers across Australia administer thousands of breath tests to drivers under legislat ion that empowers them to carry out random roadside breath-testing. The tests tend to be administered at test sites identified as hot spots of drink driving and collisions causing serious injury. These police actions are justifiable as both legal and evidence-based. The researchers at the Australian Research Council Centre of Excellence in Policing and Security, in partnership with Queensland police, set out to see whether they could significantly enhance the impact of the testing regime so that the testing not only checked for alcohol on the driver's breath but also increased public confidence in the police and support for the enforcement of drink driving legislation.

In QCET, the testing sites were randomly allocated either to a control — the standard police procedure — or to a "legitimacy treatment." In the control, drivers were stopped, given a short legal warning, and required to provide a breath test. The legal minimum process and time were taken to provide a test. In contrast, in the "legitimacy treatment," the drivers were taken through a five- stage procedure that emphasized five dimensions of procedural justice: decision neutralit y, to explain that those drivers stopped had not been singled out, but that the test was being provided to drivers at random; trustworthy motives, to provide context about the reasons for the test site and the testing campaign; citizen participation, including crime prevention advice and details of local Crimestoppers numbers; redress and feedback, or an opportunity to raise any issues of concern; and dignity and respect, which included thanks to the drivers for their cooperation.

There was a very small difference in the time taken for the two approaches (around a minute extra for the legitimacy treatment), yet the drivers' perceptions of the process were very different. Drivers who experienced the legitimacy treatment "reported significantly stronger generalized perceptions of police fairness, police respect, [and] higher satisfaction" with how police do their job.[33] The caveat on these interim findings is that researchers could not see from this trial a wider increase in the respondents' general confidence in the police or a wider tendency toward compliance with the law. Given that the encounter, even in the longer, legitimacy treatment, only lasted 1 minute and 37 seconds, this may not be surprising. However, the study suggests that the deployment of legitimacy approaches in day-to-day police interactions with citizens can have a significant and measurable benefit over an approach that simply relies on the letter of the law. It also makes the point that such approaches are not only relevant in the critically difficult relationships between police and minority communities but should also be considered as an important part of wider police operations.

Conclusions and Implications for Policing

If legitimacy is as important as I have argued, then it raises the questions of how the police should incorporate this approach and what the obstacles are to implementation. I think we can make progress on answering these questions by considering three issues:

Training. Much police training, despite improvements over the last 20 years, retains a strong bias in favor of learning the rules, particularly legislation, procedure (especially constitutional criminal procedure) and departmental policies. Such training does not apply only at the initial recruitment phase. In the United Kingdom, for example, the key gateway for promotion for all first-line managers is to pass a set of examinations in the law and procedures for crime, roads policing, general duties, and evidence and procedure.[34] This kind of reliance on law and procedure as the qualification for recruits and managers is typical across most jurisdictions. As Janet Chan and her colleagues show, procedural/legal training is now frequently supported by programs to address behaviors and practical skills but almost never by an educational approach that provides officers with the means and material to understand the social science evidence for what works in policing or how approaches such as legitimacy make their practice more effective.[35] Indeed, Chan and her colleagues demonstrate how the legal valence of front line culture can undermine even the attempts to inject some "social context." Peter Neyroud has recommended a much more fundamental shift in the framework of training for recruits, specialists and managers so that police training in the

United Kingdom would be governed by a new professional body and start with a prequalification that emphasizes learning about evidence-based practice.[36] Without such a radical shift, it seems likely, from studies like that of Chan and colleagues, that police training will continue to underpin a legalistic way of thinking about problems and their solutions. There are promising signs of change, however. Chicago Police Super intendent Garry McCarthy has instituted a day-long training in police legitimacy and racial reconciliation for the entire force. To date, more than 8,000 officers and leaders have been trained.[37] Early assessments of the program are extremely positive.[38] In the United Kingdom, extensive practical training on procedural justice in particular situations is also becoming the norm.[39]

Strategies and tactics. Too often, compelled by the ever-present demand to bring crime statistics down (especially in big cities), police executives focus on strategies and tactics designed to reduce violence in too-cramped ways. If this is right, then police executives should consider problem-solving in more holistic ways that will yield approaches that are designed not only to quell violence but also to enhance safety by changing the attitudes and dispositions of those alienated from them in ways that sustain voluntary compliance. I have in mind here hot spot policing that is not only deterrence-based but also legitimacy-based. Braga, Welsh and Schnell recently found, in a review of broken windows policing strategies, a distinct break between the effectiveness of aggressive, deterrence- focused broken windows approaches, such as stop and frisk in New York City, and other more legitimacy-based approaches. Only the latter group produced large and statistically significant impacts on crime.[40] Moreover, commitment to legitimacy can also help police increase safety and, by implication, quell violence at the incident level by encouraging officers to engage in tactics that defuse violent incidents.[41]

Democracy and community participation. I agree with Loader when he notes that, "The police, in short, are both minders and reminders of community — a producer of significant messages about the kind of place that community is or aspires to be."[42] Policing makes community. It is no accident that an iconic symbol of England itself is the Bobby's hat.[43] In the United States, policing's symbolic valence is not so positive. At least one scholar has located the genesis of American policing not in the benevolent image of a kindly community protector but in the more sinister form of the slave patroller.[44] The procedural justice literature reviewed above makes clear the ways in which this dark history can and likely does undermine trust in police in the modern era. And yet this same literature provides a roadmap for a more positive relationship that not only benefits those who need help from the police but also potentially supports their participation in democratically led government. It is important for people to feel that if they call on the police (and other legal actors and institutions), not only will their security be protected, but they will also be treated with respect, their rights will be recognized, and they will be subject to fair decision-making. The fact that most people in a communit y rarely call on the police for services does not change this, because police and other legal actors are in the background in every community and shape what people think, feel and do. People want to feel comfort, not fear, when the police are present and to anticipate that they will receive help and professional treatment when they need it. When they do, they become invested in the communities in which they live. Research on popular legitimacy, to which police contribute, suggests that when people evaluate their police and court systems as procedurally fair, they identify more with their communities and engage in them socially by trusting neighbors, politically by voting , and economically by shopping and going to entertainment venues within that community.[45]

Police play a critical role in teaching the people with whom they interact (and those who observe those interactions) what it means to be a citizen.[46]

Writing recently in the Annals, Justice and Meares argue that the criminal justice system offers a curriculum of lessons on what it means to be a citizen, much as public schools do. The overt curriculum of policing, found most obviously in the text of the United States Constitution, is designed to convey concern for rights. People's interests in autonomy, privacy and bodily integrity ought not to be subject to the whim of an individual police officer. We are a government of laws designed to restrain state power against the individual. Education theorists explain that a hidden curriculum is often taught alongside the overt curriculum typically found in textbooks and official rubrics. In schools, the hidden curriculum may be found in adult/student and student/student interactions, in the enforcement of school discipline policies and behavior codes, in the deeply buried assumptions and narratives of history textbooks, in a school's choice of mascot, in who gets to sit where in the cafeteria, or in the musical selections at the prom. The hidden curriculum of policing, similarly, is a function of how people are treated in interactions and the ways in which groups derive meaning regarding their status in the eyes of legal authority resulting from that treatment. Too of ten the hidden curriculum of policing strategies sends certain citizens clear signals that they are members of a special, dangerous and undesirable class — the mirror image of the positive overt curriculum. People do not necessarily learn these lessons. What is learned depends in part on the degree and frequency of exposure and on individual and communit y resilience. As Justice and Meares note:

> [T]he hidden curriculum flourishes in those contexts where democracy is dislocated. In high - performing public and private schools, teachers and students work together toward common goals that honor the social contract between the school, the student, the family, and the community; punishment is appropriate and merciful, and offers forgiveness; interpersonal interactions encourage success and reaffirm belonging; trust is endemic. Remove the confluence of interests, the accountability of those with authority to those under it, the fundamental sense of legitimacy, and the hidden curriculum eats away at the overt.[47]

Commitment to rightful policing can help, but executives cannot be sanguine about its potential impact. The approach requires broadly conceived and coordinated efforts among a variety of contexts — crime reduction, community relations and, importantly, internal discipline[48] — to effect real change.

End Notes

[1] See Nicholas Graham, Obama on Skip Gates Arrest: Police Acted "Stupidly," Huffington Post, Aug. 22, 2009, http://www.huffingtonpost. com/2009/07/22 obama - on - skip-gates - arres_n_243250.html (last visited Nov. 13, 2014).

[2] Rachel A. Harmon, The Problem of Policing, 110 Mich. L. Rev. 761 (2011).

[3] Christopher Stone & Jeremy Travis, Toward a New Professionalism in Policing (2011), http://www.nij.gov/pubs-sum/232359.htm (last visited Nov. 13, 2014).

[4] David H. Bayley, Police for the Future 3 (1994).

[5] For one example criticizing the police- lawfulness tradeoff, consider the discussion by Meares and Kahan of the legal struggle regarding searches for guns in Chicago public housing. See Tracey L. Meares & Dan M. K ahan, Urgent Times: Policing a nd R ights in Inner City Communities (1999).

[6] See id. at 18–22.

[7] Stone & Travis, supra note 3, at 1 (noting that accountability is a critical aspect of what they call the "new professionalism," along with legitimacy, innovation and national coherence).

[8] See id. at 12. ("The best chiefs speak confidently about 'the three C's: crime, cost and conduct. Police departments today are accountable for all three.")

[9] Id. at 12–15.

[10] See Anthony Braga & Dav id Weisbur d, Policing Problem Places: Crime Hot Spots and Effective Prevention (2010).

[11] See National Research Council, Fairness and Effectiveness in Policing: The Evidence 297 (Wesley Skogan & Kathleen Frydl, eds., 2004); Anthony A. Braga, Brandon C. Welsh & Cory Schnell, Can Policing Disorder Reduce Crime? A Systematic Review and Meta-Analysis, J. Res. Crime & Delinq. (For t hcom i ng); Anthony A. Braga, Problem-Oriented Policing and Crime Prevention (2d ed., 2008).

[12] See Transcript, Bloomberg Vows to Appeal Federal Judge's Ruling That Stop- and-Frisk Policy Violated Civil Rights in Press Conference, N.Y. Daily News, Aug. 12, 2003, http://www.nydailynews.com/news/polit ics/bloomberg- vows-appea l-federa l-judge-ruling-stop-stop-and-frisk-policy-article-1.1424630 (last visited Nov. 13, 2014); John Eterno & Eli Silverman, Mike Bloomberg's Fact-Free Defence of Stop-and-Frisk, The Guardian, Sept. 11, 2013, http://www.theguardian.com/commentisfree/2013/sep/11/ stop-and-frisk-michael-bloomberg (last visited Nov. 13, 2014).

[13] See Tracey L. Meares & Dan M. Kahan, Law and (Norms of) Order in Inner City, 32 Law & Soc'y Rev. 805, 830–32 (1998) (discussing community empowerment through law enforcement).

[14] Tracey L. Meares et al., Lawful or Fair? How Cops and Laypeople View Good Policing (Social Science Research Network) (2012), http:// papers.ssrn.com/abstract=2116645 (last visited Nov. 13, 2014).

[15] See Tom R. Tyler & Jeffrey Fagan, Legitimacy and Cooperation: Why Do People Help the Police Fight Crime in Their Communities?, 6 Ohio St. J. Crim. L. 231, 262 (2008); Tom R. Tyler & Cheryl Wakslak, Profiling and Police Legitimacy: Procedural Justice, Attributions of Motive, and Acceptance of Police Authority, 42 Criminology 253, 255 (2004); Tom R. Tyler, Trust in the Law: Encouraging Public Cooperation With the Police and Courts (2002); Raymond Paternoster et al., Do Fair Procedures Matter? The Effect of Procedural Justice on Spouse Assault, 31 Law & Soc'y Rev. 163 (1997).

[16] See Tom R. Tyler, Enhancing Police Legitimacy, 593 Annals Am. Acad. Pol. & Soc. Sci. 84, 94 (2004).

[17] See id.

[18] National Research Council, supra note 11, at 297.

[19] See generally Legitimacy and Criminal Justice: International Perspectives (Anthony Braga et al., eds., 2007) (exploring the impact of perceptions of legitimacy in criminal justice systems across the globe).

[20] Tom R. Tyler, Why People Obey the Law (reprint, 2006).

[21] See Tracey L. Meares, The Good Cop: Knowing the Difference between Lawful or Effective Policing and Rightful Policing — And Why It Matters, 54 Wm. & Mary L. Rev. 1865, 1879 (2012) (providing this illustrative figure).

[22] See, e.g., Tracey L. Meares, Inaugural Barrock Lecture on Criminal Law: The Legitimacy of Police Among Young African American Men, 92 Marq. L. Rev. 651 (2009).

[23] See Andrew V. Papachristos, Tracey L. Meares & Jeffrey Fagan, Attention Felons: Evaluating Project Safe Neighborhood s in Chicago, 4 J. Empirical Legal Stud. 223 (2007).

[24] Lorraine Mazerolle et al., Procedural Justice, Routine Encounters and Citizen Perceptions of Police: Main Findings from the Queensland Community Engagement Trial (Q C ET), 8 J. Experimental Criminology 3 43 (2012) [hereinafter Mazerolle et al., Procedural Justice]; Lorraine Mazerolle et al., Shaping Citizen Perceptions of Police Legitimacy: A Randomized Field Trial of Procedural Justice, 51 Criminology 33 (2013) [hereinafter Mazerolle et al., Shaping Citizen Perceptions].

[25] See Mazerolle et al., Procedural Justice, supra note 24.

[26] See Papachristos et al., supra note 23 (describing the federal initiative).

[27] See Evaluating Gun Policy: Effects on Crime and Violence (Jens Ludw ig & Philip J. Cook, ed., Brookings Institution Press, 2003) (evaluating Project Exile).

[28] See David M. Kennedy, Deterrence and Crime Prevention: Reconsidering the Prospect of Sanction (Rout ledge, 2 0 0 8) (describing the inter vention). For an analysis of the crime control impacts of this and similar programs, see Anthony A. Braga & David L. Weisburd, The Ef fects of Focused Deterrence Strategies on Crime: A Systematic Review and Meta-Analysis of the Empirical Evidence, 49 J. Res. Crime & Delinq. 323 (2011).

[29] See Papachristos et al., supra note 23, at 223.

[30] See id. at 258–59.

[31] See Andrew V. Papachristos et al., Desistance and Legitimacy: The Impact of Offender Notification Meetings on Recidivism Among High Risk Offenders (Social Science Research Network, 2013), http://papers.ssrn.com/abstract=2240232 (last visited Nov. 13, 2014).

[32] Lorraine Mazerolle, Sarah Bennett, Emma Antrobus & Elizabeth Eggins, Key Findings of the Queensl and Community Engagement Trial (Austl. Res. Council Centre of Excellence in Policing and Security Briefing Paper Series No. 8, 2011).

[33] See id. at 7.

[34] Peter W. Neyroud, Review of Police Leadership and Tr aining (Report to Home Sec'y, 2011).

[35] See Janet B.L . Chanetal., Fair Cop: Learning the Art of Policing (Universit y of Toronto Press, 2003).

[36] See Neyroud, supra note 34.

[37] See Pam Grimes & Gaynor Hall, Respectful Policing in Chicago: Changing the Us vs Them Mentality (WGN-TV television broadcast, Sept. 9, 2013), http://wgntv.com/2013/09/09/respectful- policing-in-chicago (last visited Nov. 13, 2014).

[38] Wesley G. Skogan, The 2013 Officer Training Experiment (Oct. 2014) (unpublished manuscript), http: //www skogan.org/files/Executive_Summary_2013_Training_Experiment.pdf (last visited Nov. 13, 2014).

[39] Levin Wheller, Paul Quinton, Alistair Fildes & Andy Mills , The Greater Manchester Police Procedural Justice Training Experiment: Technical Report (2013), http://library.college.police.uk/docs/college-of-policing/Technical-Report.pdf (last visited Nov. 13, 2014).

[40] See Anthony Braga, Brandon Welsh & Cory Schnell, Broken Windows Policing to Reduce Crime in Neighborhoods: Findings from a Campbell Collaboration Systematic Review and Meta-Analysis (Paper presented at the annual meeting of the American Society of Criminology, Chicago, IL, Nov. 22, 2013).

[41] John D. McCluskey, Police Requests for Compliance: Coercive and Procedurally Just Tactics (2003).

[42] Ia n L oader, Policing , Recog nit ion , and Belonging, 605 Annals Am. Acad. Pol. & Soc. Sci. 202, 211 (2006) (citation omitted) (citing Neil Walker, Policing and the Supranational, 12 Policing & Soc'y 307, 315 (2002)).

[43] See Ian Loader & Aogán Mulcahy, Policing and the Condition of Engl a nd: Memory, Politics and Culture (2003). Another primary iconic symbol is the red telephone box, not to be confused with the blue police box.

[44] Markus Dirk Dubber, The Police Power: Patriarchy and the Foundations of American Government (2005).

[45] Tom R. Tyler & Jonathan Jackson, Popular Legitimacy and the Exercise of Legal Authority: Motivating Compliance , Cooperation and Engagement, 20 Psychol., Pub. Pol'y & L. 78 (2014).

[46] Benjamin Justice & Tracey L. Meares, How the Criminal Justice System Educates Citizens, 651 Annals Am. Acad. Pol. & Soc. Sci. 159 (2014).

[47] Id. at 175.

[48] Bernard K. Melekian, Values-Based Discipline: T he Key to Organizational Transformation Within Law Enforcement Agencies (July 24, 2012) (unpublished Ph.D. disser tat ion, Universit y of Southern California) (on file with the Price School of Public Policy, University of Southern California).

AUTHOR NOTE

Tracey L. Meares is Walton Hale Hamilton Professor of Law and Director of the Justice Collaboratory at Yale Law School. Peter Neyroud CBE QPM, who is Affiliated Lecturer and Resident Scholar at the Jerry Lee Centre for Experimental Criminology, Institute of Criminology, University of Cambridge, contributed to an earlier version of this paper.

In: Perspectives on Policing
Editor: Holly Wheeler
ISBN: 978-1-63484-555-7

Chapter 4

FROM WARRIORS TO GUARDIANS: RECOMMITTING AMERICAN POLICE CULTURE TO DEMOCRATIC IDEALS*

Sue Rahr and Stephen K. Rice

> "In Plato's vision of a perfect society — in a republic that honors the core of democracy — the greatest amount of power is given to those called the Guardians. Only those with the most impeccable character are chosen to bear the responsibility of protecting the democracy." [1]

INTRODUCTION

Beginning in the 1960s, and more recently fueled by post 9-11 fear, American policing has slowly drifted away from Plato's vision of guardians and Socrates' view of guardian education as expressed in Plato's *Republic*. This view of guardian education is humanistic. It takes shape through criminal justice education that is not only vocational but also stresses ethics, theory and the nature of virtue.[2] As a profession, we have veered away from Sir Robert Peel's ideal, "the police are the people, and the people are the police," toward a culture and mindset more like warriors at war with the people we are sworn to protect and serve.[3] As a nation, we have tended to relinquish some of our sacred constitutional rights in favor of the perception of improved safety and security.[4] Constitutional rights are now viewed by some, including some police, as an impediment to the public safety mission. Sadly, many have forgotten that protecting constitutional rights is the mission of police in a democracy. As New York University law professor Stephen Schulhofer argues in a review of the Constitution and the police: "The future of individual liberties in this country depends on reinvigorating the system of vigorous checks and balances built into our Bill of Rights."[5] Such a call for

* This is an edited, reformatted and augmented version of a paper, NCJ 248654, in the New Perspectives in Policing series, issued by the U.S. Department of Justice, National Institute of Justice, April 2015.

reinvigoration of the civil religion of the state has strong historic precedent. As Lincoln argued before the Springfield Young Men's Lyceum in 1838:

> Let reverence for the laws, be breathed by every American mother to the lisping babe ... let it be taught in schools, in seminaries, and in colleges; let it be written in Primers, spelling books, and in Almanacs; let it be preached from the pulpit, proclaimed in legislative halls, and enforced in courts of justice. And, in short, let it become the political religion of the nation; and let the old and the young, the rich and the poor, the grave and the gay, of all sexes and tongues, and colors, and conditions, sacrifice unceasingly upon its altars.[6]

RECAPTURING THE FABRIC OF COMMUNITY

Despite two decades of aspiring to effective community policing, American law enforcement seems to have drifted off the course of building close community ties toward creating a safe distance from community members, in some cases substituting equipment and technology as the preferred means of gathering information about crime and addressing threats to public safety. In some communities, the friendly neighborhood beat cop — community guardian — has been replaced with the urban warrior, trained for battle and equipped with the accouterments and weaponry of modern warfare. Armed with sophisticated technology to mine data about crime trends, officers can lose sight of the value of building close community ties.

Largely stripped of a nuanced understanding of how communities operate, crime tracking and crime prediction software minimizes the utility of hard-earned intelligence provided by line officers who know their beats. After all, one's ability to glean meaning from algorithms is only as good as its sourcing: the accumulated body of knowledge of officers who have come to understand that there are few "straight lines" in policing — that (sometimes visceral) personto-person contact is typically not well-suited to statistical models.[7]

Most law enforcement leaders recognize that creating stronger human connections and community engagement will lead to improved public safety and more effective crime fighting. So how do we build the foundation of trust necessary to form a true partnership between the police and the people we serve? The research tells us that, despite three decades of falling crime rates — and improved training, technology and tactics — public trust in the police has not improved. Instead, empirical assessments of trust and confidence in the police have remained generally unchanged in recent years.[8]

It turns out that people don't care as much about crime rates as they do about how they are treated by the police.[9]

This phenomenon, known in academic circles as procedural justice, is regularly practiced and understood by effective and respected beat officers. The public knows it when they see it. But neither has likely heard of or used the term. Both beat officers and members of the public would describe procedural justice in action as being a good cop and doing the right thing.

More formally, Tom Tyler of Yale University explains that procedural justice focuses on perceived impartiality during interactions between police and the communities they serve, participation ("voice") from the public during these interactions, fairness, and consistency of treatment. Fairness relates to the protection of human rights and goals to include equal treatment, nondiscrimination, and nonpartisanship.[10]

As Tyler and colleagues explain, procedural justice relates directly to legitimacy. "If legal authorities exercise their authority fairly, they build legitimacy and increase both willing deference to rules and the decisions of the police and the courts and the motivation to help with the task of maintaining social order in the community."[11] Put another way, procedural justice refers to the set of procedures by which agents of social control such as police meet, or fail to meet, standards of consistency, suppression of bias, accuracy of information, mechanisms of rectification, and ethicality of standards in their interactions with the public.[12]

Few police leaders would disagree that community trust would improve if police officers routinely employed procedural justice during their interactions with the public. Training in these principles is under way in a number of locations around the nation.[13]

Elaborating on the specific behaviors of a good cop doing the right thing, the theory of procedural justice was simplified and operationalized for training street officers through a model developed in 2011 by then King County, Wash., Sheriff Sue Rahr (and first author of this paper), using the acronym LEED — Listen and Explain with Equity and Dignity. Using the LEED model, officers are trained to take the time to listen to people; explain what is going to happen and how the process works; explain why that decision was made so the equity of the decision is transparent; and leave the participants with their dignity intact.

Positive police contact facilitates public confidence.[14] People tell good cops what is going on in their neighborhoods and work with them to keep it safe. They view good cops as part of their community — one of the key distinguishing characteristics between cops with a guardian mindset and cops who operate with a warrior mindset. The guardian operates as part of the community, demonstrating empathy and employing procedural justice principles during interactions. The behavior of the warrior cop, on the other hand, leads to the perception of an occupying force, detached and separated from the community, missing opportunities to build trust and confidence based on positive interactions. Police leaders dedicated to establishing practices in their agencies based on procedural justice principles must ensure that their organizational culture is not in conflict with these same principles. As Stephen K. Rice and Karen Collins Rice explain, "Organizational systems, such as training, are nested within cultures that tend to go under-acknowledged but have tangible, and even visceral, impacts on the people working within them and their likelihood for embracing change."[15]

The current culture in some American law enforcement agencies tends toward the warrior mentality. The seeds of that culture are planted during recruit training, when some recruits are trained in an academy environment that is modeled after military boot camp, a model designed to produce a warrior ready for battle and ready to follow orders and rules without question. As Radley Balko points out in his noted book, *Rise of the Warrior Cop,* the warrior mentality threatens Fourth Amendment principles and casts the relationship between officers and citizens as a battle between "us" and "them." Balko pulls no punches in describing the Department of Justice under Attorney Generals William French Smith and Edwin Meese during the Reagan era:

> This would be a rough decade for the Symbolic Third Amendment [what Balko characterizes as strong American resistance to armies policing American streets]. Reagan's drug warriors were about to take aim at posse comitatus, utterly dehumanize drug users, cast the

> drug fight as a biblical struggle between good and evil, and in the process turn the country's drug cops into holy soldiers (p. 139).[16]

One of the many problems with the military boot camp model used in some academies is that it has little to do with the daily reality of policing. Whereas attention has been focused on the best span of control of supervisors to patrol officers,[17] in reality, few officers working the street have consistent or even regular supervision. No one is giving them orders or making decisions for them, and police executives cannot generate enough rules to cover the variety of situations they will face on the street. Plus, even if we were to create "enough" rules for officers to memorize, the effort conflicts with what cognitive science tells us about limits on working memory: young adults generally can keep no more than three to five items in mind at a time.[18] Given the realities of policing, critical thinking and decision-making, not memorization, should be a top goal of any training strategy.

Another, more insidious problem in a military-style academy is the behavior modeled by the academy staff. Those without power (recruits) submit without question to the authority of those who have power (academy staff). Rule violations are addressed by verbal abuse or physical punishment in the form of pushups and extra laps.

Day-to-day power differentials may be reinforced more subtly. As Chief David Couper relays on his more than 20 years in the Madison (Wisc.) Police Department:

> When I was introduced to the academy class that was already in training before I was appointed, the class stood at attention when I entered the room. In fact, I found that not only did they stand at attention when I entered, but that they did so for every supervisor who came into their class.
>
> A coercive, top-down leadership model had no place within a police department that was seeking highly educated people to come and join it. Some of the people we were trying to attract into a police career were currently in business, law, social work, or teaching. And most of them wouldn't choose to remain in a police department that ran like an 18th century British warship (p. 150).[19]

Upon graduation, we send our newly trained recruits out into the community — they finally have power. Despite the way they were treated during their training, we expect them to treat the powerless people they encounter in the community with dignity and respect. One example of requiring the most from the least experienced has been in New York, where for years newly credentialed officers have been placed in "Operation Impact" assignments in many of the city's most stressed neighborhoods.[20] Why are we then surprised when some officers treat both suspects and citizens with the disdain and detachment they saw modeled by those in power at the academy?

According to the lead author's experience working with police academies across the nation, much recruit training focuses on physical control tactics and weapons, with less attention given to communication and de-escalation skills. The reasoning for this approach is the sacred mantra of officer safety. We train relentlessly — as we should — in physical tactics for the high-risk, low-frequency attacks.[21] Less instructional attention is focused on human behavioral science. Yet seasoned cops and statistics tell us that the officer's intellect and social dexterity are often the most effective officer safety tools. For the sake of safety, voluntary compliance should be the primary goal in resolving conflict, with physical control reserved for those who present an immediate threat and cannot be managed any other way.

Don't misunderstand — we are not advocating a reduction in tactical training or equipment.

Officer safety is critical, and we must maintain vigorous instruction on physical control tactics and weapons. Those skills will always be necessary for dealing with individuals who refuse to comply and present an immediate threat. But we need to significantly increase the level of training and importance placed on communication skills and human behavioral science if we truly care about the safety of our officers. As Lt. Jim Glennon of the popular Calibre Press tactical training programs explains in his engaging book, *Arresting Communication,* "Mastering the skill of communication provides an officer with deep insight into what the public wants, who they are, and what their intentions might be."[22]

This leads to another great conundrum for leaders. A "physical control as last resort" maxim places immense importance on officer discretion, an orientation that can run counter to longstanding tendencies to regulate officer actions through operational control in the form of complex policies, rules and procedures.[23] To reduce the need for officers to use physical force, it may be necessary to increase their discretion and to trust their critical thinking and decision-making skills.[24]

What stands in the way of adopting a training model and culture that supports the development of critically thinking leaders with enhanced skills in managing human behavior? Tradition. Some perceive moving away from the boot camp model as coddling recruits, making them weak and diminishing officer safety. Worse yet, it could be perceived as "soft on crime," a political death knell to leaders since the 1960s.

However, there appear to be no clearly logical or evidence-based reasons that we should train police officers as we do soldiers. Although police officers wear uniforms and carry weapons, the similarity ends there. Their missions and rules of engagement are completely different. The soldier's primary mission is that of a warrior: to conquer. The rules of engagement are decided before the battle. The police officer's mission is that of a guardian: to protect. The rules of engagement evolve as the incident unfolds. In war, collateral damage is expected and accepted. Not so in policing. On the battlefield, the soldier acts on orders from a superior. In the community, the officer is the leader, rarely operating with the luxury of direct supervision.

Why aren't more police executives clamoring to train police officers to be more independent, critically thinking leaders? Because it is not consistent with the culture that exists in many American police agencies. The hierarchical, top-down control model remains the predominant structure both in the station and on the street. We do not encourage the rank and file to question authority. We cling to the belief that fear of punishment for rule violations leads to greater rule adherence and better police performance. Many still believe that an abundance of rules leads to fewer mistakes and greater accountability. Though well-intentioned, this style of leadership has the unintended but powerful consequence of conveying a distrust of officers by their leaders. It is no wonder that one of the hallmarks of law enforcement culture is the reciprocated distrust and disdain of police leadership by rank-and-file officers.

As David Bayley explains, "Authority is very much top-down, but perhaps for good reason. Policing needs to be accountable to law and morality, so supervisors double-down on discipline so as to minimize mistakes, they hope. Not only do officers not trust the community, but senior officers don't trust their officers. They don't know how to minimize mistakes except by minimizing discretion."[25]

This culture is mirrored on the street when police actions focus primarily on aggressive enforcement (zero tolerance) in the belief that fear of arrest is the best way to prevent criminal behavior. Just as it does internally, this overfocus on enforcement conveys the same level of distrust between those in power (police) and those under their authority (the public). Just as we measure internal organizational success by employee adherence to rules, we measure external operational success through crime rates and arrest statistics. We do both to the detriment of building trust and legitimacy, because they ignore what the research tells us and what the public and the rank and file tell us. Both the public and rank-and-file officers want to be treated fairly by those in authority. We should not be surprised that we end up with poor morale among our officers echoed by the lack of trust from the community.

Changing the Police Culture from Warriors to Guardians

Perhaps it is time to reassess the predominant mindset of our profession, to change our culture — or rather recommit our culture — to democratic ideals. Perhaps it is time to revisit the wisdom of Plato and Sir Robert Peel and strive to become the trusted guardians of democracy. This will not be easy. In the first author's 35 years of experience, there are two things cops hate: the way things are, and change. When we add the emotional implications of changing culture, we must be prepared for strong resistance. That resistance will be intensified because we are challenging the very core of the warrior identity that many have embraced in the popular culture of policing. Furthermore, we are challenging the strict paramilitary organizational structure that is a hallmark of many police agencies. The challenge seems insurmountable.

There is good news. Change is afoot, and instructive examples are emerging around the country. One such transformation in training is taking place at the Washington State Criminal Justice Training Commission (WSCJTC). This transformation began in 2012, when Sue Rahr took over as the Executive Director. She brought with her the hard lessons from the street, the courts, and the political arena after serving 33 years with the King County Sheriff's Office, the last seven as the elected Sheriff. The following summary chronicles the transformation that occurred from 2012 to 2014 and continues today. This example is instructive for law enforcement leaders who are ready to transform their agencies from a culture of warriors to a culture of guardians.

Transforming Police Training in Washington State

The WSCJTC sets training standards, issues peace officer certifications, and conducts all mandated basic and advanced training for police, local corrections and a wide variety of other criminal justice system professionals. The Commission oversees the training of approximately 10,000 police officers and deputies from across the state, serving in 39 counties, 243 cities and a variety of tribal and state agencies. Each year, more than 600 police recruits receive 720 hours of basic training in programs that last 5 months. Figure 1 shows the courses and hours of training.

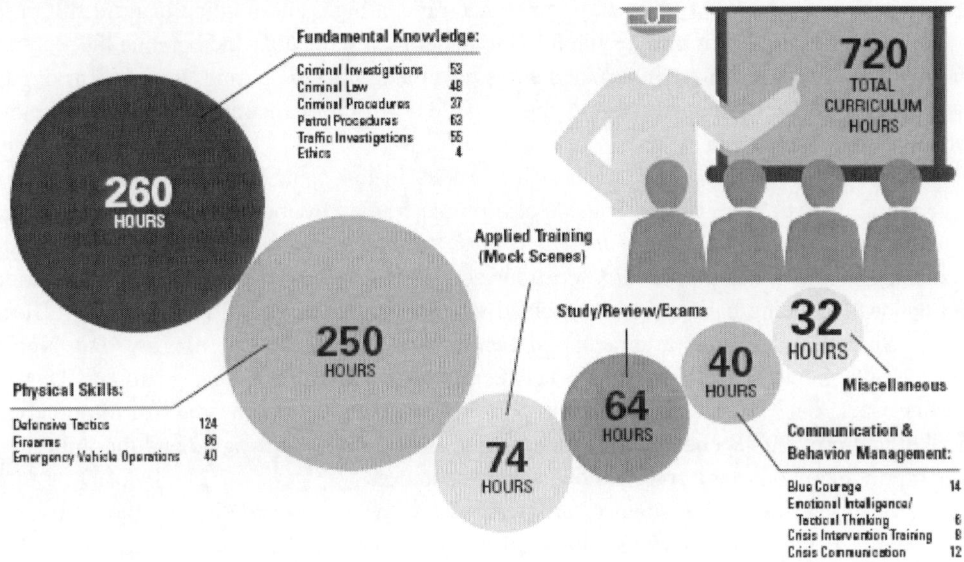

*Elements of the Communications and Behavioral Management training have been extensively integrated into the Fundamental Knowledge and Physical Skills blocks of training and must be demonstrated in Mock Scenes.

Figure 1. Basic Law Enforcement Academy Curriculum.

Before 2012, basic training was conducted according to a paramilitary "boot camp" model that employed a deterrence strategy to maintain discipline and control. Referred to as a "tune-up," starting the first day, training officers yelled at and berated new recruits for failing to complete drills designed to be impossible. Recruits were required to brace (salute) and remain silent whenever they encountered an academy staff member. Minor rule violations resulted in physical punishment in the form of extra pushups and running laps.

Despite the offering of behavioral and communications instruction in the classroom, the majority of the five-month training regimen emphasized physical skills training accompanied by a steady stream of fear-provoking stories about officers killed in the line of duty. Few classes effectively integrated communication skills and physical tactics. Physical control was emphasized over de-escalation. Conquering was emphasized over serving.

Most of the posters and visual aids in the classrooms carried themes related to deadly threats on the lives of officers. Skulls and crossbones were featured prominently. The lobby was decorated with display cases featuring the "tools of the trade." Legacy mementos from previous classes reflected a consistent theme of warriors, battles and survival. Noticeably absent from both the physical environment and curriculum was any reference to service and the noble and historical role of policing in a democracy.

What changed? The first change was the elimination of the protocol requiring recruits to brace. The new protocol requires recruits to initiate a conversation any time they come in contact with a staff member, taking care to make eye contact, show respect and address the person as "sir" or "ma'am."

The artificially imposed fear and humiliation from the "tune-up" day has been replaced by coaching. The standards for physical performance remain high, and training officers still push the recruits far beyond their physical limits. But, rather than screaming and berating the recruits, the training officers vigorously coach and encourage them to keep pushing. Instead of trying to instill a sense of fear, training officers strive to build a sense of camaraderie and pride for the success of the whole team.

The displays containing the "tools of the trade" in the main lobby were replaced by a large mural depicting the United States Constitution, framed by the following words in large relief: *"In These Halls ... Training the Guardians of Democracy,"* as shown in Figure 2. This theme has been replicated in several locations across the campus. Posters depicting the pride and honor of policing have been interspersed with the more traditional posters about officer safety. Speeches delivered at graduation ceremonies emphasize the nobility and higher purpose of policing and the distinction between the roles of warriors and guardians. During the first week, each recruit is presented a pocket-sized book containing the Constitution and the Declaration of Independence. A vigorous discussion about civil rights and the important role of policing in our democracy follows the presentation.

Behavioral and social science programs have been integrated into the 720-hour curriculum. Although intertwined, each of these programs has a distinct purpose that supports the others and contributes to better officer safety and improved public trust — two areas that, in the past, have been incorrectly viewed as mutually exclusive. They are:

- *Blue Courage.* Developed through a Bureau of Justice Assistance grant, this motivational program instills pride and supports values about the nobility of policing and the importance of maintaining physical, emotional and spiritual health. It has also been implemented at the Arizona Law Enforcement Academy and is currently being introduced to the rank and file at the New York Police Department and many other agencies across the nation.
- *Justice Based Policing.* This program, developed by the King County Sheriff's Office with funding from the Office of Community Oriented Policing Services, teaches the principles of procedural justice using the LEED model (Listen and Explain with Equity and Dignity).
- *Crisis Intervention Training.* This program teaches recruits to recognize behavioral cues associated with mental illness and traumatic brain injury and helps recruits develop strategies to de-escalate conflict and gain compliance. More than half of the "mock scenario" training and testing activities have been modified to include options and requirements for using crisis intervention techniques.
- *Tactical Social Interaction.* Academy personnel worked in partnership with Defense Advanced Research Program Administration (DARPA) researchers to create a program that teaches students specific, measurable actions that increase rapport between strangers and lead to positive social interaction. Although the program was developed to train Marine recruits how to conduct peacekeeping missions in foreign villages, it has shown great utility for police officers and is currently being adapted for both basic and in-service training.

- *"The Respect Effect."* Lessons from the book by Paul Meshanko about the neuroscience behind the acts of respect and disrespect to either motivate or antagonize[26] were integrated into the basic academy curriculum. At the same time, the entire WSCJTC staff completed the program as a demonstration of the effectiveness of this organizational strategy to begin cultural transformation.

Figure 2. A 6' x 9' Mural of the United States Constitution.

What has not changed? Moving away from the "boot camp" model has not led to softening of the training. Recruits still must demonstrate a high level of proficiency in defensive tactics and firearms. In fact, additional firearms training time and tools have been added, and the defensive tactics program has been expanded to include more realistic and challenging scenarios.

Discipline standards have not been relaxed. The use of formal titles and deference to senior officers and staff are still required. The changes made at the academy do not resemble previous experiments with "non-stress" academies, nor has the environment been changed to mirror a community college. The military protocols that have been retained (marching and formal flag ceremonies) are focused on patriotism and honor rather than power and submission. Behavioral strategies and decision-making have been integrated into physical control scenarios to better reflect the reality of policing.

A five-year longitudinal study of the effectiveness of the new training is now under way, having been launched in the fall of 2014. Researchers will follow cohorts of recruits for five years, conducting interviews and administering surveys at various intervals. The study is designed to determine if the guardian philosophy, the Blue Courage program and the Tactical Social Interaction program positively influence officers' attitudes about their job and the public. It will also measure whether or not officers trained under those programs are more likely to use crisis intervention strategies and de-escalation skills in the field than officers trained under the old warrior philosophy.

CONCLUSION

As this paper was being written, media images of officers atop armored personnel carriers, dressed in military fatigues and armed with rifles, have proven to be a powerful catalyst for vigorous discussion about the militarization of police in this country.[27] This debate should generate introspection by police leaders about cultures created within police agencies. This introspection should lead to a robust conversation with community members to assess whether police cultures reflect the values and expectations of the communities they serve.

AUTHOR NOTE

Sue Rahr is Executive Director of the Washington State Criminal Justice Training Commission and former King County Sheriff, Seattle, Wash. Stephen K. Rice, Ph.D., is Associate Professor of Criminal Justice at Seattle University.

The authors would like to thank Dr. David Bayley, Distinguished Professor Emeritus at the University at Albany, and Christine Cole, Vice President and Executive Director of the Crime and Justice Institute at Community Resources for Justice, for their thoughtful comments on earlier versions of this paper.

End Notes

[1] Nila, Michael and Stephen R. Covey, *The Nobility of Policing,* West Valley City, Utah: Franklin Covey Publishing, 2008: 7.

[2] See Holland, Kenneth, "Socrates: The First Criminal Justice Educator," *Criminal Justice Review,* 5(2) (1980): 1-4.

[3] As a kind of "policing originalism," Sir Robert Peel has received newfound attention in his impact on New York Police Commissioner William Bratton. See Goldstein, Joseph and J. David Goodman, "A London Guide for 1 Police Plaza," *New York Times,* April 15, 2014, http:// www.nytimes.com/2014/04/16/nyregion/alondon-guide-for-1-police-plaza.html.

[4] Within the context of homeland security and the risk of profiling, see, e.g., Rice, Stephen K. and William Parkin, "New Avenues for Profiling Research: The Question of Muslim Americans," in *Race, Ethnicity and Policing,* ed. S.K. Rice and M.D. White, New York: New York University Press, 2010.

[5] Schulhofer, Stephen J., "The Constitution and the Police: Individual Rights and Law Enforcement," Washington *University Law Quarterly* 66 (1) (1988): 11.

[6] Lincoln, Abraham, "Address Before the Springfield Young Men's Lyceum," in *The Political Thought of Abraham Lincoln,* ed. R.N. Current, Indianapolis, Indiana: Bobbs-Merrill, 1967.

[7] For a useful conversation about the challenges and advantages of predictive policing software, see Vlahos, James, "The Department of Pre-Crime," *Scientific American,* January 2012.

[8] Tyler, T.R., "Trust and Legitimacy in the USA and Europe," *European Journal of Criminology* 8 (2011): 254-266.

[9] See Meares, Tracey L., *Rightful Policing,* New Perspectives in Policing Bulletin, Washington, D.C.: U.S. Department of Justice, National Institute of Justice, 2015. NCJ 248411; Meares Tracey L., Tom R. Tyler and Jacob Gardener, "Lawful or Fair? How Cops and Laypeople View Good Policing," Social Science Research

Network, 2012, http://papers.ssrn.com/abstract=2116645 (last visited Nov. 13, 2014); Paternoster, Raymond, Ronet Bachman, Robert Brame, and Lawrence W. Sherman, "Do Fair Procedures Matter? The Effect of Procedural Justice on Spouse Assault," *Law and Society Review* 31 (1997): 163-197; Tyler, Tom R. and Yuen J. Huo, *Trust in the Law: Encouraging Public Cooperation With the Police and Courts,* New York: Russell Sage Foundation, 2002; Tyler, Tom R., "Enhancing Police Legitimacy," *Annals of the American Academy of Political & Social Science* 593 (2004): 84-99; Tyler, Tom R. and Jeffrey Fagan, "Legitimacy and Cooperation: Why Do People Help the Police Fight Crime in Their Communities?" *Ohio State Journal of Criminal Law* 6 (2008): 231; Tyler, Tom R. and Cheryl Wakslak, "Profiling and Police Legitimacy: Procedural Justice, Attributions of Motive, and Acceptance of Police Authority," *Criminology* 42 (2004): 253.

[10] See Hickman, Matthew J., "Democratic Policing: How Would We Know It If We Saw It?" in *Race, Ethnicity and Policing: New and Essential Readings,* ed. S. K. Rice and M.D. White, New York: New York University Press, 2010.

[11] See Tyler, Tom, Jonathan Jackson, and Ben Bradford, "Psychology of Procedural Justice and Cooperation," in *Encyclopedia of Criminology and Criminal Justice,* ed. G. Bruinsma and D. Weisburd, New York: Springer-Verlag, 2013.

[12] Leventhal, F.S., J. Karuza, Jr., and W.R. Fry, "Beyond Fairness: A Theory of Allocation Preferences," in *Justice and Social Interaction,* ed. G. Mikula, New York: Springer-Verlag, 1980: 167-218.

[13] One such effort is the Chicago Police Department's goal of training its 11,000 officers in procedural justice principles. See Fox, Aubrey, "Work in Progress: Can Police Officers Be Trained in Procedural Justice Principles?" *Augustus: The Latest Research* and *Commentary About Criminal Justice Reform,* Apr. 16, 2013.

[14] Bradford, Ben, Jonathan Jackson, and Elizabeth A. Stanko, "Contact and Confidence: Revisiting the Impact of Public Encounters With the Police," *Policing and Society: An International Journal of Research and Policy* 19(1) (2009): 20-46.

[15] Rice, Stephen K. and Karen Collins Rice, "How to Change the Culture of the Seattle Police Department," *Seattle Times* (June 20, 2014), http:// seattletimes.com/html/opinion/2023892606_ stephenkarencollinsriceoped policereform23xml. html.

[16] Balko, Radley, *Rise of the Warrior Cop: The Militarization of America's Police Forces,* New York: Public Affairs Books, 2013.

[17] See Johnson, O'Ryan, "Police Supervisors Push Marty Walsh to Add 40 to Staff," *Boston Herald,* May 24, 2014, http://bostonherald. com/news_opinion/local_coverage/2014/05/ police_supervisors_push_marty_walsh_to_ add_40_to_staff (accessed May 25, 2014).

[18] See Cowan, Nelson. "The Magical Mystery Four: How Is Working Memory Capacity Limited, and Why?" *Current Directions in Psychological Science* 19 (2010): 51-57.

[19] Couper, D.C., *Arrested Development: A Veteran Police Chief Sounds Off About Protest, Racism, Corruption and the Seven Steps Necessary to Improve Our Nation's Police,* Indianapolis, Indiana: Dog Ear Publishing, 2011.

[20] The tide may be shifting, however. As New York Police Commissioner William Bratton explained recently, "I want to change the dynamic of kids coming out of the academy and immediately being put into Operation Impact assignments, where they really have an almost single-minded focus and really don't get a full flavor of the job." Goodman, J. David, "Bratton Says Rookies' Role in Anticrime Effort Will End." *The New York Times,* Feb. 1, 2004, http://www.nytimes. com/2014/02/01/nyregion/bratton-tells-chiefshell-stop-sending-rookies-to-high-crime-areas. html (accessed May 25, 2014).

[21] Methodologically, this "high risk, low frequency" operational environment has been assessed by way of "danger ratios" and similar tools (see, e.g., Garner, Joel and Elizabeth Clemmer, *Danger to Police in Domestic Disturbances,* Washington, D.C.: U.S. Department of Justice, National Institute of Justice, 1986. Garner and Clemmer's formula uses the ratio of violent incidents divided by the total police activity in the area of focus).

[22] Glennon, Jim, *Arresting Communication: Essential Interaction Skills for Law Enforcement,* Villa Park, Illinois: LifeLine Training, 2010: 35.

[23] See Alpert, Geoffrey P. and William C. Smith, "Developing Police Policy: An Evaluation of the Control Principle," *American Journal of Police* 13 (1994): 1.

[24] For an excellent review of cutting-edge research on decision-making and problem-solving, see Brockman, John (ed.), *Thinking: The New Science of Decision-Making, Problem-Solving, and Prediction,* New York: Harper Collins, 2013. Of particular relevance to policing is *Thinking's* discussion of the smart heuristics that expert performers use to make good decisions. As Brockman explains, "In order to make good decisions in an uncertain world, one sometimes has to ignore information. The art is knowing what one doesn't have to know" (p. 40).

[25] Bayley, David, personal correspondence, June 15, 2014.

[26] Meshanko, Paul, *The Respect Effect: Using the Science of Neuroleadership to Inspire a More Loyal and Productive Workplace,* Columbus, Ohio: McGraw-Hill Education, 2013.

[27] Militarization of the police within the context of Ferguson has received explicit attention. See, e.g., http://www.msnbc.com/andrea-mitchell-reports/watch/ police-militarization-adds-to-fergusonchaos-319148099539.

In: Perspectives on Policing
Editor: Holly Wheeler
ISBN: 978-1-63484-555-7

Chapter 5

RACE AND POLICING: AN AGENDA FOR ACTION*

David H. Bayley, Michael A. Davis and Ronald L. Davis

American police confront issues of race, daily, in almost everything they do. They confront race in the geographic distribution of criminality and the fear of crime as well as in assumptions about what criminals look like. They confront race in the suspicion and hostility of many young African American men they encounter on the street. They confront race in complaints from ethnic communities about being either over- or under-policed. They confront race in charges of racial profiling and unequal justice. And they confront race in decisions about hiring, promoting and assigning police officers. In short, race remains an "American dilemma," as Gunnar Myrdal famously observed in 1944 (Myrdal, 1944), especially and inescapably for today's police.

The importance of race in policing has been demonstrated in discussions held since 2008 at the Second Executive Session on Policing and Public Safety at Harvard University. At almost every session, race emerged as a troubling preoccupation for police executives. Although many suggestions for dealing with the issue were discussed, the Executive Session did not try to formulate policies to deal with the various issues involving race. Concern about race seemed to become stalled in discussion rather than advancing to action. So, the authors of this article suggested to the Session members that we try to cull an agenda for action from the years of frank, insightful and sometimes passionate conversation. The Session readily agreed. These are the ideas we think are most promising in terms of what police executives might do to alleviate the problems of race in contemporary policing. They reflect what we have learned that might help the most. We alone are responsible for the contents of this agenda.

Readers should also understand that the agenda consists of suggestions, not directions. Although some of these ideas have been tried, few, if any, have been evaluated. Furthermore,

* This is an edited, reformatted and augmented version of a paper, NCJ 248624, in the New Perspectives in Policing series, issued by the U.S. Department of Justice, National Institute of Justice, June 2015.

many of them are controversial. We include them nonetheless in order to provoke thought, often explicitly acknowledging their shortcomings. We hope that this agenda will move discussions about race from anger and yearning to concrete action by police leaders, and beyond. This is also not a "scholarly" paper that cites and explores all the writing that has been done on the activities suggested. That is beyond our ability. Therefore, before following any of our leads, readers should do their homework. Others, often more experienced than we, have thought about these issues before.

The agenda is organized into two parts — Strategic Voice and Tactical Agency. Strategic Voice argues that problems of race in policing cannot be resolved by the police alone. Other people must help by understanding and ameliorating the social conditions that cause race to be associated with crime and hence become a dilemma for American policing. Rather than accepting these conditions as givens, police leaders with their powerful collective voice should actively call attention to what needs to be changed.

Tactical Agency outlines what the police can do on their own initiative to deal with the operational dilemmas of race — in the communities they serve and in their own organizations.

Strategic Voice

We believe there are two messages that police leaders must find the voice to deliver: (1) Police need to be supported by policies that address conditions causing criminality and disorder to be concentrated in particular places, especially in communities of color; and (2) police strategies must expand freedom and justice, not just provide safety.

Strategic Voice One

Police officers know, through hard-won experience, that crime is not randomly distributed in society. It is concentrated in particular places. Any good cop can drive immediately to the neighborhoods where crimes rates are the highest and 911 calls are most common. Most of the rest of their jurisdictions are virtually free of reported crime.

The problem is that the highest rates of violent crime are in minority neighborhoods — those where African Americans, Latinos and new immigrants live. This creates the impression that race or ethnicity is implicated in criminality and that serious crime in America is particularly a "black problem" (Braga and Brunson, 2015). However, this reasoning gets the causality backward. Race does not generate criminality but, rather, the circumstances that create compacted disadvantage for minority groups also create criminality. As the police who work in minority communities know, people of color are no more tolerant of crime and disorder than others. It also obscures the fact that minority people are more likely than the majority of white people to be victims of crime.

Police also know that their ability to reduce crime where it matters most, as in disadvantaged neighborhoods, is limited through both reactive law enforcement and proactive crime prevention programs. This is not to say that the police cannot do anything, although it is generally agreed that deterrence alone will not reduce crime for people most at risk from it.

Police officers are often frustrated by what little they can achieve as they respond over and over to the same problems among the same people in the same places. They feel that they are only "a band-aid on a cancer."

So, our first recommendation is that police leaders call attention publicly to the conditions of economic and social disadvantage that generate crime and disorder and undermine the ability of communities to protect themselves. They should speak loudly about the connections they see in their own experience between serious crime and conditions of unemployment, poverty, truancy, education attrition, teen pregnancy, housing segregation, inadequate health care, crowded and unsanitary housing, homelessness, underfinanced public services, and a lack of civic amenities such as parks, public transportation and street lighting. They should say publicly, out loud, as one commentator said almost 40 years ago, that police can only "perform a holding operation until other institutions attack such problems with an array of resources" (Robinson, 1975: 278).

Of course, it is one thing to be critical of, even outraged by, persistent, self-perpetuating conditions associated with high crime rates. It is another to frame policies that will successfully remedy them. Doing this will take the finest minds the country has. All we can do is suggest the sorts of policy changes that should be considered:

1) Recognize that race endures as an issue in America, not just because people are prejudiced but also because they fail to support structural changes that equalize opportunity. Law enforcement should not be viewed as a morality play between good guys and bad guys. It is about circumstances that put people on different life courses. Police, black communities and even street gangs are, as David Kennedy (2011) has said:

> all, all of them, in their own ways strong and aspirational and resilient. They are, all of them, dealing as best they can with a world they did not make. They are all doing profoundly destructive things without understanding what they do.
>
> There is, on all sides, malice, craziness, and evil, but not much, it turns out, not much at all. There is, on all sides, a deep reservoir of core human decency. (p. 17)

2) Focus crime prevention programs on communities and neighborhoods, not just on individuals. In particular, improve physical environments, fix the famous "broken windows," and develop the capacity of communities to organize for the advancement of common interests, whether using their own resources or mobilizing wider public and private help.
3) Mobilize and coordinate all government services bearing on public safety rather than assigning responsibility exclusively to the police. If criminality is rooted in social conditions, especially chronic deprivations, then more than police action is required to prevent it. Effective crime prevention requires that all the resources of government — welfare, education, health, sanitation, recreation, public transport — be focused where criminality is concentrated. It requires wholeof-government planning and implementation.

Strategic Voice One may be sensible and righteous, but it poses risks for police. It puts them squarely into politics by challenging the policy shortcomings of the very governments that hired them. Furthermore, these brave words undermine what police chiefs promise and what the public expects from the police — safety represented by effective crime control.

They challenge the very raison d'etre of police. Although social policies undoubtedly contribute to crime, the police have been created precisely to minimize their effects.

Strategic Voice One is also out of sync with American public opinion about structural inequality, according to an NBC/*Wall Street Journal* poll in June 2013 (Blow, 2013). Asked to explain poverty in the U.S., most people (24 percent) blamed the individuals themselves, especially citing receipt of welfare that eroded individual initiative. Only 4 percent blamed "lack of government money." They did implicate unemployment (18 percent) and poor schooling (13 percent), although one wonders where they thought the remedies would come from, if not from government. The article concludes that "the stereotypes of poor people in the United States are among the most negative prejudices that we have ... . It seems like Washington is a place without pity right now" (Blow, 2013). That these uncharitable views may be laced with racism goes without saying.

Scholars, too, have been complicit in fostering doubts about the efficacy of structural interventions. In his 1975 book, *Thinking About Crime,* James Q. Wilson argued that government was ill-equipped to remedy the root causes of crime, even if they could be identified with certainty (Wilson, 1975). He believed that public policy should focus on changing the incentives for crime by increasing the risk to offenders and lowering the relative rewards. Criminology in the following years seemed to follow his lead, focusing more on exploring factors that facilitated criminality (such as "routine activity theory," Cohen and Felson, 1979) or changing criminal trajectories of individuals than on macrosocial correlates (Sampson, 2012). Advocates for structural reform have been very few (Currie, 2010). Intellectual predispositions, it would seem, may shape scholarship just as ideology does politics.

Asking police leaders to speak with Strategic Voice One is asking a lot. It requires them to articulate a larger vision of the social forces and structural factors linked to crime, even as they direct the everyday efforts of their police officers to address specific incidents of crime. As one member of the Executive Session said, "I feel like if we are going to be the canaries in the coal mine about this issue [race] from a macro level, we are going to really injure our ability to do any good at the micro level."

Strategic Voice Two

The primary purpose for which police have been created is to safeguard life and property. This should continue to be their operational focus because public safety is not only a human right; it is fundamental to any constructive social activity, including the kind of community reconstruction suggested by Strategic Voice One. Implementing this purpose is more complex in the United States, however, because public safety must be created in a particularly demanding way, namely, within a rule of law that protects individuals from unjustified intrusions of governmental power. American policing is not just about crime fighting; it involves enhancing human freedom at the same time. Policing in America has two goals, both equally important (Manning, 2011).

Accordingly, we recommend that police leaders explain, publicly and repeatedly, what is involved in combining effective law enforcement with liberty. It begins with finding the voice to criticize criminal justice policies that produce high rates of black male incarceration, perceptions of racial profiling, unequal enforcement of drug laws, and justice outcomes affected by race and class.

But it goes farther. It requires police, through word and deed, to obtain the public's consent for their actions. Policing with consent is an old theme in the democratic police tradition. Sir Robert Peel, considered the founding father of modern Anglo-American policing (1829), is credited with formulating nine principles of policing, three of which involve policing with communities (CIVITAS, 2014):

- "To recognise always that the power of the police to fulfil their functions and duties is dependent on public approval of their existence, actions and behaviour and on their ability to secure and maintain public respect."
- "To recognise always that to secure and maintain the respect and approval of the public means also the securing of the willing co-operation of the public in the task of securing observance of laws."
- "To maintain at all times a relationship with the public that gives reality to the historic tradition that the police are the public and that the public are the police, the police being only members of the public who are paid to give full[-]time attention to duties which are incumbent on every citizen in the interests of community welfare and existence."

These principles became meaningful at first through the encouragement of the public to contact police directly whenever something is wrong that needs authoritative intervention, such as the commission of crime. Operationally, this became the 911 dispatch system developed during the 20th century. The importance of public input in creating the police agenda was reaffirmed by the First Executive Session on Police and Public Safety, 1986–1992, but with a new wrinkle. Rather than having police work defined by individuals as well as the police themselves, the First Session stressed the importance of police consulting with, as well as mobilizing, communities with common interests. This was called community policing. Two of the recommendations were to create neighborhood advisory boards and for police officers to conduct periodic visits to individual homes and businesses. In effect, community policing introduced a new level of social organization into policing by consent — groups of individuals organized by interest and/ or geography.

Together, 911 and community policing empowered the public to shape what police do through individual and neighborhood instigation. Through them, policing by consent became radically democratized. It shifted the authority for determining what police do away from formal government, represented by the police, and directly to the public. As a result, police in the United States and in other democratic countries became more than agents of government. They became the citizens' police (Bayley, 1985). "Consent" in democratic countries means more than acceptance by the public of what the police are doing; it also means the ability to shape that activity directly through personal contact. This represents a radical change in the relation of security institutions to the public — one that has become the distinguishing characteristic of democratic policing. Policing by consent, in this sense, exists in only a handful of countries worldwide.

Policing with consent has another dimension, one more recently discovered: namely, how the police act in their encounters with the public. Beginning in the early 1990s, Professor Tom Tyler showed that when people are treated by the police in ways they regard as respectful and fair, they are less likely to resist and more likely to conform to what the law requires (Tyler, 2006). Robert Peel, in fact, made much the same point in one of his nine principles of policing (CIVITAS, 2014):

> [Police should] seek and preserve public favour, not by pandering to public opinion[,] but by constantly demonstrating absolutely impartial service to law, in complete independence of policy, and without regard to the justice or injustice of the substance of individual laws[;] by ready offering of individual service and friendship to all members of the public without regard to their wealth or social standing[;] by ready exercise of courtesy and friendly good humour; and by ready offering of individual sacrifice in protecting and preserving life.

Tyler's research moved significantly beyond Peel's generalities by showing that police behavior, both in attitude and procedure, could improve law enforcement outcomes even with people who have violated the law. "Procedural justice," as he calls it, undercuts a common belief among police that authority has to be visibly demonstrated to actual and potential lawbreakers and that adhering to technicalities of legal procedure undermines deterrence. Procedural justice challenges the mindset that there are tradeoffs between effectiveness in controlling crime and observance of civil rights guaranteed by the Constitution.

Giving voice to policing by consent is probably less controversial than the social reforms of Strategic Voice One. Priorities in police work and the behavior of officers are ongoing topics of conversation within contemporary police agencies, well within the "police line of work." Moreover, police officers understand from their own experience the importance of having the public "on their side." Exercising "discretion" in applying the law is an accepted part of police professionalism. Police officers know that different folks need different strokes. The crucial question is, which folks?

At the same time, some of the issues embedded in policing with consent are controversial among police, and discussing them in public is not something they may be comfortable doing.

Responding to calls for service in a timely manner, for example, is enormously popular with the public and politicians alike. It is costly, however, and may divert resources that might be more effectively employed in proactive crime prevention. Some of the popular new strategies, such as predictive and hot spots policing, depend on analyses done by headquarters staff, not input from the public. Police may also know better, in some cases, about how to deal with particular forms of crime. Furthermore, police are increasingly expected to address not just crimes that affect individuals (street crime) but also crimes that affect the society as a whole, such as terrorism, drug markets, human trafficking and violent youth gangs. Within this crowded agenda, encouraging and facilitating direct public input may seem a luxury from a bygone age (Bayley and Nixon, 2010).

So, too, with procedural justice. Many police officers believe that respect comes from a display of authority. They believe that they are the best judges of people who are deserving of soft or hard treatment, and they resent having their decisions challenged. The public, too, is ambivalent about procedural justice. Many people believe strongly in being "tough on crime" and not "coddling criminals," and they are willing to excuse intrusive and punitive policing when they fear the crime is close at hand.

Selling procedural justice will be much easier in the abstract than in the particular. In areas experiencing high levels of violence, police and the public may doubt that procedural justice will gain enough consent, especially from troublemakers, to improve safety significantly. Perhaps in those situations, consent is more likely to come from being "tough on crime" rather than from procedural justice (Tankebe, 2009). Issues like these are being explored and tested in a departmentwide training program developed by the Chicago Police Department in 2011. It has already been given to over 3,000 employees (Meares and Neyroud, 2015)

Finally, supporting policing by consent involves taking a stand on another development that is very controversial among police, namely, civilian review. In the U.S., racial minorities have repeatedly criticized the willingness of police agencies to investigate themselves. Their consent to be policed turns, to a considerable degree, on whether they believe police are being held to account. Civilian review is supposed to provide that assurance. Civilian review panels have been used to evaluate both the crime-control effectiveness of the police and the behavior of police in carrying out assigned duties.

The questions for American police are not "whether" to allow civilian review but, instead, "when" and "how." More than 100 American cities have already developed some form of it. All Canadian provinces and all Australian states have; so, too, has Great Britain (Stenning, 2011; Walker, 2010). Civilian review is being advocated by both the United Nations and the U.S. government as fundamental to police reform in countries emerging from civil strife. For many people in democratic countries, civilian review is essential for ensuring that police are practicing procedural justice.

What is often not recognized in debates about civilian review is that it is not unidimensional. It varies from place to place in membership, powers and ambit of oversight. Some civilian review boards, for example, only evaluate the rigor with which the police receive, investigate and discipline allegations of misbehavior and then publish the results. Others have the power to oversee particular investigations and provide advice about them. Still others completely remove investigations and the determination of sanctions from police authority. Being either in favor or opposed to civilian review in principle is naive — especially when one considers that, in democratic countries, civilian review already occurs by elected officials, courts and the media. "Civilian review" may be new, but review by civilians is not.

In sum, speaking with Strategic Voice Two is easy to do in normative generalities. It fits America's democratic heritage. The difficulty comes in convincing police officers and the public that policing with consent improves the effectiveness of crime control. Scholars and many police officers believe that it does. Strategic Voice Two requires police leaders to participate in a public discussion about the importance of policing with consent in achieving public safety. In particular, it challenges them to discuss openly whether small encroachments on civil rights enhance public safety or, at the very least, to explain when exceptions are justified.

TACTICAL AGENCY

Police may do important things to address the dilemmas of race in policing without waiting for outside support in the form of either additional resources or progressive social policies. Indeed, many departments have courageously accepted the need to confront issues of race, instituting new programs and revising customary ways of doing business. We provide references to some active programs (see "References"). However, given the number and variety of American police agencies, the implementation of such actions has been uneven. To encourage and assist in reform, we make the following suggestions, drawing on the growing experience of police themselves and on the research by scholars. Our suggestions are divided into two parts — engaging the community and managing police agencies.

Engaging the Community

1) Reorient the culture of policing from going to war against lawbreakers to engaging with communities to help those at risk and in need. One way to do this is to take the time to educate police officers about the history of the communities to which they are assigned, stressing the fact that their inhabitants, especially the children, have no control over that history.
2) Embrace community policing as the primary strategy for policing. This is not an uncomplicated suggestion. Community policing has been consistently advocated as a philosophy applicable throughout policing (see, e.g., Bayley and Skolnick, 1988). Views differ considerably, however, about its programmatic elements (Maguire et al., 1997). As a result, officers have been confused about what it means for their work, frequently dismissing it with the comment, "community policing, whatever that means." For this reason, many officers have come to the conclusion that it was largely a matter of rhetoric, a flavor-of-the-month whose time had passed. Problem-oriented policing (POP), often associated with community-oriented policing, has enjoyed greater staying power precisely because it has a clear implementation program. POP quickly became identified as a set of activities — scanning, analysis, response and assessment — identified by the acronym SARA.
3) Police officers should develop the habit of explaining what they are doing whenever they act (Fridell et al., 2001). This is particularly important when an encounter has occurred as a result of the initiative of the police officer, especially when African Americans are the target.
4) Patrol supervisors should regularly assess how people contacted by the police feel about the treatment they received. This may be done systematically through surveys or by direct contact with individuals who have solicited help or have been contacted proactively.
5) A simple, user-friendly system for receiving complaints from the public about police behavior should be created. Its receptiveness should be tested periodically by sending civilians or plainclothes police officers to file complaints. For example, the Charlotte- Mecklenburg police in North Carolina have created a website for filing

complaints online (http://charmeck.org/city/charlotte/CMPD/Pages/Complaints.aspx).

6) Routinely collect and publish information about allegations of police misbehavior, the results of investigations into them, and their disciplinary outcomes. This kind of transparency is important for reassuring communities that police are serious about investigating and punishing misbehavior. It makes the issue of police discipline discussable publicly.

Managing the Organization

Police organizations are themselves microcosms of the community they ser ve, where larger societal issues have very real implications for running an effective organization. In order to make progress externally, the police need to improve race relations internally.

1. Officers in supervisory positions must demonstrate, by word and action, that protection of human rights should permeate all aspects of policing. Their performance in this regard should be part of their annual evaluations. In particular, supervisors at all levels must never tolerate attitudes (often revealed in denigrating language) that excuse differential treatment of particular groups, such as "We have to be tough with those people" and "Those people only respect force."
2. Managers must search out and confront racial and ethnic tensions among offcers, especially perceptions by minorities that they have not received equitable treatment in assignments or promotions. Frank discussions with organizations representing minority offcers can be very helpful.
3. In place of detailed regulations, statements of values should be developed that guide all aspects of policing that involve the public. Having clear statements about standards of behavior is necessary in order to empower supervisors in taking corrective action. As one participant at the Executive Session remarked, It's easier to act your way to right thinkingthan to think your way to right acting." Right behavior is ensured when it is required by the immediate supervisors. The Madison, Wis., police department pioneered this approach in the early 1980s. The Milwaukee Police Department has a detailed code of conduct specifying the depa rtment's mission, values and disciplinary guidelines. (See http://city. milwaukee.gov/police under "About MPD/Code of Conduct & Standard Operating Procedures").
4. Take time to explain the importance of neighborhood histories so that officers understand the people they will be dealing with. This is usually done through "cultural sensitivity" programs featuring presentations by members of racial and ethnic communities. A better way is to show recruits what the world looks like from subcultural points of view. This can be done by assigning recruit officers to live among and with minority families for short periods of time or to serve as interns for neighborhood nonprofit organizations.
5. Develop procedures for evaluating whether officers engage effectively with communities, and reward them in recognizable ways.
6. Create early warning systems for detecting patterns of behavior, such as complaints filed against officers, that indicate potential vulnerabilities for the officer and the

department. The primary purpose of such systems is not to punish but to provide counseling to officers so as to reduce their level of risk. The creation of such a system was a key recommendation in the 1997 consent decree between the U.S. Department of Justice and the Pittsburgh police department, and many other accords since then.

CONCLUSION

The purpose of this article has been to move the discussion about the dilemmas of race in policing from talk to action. Although we think these actions will help to ease tensions at the intersection of policing and race, race will remain difficult to talk about. However, at some point in the career of every senior officer, the need to do so will almost inevitably arise. It will occur when a white officer shoots a black man, when police of any color arrest distraught minority women amid a jeering crowd, and when crime-control activities in high-crime neighborhoods weigh more heavily on minority people. In situations like these, race becomes "the third rail" in discussions between police leaders and their communities, leading to an angry disconnect. Because of its sensitivity, therefore, police leaders should think carefully about what they should say when race-infused events occur.

The key is for police leaders to remember that they are not trying to change the minds of the people who are either irretrievably bigoted or already open-minded. Some people are attuned to expect prejudice in all dealings with the police, others reflexively defend the police and discount charges of unequal treatment, and still others wave the "bloody flag" of race for their own purposes. The target audience is not these, but the vast majority who know little about either policing or race. For these people, the discussion needs to move away from charge and countercharge to an understanding of what police work requires and what minority status compels with regard to treatment.

If approached with forethought and no small amount of courage, controversial race-implicated events should be seen as opportunities to develop new understandings and not just as inevitable public relations disasters. Police officials should not speak hastily before they have basic facts about what occurred. And they must be willing to "let the chips fall where they may" if mistakes, individual or organizational, have been made. This requires police leaders to do a tricky two-step — reassuring their officers that there will be communities that justice will be done.

Police officials should use these occasions to point out that confrontations between police and minorities do not arise primarily out of differences in values. Minority individuals, except for a few unredeemable criminals, want safety and order as much as the majority of people. Sadly, however, many minority individuals have been raised within a structure that limits their ability to have stable families, obtain necessary education, and be gainfully employed. Their culture is not at fault, but the circumstances into which they were born are.

On the other hand, most police officers are not prejudiced against minorities, although some are. Most act according to inherited understandings that focus enforcement attention on minority people, especially young males. Police officers are required to prevent crime by acting on suspicion within a society where many people, white as well as black, identify young, black males as likely threats and stereotype them as criminals.

Developing this kind of empathic voice in contemporary policing is a tall order. But words can shape events, creating new and more positive directions as scenarios unfold. In particular, they can diminish the perception that race is the sole or primary issue affecting police-minority relations.

REFERENCES

Bayley, David H. 1985. Patterns of Policing: *A Comparative International Analysis*. New Brunswick, New Jersey: Rutgers University Press.

Bayley, David H., and Christine Nixon. 2010. *The Changing Environment for Policing, 1985–2008*. Cambridge, Massachusetts: Harvard Kennedy School.

Bayley, David H., and Jerome H. Skolnick. 1988. Community Policing: Issues and Practices Around the World. Washington, D.C.: U.S. Department of Justice, National Institute of Justice.

Blow, Charles M. "A Town Without Pity," The New York Times, Aug. 10, 2013, A19. *Report of NBC News/Wall Street Journal poll*, June 2013.

Braga, Anthony, and Rod K. Brunson. 2015. The Police and Public Discourse on "Black-on-Black" Violence. New Perspectives in Policing Bulletin. Washington, D.C.: U.S. Department of Justice. NCJ 248588.

CIVITAS (The Institute for the Study of Civil Society). 2014. The Nine Principles of Policing. Based on "General Instructions" to British Metropolitan Police, 1829, by Sir Robert Peel, and republished 1956 as appendix in A New Study of Police History, by Charles Reith (London: Oliver and Boyd). www.civitas.org.uk/pubs/policeNine. php.

Cohen, Lawrence E., and Marcus K. Felson. 1979. Social change and crime rate trends: A routine activity approach. *American Sociological Review* 44: 588–608. http://dx. doi.org/10.2307/2094589.

Currie, Elliott. 2010. "On Being Right, but Unhappy." *Criminology and Public Policy* 9(1): 1–10. (Vollmer Award Address, American Society of Criminology, 2009).

Fridell, Laurie, Bob Lunney, Drew Diamond and Bruce Kobe. 2001. Racial Profiling — A Principled Response. Washington, D.C.: Police Executive Research Forum.

Kennedy, David. 2011. Don't Shoot: One Man, a Street Fellowship, and the End of Violence in Inner-City America. New York: Bloomsbury.

Maguire, Edward R., Joseph B. Kuhns, Craig D. Uchida and Stephen M. Cox. 1997. "Patterns of Community Policing in Nonurban America." *Journal of Research in Crime and Delinquency* 34 (3): 368–394.

Manning, Peter K. 2011. Democratic Policing in a Changing World. Boulder, Colorado: Paradigm Publishers.

Meares, Tracey L., with Peter Neyroud. 2015. Rightful Policing. New Perspectives in Policing Bulletin. Washington, D.C.: U.S. Department of Justice. National Institute of Justice. NCJ 248411.

Myrdal, Gunnar. 1944. An American Dilemma: The Negro Problem and Modern Democracy. New York: Harper & Bros.

Robinson, Cyril D. 1975. "The Mayor and the Police — the Political Role of the Police in Society," in George L. Mosse (ed.), *Police Forces in History,* vol. 2. Beverly Hills, California: Sage Publications.

Sampson, Robert J. 2012. Great American City: Chicago and the Enduring Neighborhood Effect. Chicago: University of Chicago Press.

Stenning, Phillip. 2011. "Governance of the Police: Independence, Accountability and Interference." *Flinders Law Journal* 13 (2): 241–267.

Tankebe, P.J. 2009. "Public Cooperation with the Police in Ghana: Does Procedural Fairness Matter?" *Criminology* 47 (4): 1265–1294.

Tyler, Tom R. 2006. Why People Obey the Law. Princeton, New Jersey: Princeton University Press.

Walker, Sam. 2010. "Police Accountability and the Central Problem of American Criminal Justice," in Candace McCoy (ed.), Holding Police Accountable. Washington, D.C.: The Urban Institute.

Wilson, James Q. 1975. *Thinking About Crime*. New York: Basic Books.

AUTHOR NOTE

David H. Bayley is Distinguished Professor Emeritus in the School of Criminal Justice at the State University of New York, Albany.

Michael A. Davis is the Chief Law Enforcement Officer for Northeastern University and former Chief of Police for Brooklyn Park, Minnesota.

Ronald L. Davis is the former Chief of Police for East Palo Alto, California.

In: Perspectives on Policing
Editor: Holly Wheeler
ISBN: 978-1-63484-555-7

Chapter 6

THE POLICE AND PUBLIC DISCOURSE ON "BLACK-ON-BLACK" VIOLENCE*

Anthony A. Braga and Rod K. Brunson

INTRODUCTION

Police departments, especially in urban jurisdictions, are often called on to quell outbreaks of serious violence such as sudden increases in homicides, aggravated assaults and robberies. Inner-city residents and their children usually suffer the most serious harm when violent crime waves occur. Unfortunately, due to a long history of exclusion from important economic and social opportunities, residents of disadvantaged urban neighborhoods are primarily minorities and often black. Research has long documented that most violence occurs within racial groups and that black Americans, often victimized by black offenders, experience disproportionately high levels of violent crime. The term "black-on-black" violence, while statistically correct, is a simplistic and emotionally charged definition of urban violence that can be problematic when used by political commentators, politicians and police executives. To the vast majority of urban black residents who are not involved in violence or criminal behavior, the term invokes visions of indiscriminate and aggressive police enforcement responses applied to a broad range of black people. The term also seems to marginalize serious urban violence as a "black problem" that, in the minds of some black residents, may only receive a cursory response or, worse yet, be ignored by police departments entirely.

We believe that most police departments in the U.S. are dedicated to reducing violence, investigating crimes, and protecting victims irrespective of race. However, poor analyses and inappropriate descriptions of urban violent crime problems can sometimes lead to the adoption of problematic policing policies and programs. Moreover, careless discussions of the nature of urban violence can further alienate law-abiding black residents who need and desperately want to partner with the police to create safer communities. In this paper, we

---

* This is an edited, reformatted and augmented version of a paper, NCJ 248588, in the New Perspectives in Policing series, issued by the U.S. Department of Justice, National Institute of Justice, May 2015.

briefly describe how news media coverage sometimes distorts racial issues, present a (hopefully) more cool-headed analysis of black-on-black violence (measured as a homicide problem), and consider how misconceptions of black-on-black violence coupled with over- and/or under-policing of black neighborhoods can further erode citizen confidence in the police.

THE DISTORTING ROLE OF MASS NEWS MEDIA COVERAGE OF URBAN VIOLENCE

As Surette (1998) suggests, what most Americans know about crime and justice comes from popular media's portrayal of these subjects. Unfortunately, media outlets have an interest in presenting crime and justice issues in a way that captivates audiences and stimulates passions. Even though crime has steadily decreased over the last two decades, personal safety remains high on the list of public concerns, in part, because citizen perceptions are influenced by news media sources intentionally designed to make us feel passionately about the subject (Surette, 1998; Crayton and Glickman, 2007). Obviously, there are many positive aspects of intensive, fervent coverage of crime and justice issues: untended crime problems may be addressed, miscarriages of justice may be corrected, victims and their families may receive relief, and other public goods may be generated.

However, the media can also distort crime and justice issues by constructing attitudes and perceptions that do not match the reality of contemporary crime problems. Media distortions of the reality of black-on-black violence in cities can take many forms. Persistent coverage of homicides and shootings in black neighborhoods without appropriate contextual information can perpetrate inaccurate stereotypes of blacks as innately violent people. When media outlets provide extensive coverage of homicides involving white victims, especially white female victims, but little ongoing coverage of homicides involving black victims, it promotes a perception among black citizens that killings of black people are less important than killings of white people. And, by unfortunate association, that the police are not devoting, or do not think they need to devote, sufficient resources to investigate black victim homicides.

A casual sampling of characterizations of blackon-black violence in the media by political commentators, politicians and police chiefs reveals persistently vague definitions of the phenomenon and occasionally problematic associations with ideas about morally bankrupt behaviors in black families and communities.

Jason Riley, Columnist, Wall Street Journal[1]

"The black crime rate in 1960 was lower than it is today ... Was there less racism or less poverty than in 1960? This is about black behavior. It needs to be addressed head-on. It's about attitudes toward the criminal justice system in these neighborhoods, where young black men have no sense of what it means to be a male or what it means to be black."

Chris Wallace, Political Commentator, Fox News[2]

"The president talked ... about black-on-black crime. And as I looked into this, the numbers are just staggering ... should the African American community be focusing on that, the black-on-black crime, the carnage in our inner cities and not on George

Zimmerman? ... When you have people demanding, 'Let's go after George Zimmerman,' hate crimes, economic boycotts of Florida, that isn't talking about the real problems in the inner city."

Rahm Emanuel, Mayor, City of Chicago[3]

"The issue of gun violence is not limited to Chicago ... It's an urban problem." The urban violence, Emanuel said, "gets put in a different value system. These are our kids, these are our children, and the worst thing for us to do in my opinion would be to say, 'Let's not discuss this.' We need to make sure that once a crime is committed, we don't allow them back on the street to become perpetrators or victims. ... A piece of this is the culture ... Part of this is having an honest conversation, given the lion's share of the victims and the perpetrators are young African-American men."

Michael Bloomberg, former Mayor, City of New York[4]

"Ninety percent of all people killed in our city — and 90 percent of all those who commit the murders and other violent crimes — are black and Hispanic. It is shameful that so many elected officials and editorial writers have been largely silent on these facts ... Instead, they have argued that police stops are discriminatory because they do not reflect the city's overall census numbers. By that flawed logic, our police officers would stop women as often as men, and senior citizens as often as young people ... To do so would be a colossal misdirection of resources and would take the core elements of police work — targeting high-crime neighborhoods and identifying suspects based on evidence — out of crime-fighting ... . The absurd result of such a strategy would be far more crimes committed against black and Latino New Yorkers. When it comes to policing, political correctness is deadly."

Ray Kelly, former Commissioner, New York Police Department[5]

"The stark reality is that crime happens in communities of color ... About 70% to 75% of the people described as committing violent crimes — assault, robbery, shootings, grand larceny — are described as being African-American." ... "The percentage of people who are stopped is 53% African-American ... So really, African-Americans are being under stopped in relation to the percentage of people being described as being the perpetrators of violent crime."

There are certainly other concerning perspectives put forth in the popular media on this issue. It is important to recognize, however, that some police chiefs steer clear of vague black-onblack violence descriptions by focusing on "disparate victimization" in black disadvantaged neighborhoods. For instance:

Edward A. Flynn, Chief, Milwaukee Police Department[6]

"Here's what's disproportionate to me ... With about 40 percent of Milwaukee's population, African-Americans represent 80 percent of our homicide victims. They represent 60 percent of our robbery victims and 80 percent of our aggravated assault victims." ... "It's as though the arresting of African-Americans takes place in a vacuum ... If I draw an ellipse over our poorest neighborhoods and then find an ellipse and draw it where our most 911 calls are, and then draw the ellipse over where most of our crime victims are ... it's the same neighborhoods and the same zip codes."

Nevertheless, the explicit and implicit promotion of inaccurate and vague descriptions is generally offensive to black Americans.

Before we begin to analyze the issue more closely, it is worth noting what black-on-black homicide is not. We believe the following ideas are wrong and ultimately not helpful.

- *Black-on-black homicide is random.* The term "random" is commonly defined as "proceeding, made, or occurring without definite aim, reason, or pattern."[7] The perspective that black-on-black homicide is not patterned lends itself to an interpretation that any citizen could spontaneously be the victim of a horrendous crime at any place or any time. The promotion of this misunderstanding may result in heightened fear of violence among black residents and visitors to majority black neighborhoods. Increased fear of violence may undermine the full participation of black residents in neighborhood life and lead to weakened community control over local youth and public spaces.
- *Black-on-black homicide problems are symptomatic of persistent lawless behavior by black people.* This wrongheaded idea leads to an implicit assumption among the public that a high proportion of black residents are involved in crime and disorder. This misperception promotes uncertainty regarding whether blacks share the moral standards of mainstream society and, as a result, diminishes levels of mainstream concern and determination to find evidence-based responses to the problem.
- *Black-on-black homicide problems are driven by black people's tolerance for criminal and immoral behavior.* This false perspective can influence police officers to mistakenly view entire black neighborhoods as supportive of criminal behavior and exacerbate an already fragile relationship.

Black Homicide Victimization and Black Homicide Offending Rates

In this section, we focus on black and white comparisons. This crude categorization stems from a lack of crime data that consistently classify information for Hispanics and non-Hispanics as well as for Asians and Native Americans (Lauritsen and Sampson, 1998). Consequently, most analysis of disparity and discrimination in crime and criminal justice has focused on comparisons between blacks and whites. In general, the available scientific evidence on crime victimization suggests the following patterns:

- Blacks suffer much higher rates of personal violence and violent victimization than whites.[8] As discussed in greater detail below, this is particularly true for homicide victimization.
- Racial differences are reduced substantially for household crimes and personal theft victimization.
- Although whites represent the majority of suspects arrested for all crimes, blacks are disproportionately more likely to be arrested for violent crimes, especially homicide, relative to their share of the U.S. population.[9]

Between 1980 and 2008, blacks were disproportionately represented as both homicide victims and offenders (Cooper and Smith, 2011). The homicide victimization rate for blacks (27.8 per 100,000) was six times higher than the rate for whites (4.5 per 100,000) (figure 1). Blacks accounted for slightly more than 51 percent of all gun homicide victims between 1980 and 2008, despite representing only about 13 percent of the U.S. population. The homicide offending rate for blacks (34.4 per 100,000) was almost eight times higher than the rate for whites (4.5 per 100,000) (figure 2). The vast majority of homicides are intra-racial, with 84 percent of white victims killed by whites and 93 percent of black victims killed by blacks (figure 3). Black males between the ages of 18 and 24 are dramatically overrepresented in homicide. Homicides of young black males in this age category peaked at 195.9 victimizations per 100,000 in 1993 and subsequently declined to 91.1 victimizations per 100,000 in 2008. Homicides by young adult black males peaked at 365 offenders per 100,000 in 1993 and subsequently declined to 175.8 offenders per 100,000 in 2008.

Black homicide victimizations are less likely to be cleared by arrest than white homicide victimizations. A recent analysis of 2000-2007 homicide data from the National Incident-Based Reporting System (NIBRS) reported that 57.2 percent of white homicide victim cases were cleared by arrest while only 50.6 percent of black homicide victim cases were cleared by arrest (Roberts and Lyons, 2011). In general, the circumstances of homicide incidents powerfully influence clearance rates. For example, offenders in gang-related and drug-related homicides are much less likely to be arrested by homicide detectives (Wellford and Cronin, 2000), in part due to lack of witness cooperation. Further, black males are more likely than white males to be involved in these kinds of homicide incidents (Cook and Laub, 2002). Without citizens coming forward to provide detectives with much needed information, investigations of gang and drug homicides can hit dead ends quickly, with no substantive leads.

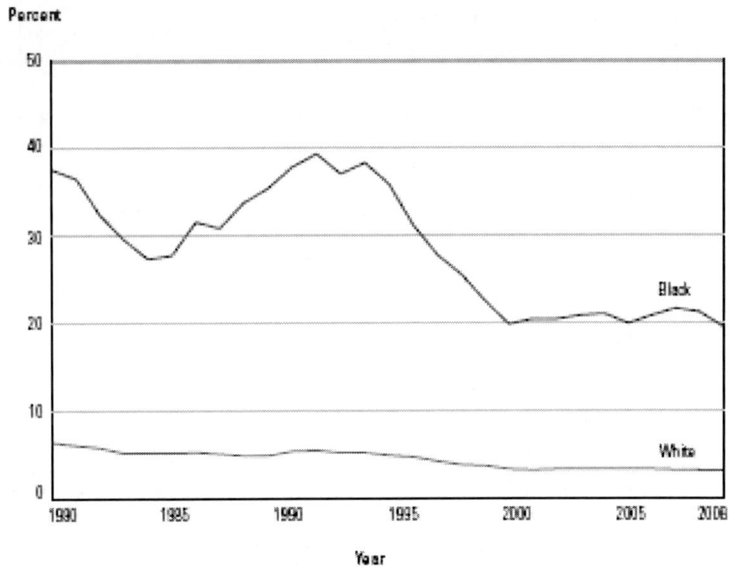

Source: Cooper and Smith (2011: 11).

Figure 1. Homicide Victimization Rates, by Race, 1980-2008.

Source: Cooper and Smith (2011: 11).

Figure 2. Homicide Offending Rated by Race, 1980-2008.

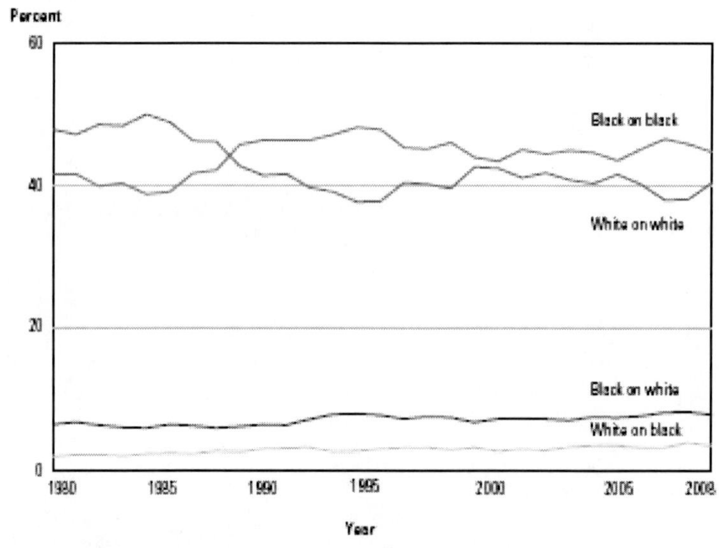

Source: Cooper and Smith (2011: 13).

Figure 3. Homicides, by Race of Offender and Victim, 1980-2008.

Some analysts suggest that the killings of black male victims receive less investigative time and effort from homicide detectives (Roberts and Lyons, 2011), whereas others suggest that white female homicide victims receive more investigative time and effort (Holcomb, Williams, and Demuth, 2004). Most available research on clearance rates finds little evidence of homicide detectives valuing or devaluing victims based on race (Puckett and Lundman, 2003; Litwin, 2004; Lundman and Myers, 2012), but there are some noteworthy exceptions.

For instance, a multivariate analysis of homicides in Los Angeles County between 1990 and 1994 suggested that white homicide victims received additional investigation attention and, as a result, their cases were more likely to be solved than those involving nonwhite homicide victims (Lee, 2005).

The extremely high homicide victimization and offending rates for young black males in the early 1990s has been tied to gun violence epidemics tipped off by the initiation of crack cocaine sales in most U.S. cities during the late 1980s (Blumstein, 1995; Braga, 2003; Cork, 1999). Although the intensity of black homicide rates has changed over the last century, the persistence of the black-white homicide rate gap has not (Hawkins, 1999). Criminologists have long considered the reasons for observed racial disparities in violence and have put forth a variety of explanations, including individual factors (most notably, IQ and self-control), family socialization, subculture of violence and economic deprivation theories (see, e.g., Wilson and Herrnstein, 1985). Unfortunately, most of these perspectives have been unsatisfactory in explaining observed differences in homicide victimization and offending rates for young black and white males. As summarized by Lauritsen and Sampson (1998: 65-66):

> Constitutional explanations are problematic on empirical grounds — the variations within any minority group are greater than the variations between them. Although there is good evidence that family socialization influences children's delinquency and aggressive behavior patterns, there is no consistent evidence that factors such as lack of supervision and erratic/harsh discipline account for race differences in crime when socioeconomic conditions are taken into account. Subcultural explanations of group variation in offending have yet to show that black and white Americans differ significantly in their values and attitudes regarding crime, or that these differences in values have an independent influence on offending disparities. Finally, research emphasizing access to the legitimate economic system typically finds that race differences persist even after controlling for socioeconomic status.

Another diagnostic approach is to examine the community-level underpinnings of racial disparities in violent crime to identify the neighborhood characteristics that lead to high rates of violence (Sampson and Wilson, 1985). Empirical evidence suggests that the capacity of neighborhood residents to achieve a common set of goals and exert control over youth and public spaces, termed "collective efficacy," protects against serious violence (Sampson, Raudenbush and Earls, 1997). The presence of community-based organizations, which draw membership from individuals within and outside specific neighborhoods, predicts collective efficacy and collective civic action (Sampson, 2012). Concentrated disadvantage in urban neighborhoods, which are often populated by black residents, undermines local collective efficacy and gravely limits the ability of residents to address serious violent crime problems (Sampson and Wilson, 1985). As a result, urban homicides, largely committed with guns and perpetrated by and against young black men, tend to concentrate in disadvantaged black neighborhoods.

Urban environments experience the largest proportion of homicides, and black Americans tend to make up larger shares of urban populations relative to suburban and rural areas. Between 1980 and 2008, nearly 58 percent of homicides occurred in U.S. cities with a population of 100,000 or more (Cooper and Smith, 2011). More than one-third of all homicides in the U.S. during that same time period occurred in cities with one million or more residents. City-level analyses provide an important opportunity to understand the nature of homicide problems better. While useful in describing objective information on homicide incidents such as age, race, sex and weapon type, national data systems, such as the Federal Bureau of Investigation's *Supplementary Homicide Reports,* are well-known to be limited in providing reliable and valid information on homicide circumstances and relationships between victims and offenders (Braga, Piehl and Kennedy, 1999; Maxfield, 1989; Riedel and Zahn, 1985). Careful within-city research on homicide facilitates a deeper understanding of the situations, dynamics and relationships associated with elevated rates of black homicide victimization and offending.

City-Level Analysis of Black Homicide Victims and Black Homicide Offenders

We use detailed data on homicides in Boston to examine the nature of black homicide victimization and offending in urban settings. Although modest differences are associated with variations in local dynamics across other U.S. cities, the basic picture of black homicide victimization as highly concentrated among a small number of active offenders involved in high-risk social networks is essentially the same. Research has consistently documented that violence driven by conflicts within and among gangs, drug-selling crews and other criminally active groups generate the bulk of urban homicide problems (see, e.g., Block and Block, 1993; Kennedy, Piehl and Braga, 1996; Papachristos, 2009; Tita et al., 2004).

According to the 2010 U.S. Census, 24 percent of Boston's estimated 618,000 residents identified themselves as black. Between 2000 and 2013, Boston experienced 836 homicides. Nearly 74 percent of Boston homicide victims were black (615 of 836), and roughly 68 percent of arrested homicide offenders were also black (294 of 430). In cleared black homicides (218, 35.4 percent of 615), 91.7 percent of the offenders were black (200 of 218). As figure 4 shows, the year-to-year variation in total homicide counts in Boston is largely driven by black homicide victimization rates.

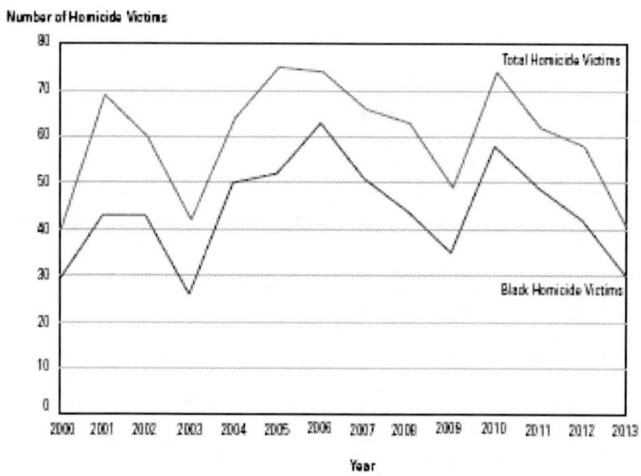

Figure 4. Total Homicide Victims and Black Homicide Victims in Boston, 2000-2013.

Circumstances of Boston Homicide Victims by Race, 2000-2013

	Non-Hispanic Black		Non-Hispanic White	
Circumstances	N	Percent	N	Percent
Gang-related	315	55.0	4	4.4
Personal dispute/argument	95	16.6	34	37.8
Drug-related	84	14.7	14	15.6
Family/domestic violence	34	5.9	11	12.2
Robbery	16	2.8	16	17.8
Other/unknown	29	5.9	11	12.2
Total	573	100.0	90	100.0

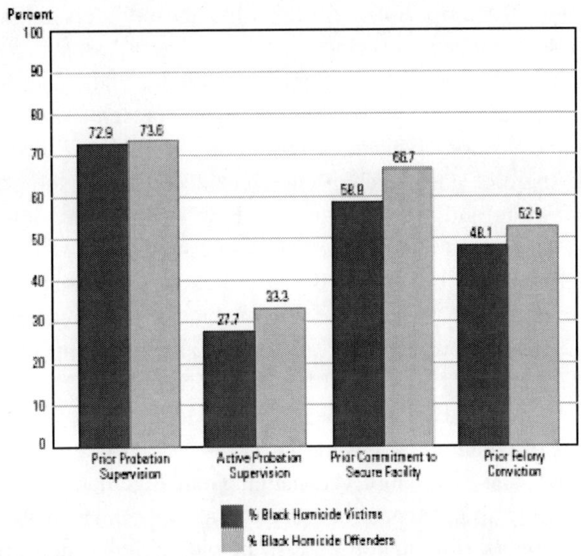

Note: N = 480 for known black homicide victims; N = 265 for known arrested black homicide offenders.

Figure 5. Criminal Justice System Involvement of Known Black Homicide Victims and Known Arrested Black Homicide Offenders in Boston, 2000-2013.

Black homicide victims were primarily young (mean age = 26.6 years, 54 percent were age 24 and younger), overwhelmingly male (91.1 percent), and usually died from gunshot wounds (84.1 percent). Arrested black homicide offenders were also primarily young (mean age = 25.0 years, 59.5 percent were age 24 and younger) and overwhelmingly male (94.2 percent). In addition, 78 percent of black homicide victims (480 of 615) and almost 90 percent of arrested black homicide offenders (264 of 294) were known to the Massachusetts criminal justice system before the homicide incident. Black homicide victims and arrested black homicide offenders known to the criminal justice system averaged, respectively, 12.4 and 12.7 prior arraignments in Massachusetts courts for a variety of violent, drug, property and disorder offenses. So these two groups — homicide offenders and victims — are essentially the same. Figure 5 (page 10) shows the previous criminal justice system involvement of known black homicide victims and known arrested black homicide offenders.

Probation supervision, commitments to secure facilities and felony convictions characterized the prior criminal justice system experiences of both of these groups.

A majority of black homicide victims (78.9 percent, 485 of 618) were killed in the Roxbury, Dorchester and Mattapan neighborhoods of Boston. Inhabitants of these areas are mostly black, and these communities are characterized by high levels of social and economic disadvantage. Homicides are not evenly spread throughout these neighborhoods, though. In fact, most streets did not experience any homicide incidents between 2000 and 2013. Rather, black homicide incidents tend to recur in very specific places, such as in and around public housing dwellings, gang turfs and street drug markets. A recent analysis by Braga, Papachristos and Hureau (2010) revealed that only 5 percent of Boston's street blocks and intersections experienced nearly 74 percent of all fatal and nonfatal shootings in the city between 1980 and 2008. The most violent 60 street blocks and intersections experienced more than 1,000 shootings during this time period.

Boston, like many cities, suffers gang-related violence that tends to generate a large number of black homicide victims. The table on page 9 presents the circumstances of 573 non-Hispanic black and 90 non-Hispanic white homicide victims killed in Boston between 2000 and 2013. The share of gang-related homicides accounts for the greatest difference in the circumstances of white and black homicides. Few Boston black male youths are gang members. The most recent estimate, in 2006, suggests that only 1 percent of Boston's population between the ages of 14 and 24 (Braga, Hureau and Winship, 2008) were members of street gangs involved in gun violence. However, black male youth participation in these high-risk social networks that promote violent norms to settle disputes puts them at elevated risk of becoming a perpetrator or a victim of fatal gun violence.

A recent study analyzed detailed police records to map the social networks of 763 individuals in one Boston community, using non-arrest observations to create links between individuals (the nodes) who were observed hanging out together (Papachristos, Braga and Hureau, 2012). The study found that 85 percent of all shootings in this community occur within the observed network (less than 3 percent of total neighborhood population)—nearly all of which are driven by 10 different gangs, also observed in the network. The risk of fatal and nonfatal gun victimization within the network spreads outward from other shooting victims to infect their friends and associates. In fact, each "handshake" closer one is to a shooting victim increases one's own probability of getting shot by approximately 25 percent (Source: Papachristos, Braga and Hureau).

Boston Police Department (BPD) homicide detectives cleared 50.9 percent of all homicide victimizations by arrest or exceptional circumstances, such as the subsequent suicide or murder of the offender, between 2000 and 2013 (426 of 836 homicide victims). Incidents involving homicides of white non-Hispanic victims had an 80.0 percent clearance rate (72 of 90 non-Hispanic white homicide victims). However, BPD homicide detectives only cleared 35.9 percent of non-Hispanic black homicide victims during this same time period (204 of 573 non-Hispanic black homicide victims). This disparity seems to be strongly influenced by very low clearance rates for gang-related homicides. Only 26.0 percent of gang-related non-Hispanic black homicides (82 of 315) were cleared by arrest or exceptional circumstances between 2000 and 2013. Data derived from qualitative interviews with BPD homicide detectives suggest that low levels of witness cooperation in gang homicide cases, driven by citizen fear of violent reprisals or participation in criminal social networks with norms against sharing information with the police, seriously limit investigators' ability to make arrests in these kinds of cases.

It is worth noting here that the criminal dynamics that characterize high levels of homicides and lower clearance rates in black neighborhoods are not race-based. Indeed, disadvantaged white neighborhoods of Boston have been known to exhibit similar patterns of violence and lack of cooperation with the police. For instance, the Charlestown, South Boston and North End neighborhoods of Boston were noted strongholds of Irish and Italian organized crime organizations during the 1960s through the 1980s that were characterized by repeated, unsolved killings by warring factions of the organizations (Lehr and O'Neill, 2000; MacDonald, 1999; O'Neill and Lehr, 1989). Criminal subcultures that embrace violent norms in settling disputes and promote anti-police attitudes exist in impoverished neighborhoods with varied racial compositions. However, black neighborhoods suffer higher rates of this kind of criminal network violence due to the more intense concentration of disadvantage in these neighborhoods (Sampson and Wilson, 1985).

How Weak Descriptions Further Erode Community Trust and Confidence

Research and analysis thus reveal that black-onblack homicide, and by extension more general black-on-black violence, is largely concentrated among a small number of criminally active individuals and occurs in a small number of high-risk settings within disadvantaged neighborhoods. It is important to remember, however, that many black homicide victims are not involved in any criminal activity. For instance, in 2009, 15-year-old Soheil Turner was waiting for his early morning school bus in Boston's Dudley Square near the Orchard Gardens (formerly Orchard Park) housing development. Turner was not involved in gangs. Nevertheless, he was shot once in the back of the head by 18-year-old Xzeniyeju Chukwuezi, a member of the Dudley Street Posse looking to send a message to the rival Orchard Park Trailblazers. Tragedies like this, involving innocent bystanders, occur too frequently in cities across the U.S. All homicide victims and offenders, regardless of their status as criminals or not, are members of someone's family. In disadvantaged neighborhoods with limited opportunities, many otherwise promising youth become involved in criminal activities. And whether they are lost to ghastly street violence or to the justice system, family and friends will grieve over their absence.

As we noted earlier, commentators routinely refer to eruptions of violence in minority, disadvantaged neighborhoods as the black-onblack violence problem. We acknowledge that this designation is undeniably statistically accurate, given that most interpersonal violence involves victims and offenders of the same race. However, this higher-level statistical view can blind us to the details of the specific problems and dynamics that drive these statistics.

Seldom are crimes involving whites described as white-on-white violence. Use of this vernacular to describe blacks' victimization of other blacks has several important consequences. First, a singular focus on a rudimentary race-based dyad characterizing black offending and victimization has the potential to devalue black life while overshadowing the importance of harmful social conditions, such as concentrated neighborhood disadvantage and low collective efficacy (Sampson, 2012) that collectively produce crime. Second, casual use of the black-on-black violence classification may lead segments of the public to implicitly assume that blacks are more tolerant of crime and disorder and do not share the moral standards of mainstream society.

Further, tensions between the police and minority communities are worsened when frustrated public officials hold press conferences following high-profile homicides, chastising residents of black neighborhoods for not coming forward with information, unwittingly calling into question the black community's fundamental sense of decency or commitment to citizenship. Such proclamations about blacks' unwavering reticence to assist the police are not only inflammatory, they are also exaggerated. In fact, blacks comprise a sizable proportion of prosecution witnesses and routinely petition criminal justice officials for increased attention to community violence, irrespective of family and friendship relationships with offenders (Donziger, 1996; Tonry, 1995).

Evolving Police Strategies to Engage Minority Communities

The evolution of policing strategies is highly relevant to the effective treatment of these issues. Through the adoption of community and problem-oriented policing, the way police departments deliver services in urban communities in general, and disadvantaged communities in particular, has changed dramatically over the last 30 years (Skogan and Frydl, 2004). By the beginning of the 2000s, nearly all large urban police departments reported having a community policing program in place (Hickman and Reaves, 2001). Police are now more open to input from communities, deal with a wider range of complex social problems, and rely on partnerships more heavily. In general, broad-based community policing initiatives have been found to reduce fear of crime and improve the relationships between the police and the communities they serve (Skogan and Frydl, 2004; Weisburd and Eck, 2004). Modern police departments are also more likely to systematically analyze the nature of crime problems, develop tailored responses to those problems, and engage a diverse set of strategies and partners in their implemented responses. Indeed, a growing body of scientific evidence confirms the crime control value of innovative police strategies such as problem-oriented policing, hot spots policing initiatives, and focused deterrence strategies (Braga and Weisburd, 2010, 2012; Weisburd et al., 2010).

Unfortunately, despite these important reforms, it remains surprisingly difficult to get residents of poor minority neighborhoods to engage constructively with police due to a history of strained relationships, continued skepticism of the sincerity of the police, and fear of reprisals from local criminals when cooperating with the police (Skogan and Frydl, 2004). Further, highly disadvantaged neighborhoods often lack the organizational infrastructure to collaborate with the police to manage crime and disorder. The available research suggests that community policing has been unevenly implemented within police departments, with responsibility for community-based initiatives sometimes relegated to specialized units comprising a small number of officers rather than spread across police departments (Skogan and Frydl, 2004; Skogan, 2006). Many police agencies still have far to go in developing real working relationships with the minority communities they serve.

Inaccurate descriptions and poor analysis of crime problems can lead to inappropriate and ineffective police responses to recurring incidents. Goldstein (1990) urged police officers to ensure adequate depth when analyzing crime problems so that interventions could be

appropriately focused, and a broader range of responses, beyond just increasing presence and making arrests, could be considered. Whereas police departments should be encouraged to pursue strategies artfully tailored to specific risks (such as hot spots, repeat victims, high-rate offenders, or gang hostilities (Braga, 2008)), how the police choose to address these recurring problems may either improve or further damage their relationships with minority residents. Police departments can adopt crime prevention strategies that seek to engage the community in changing the underlying conditions, situations and dynamics that cause violence to recur. Alternatively, police departments can simply "put cops on dots" through directed patrols or carry out enforcement blitzes aimed at potential offenders in high-violence areas. The overly simplistic "black-on-black violence" problem description seems likely to encourage officers to pursue harsher and less thoughtful approaches, concentrating intensive enforcement efforts or zero-tolerance policies on blacks in specific public spaces.

Citizens' appraisals of the police are influenced by the style of policing in their communities. Minorities living in distressed neighborhoods routinely report high levels of dissatisfaction with, and skepticism of, the police (Bass, 2001; Websdale, 2001). Police executives and city managers sometimes point to elevated crime rates to justify officers' use of aggressive policing initiatives in poor black neighborhoods. The use of what residents may consider heavy-handed and oppressive crime-control tactics has resulted in some policing strategies being compared to "urban warfare" (Brunson and Gau, 2014). For instance, when specialized units and task forces constitute the foundation of neighborhood policing efforts, it potentially suggests to bystanders that officers are involved in a fierce battle with every neighborhood resident, regardless of their law-abiding status (Brunson and Weitzer, 2009). The urban warfare mindset begets particular kinds of tactical operations and has the potential to create a rift between neighborhood residents and the police, reducing citizens' level of trust in officers and their willingness to participate in local crime-reduction efforts (Brunson and Gau, 2014). The vast majority of urban residents, of course, are not anti-police and fully recognize that officers are critical to public safety (Carr, Napolitano and Keating, 2007). Yet, what many minorities consider over-policing, combined with occasional disrespectful treatment at the hands of officers, intensifies black citizens' overall negative views of the police.

Over-policing refers to officers intervening in matters that, to everyday citizens, seemingly do not warrant law enforcement action. Over-policing typically occurs in locales that the police deem suspicious and/or dangerous due to obvious signs of disorder and perceptions that a considerable number of crime-prone individuals operate there (Klinger, 1997). Where the police consider certain places (and some of the people they encounter there) more menacing, they are likely to approach otherwise mundane situations with greater unease than they might in more tranquil settings (Klinger, 1997). Further, in extremely disadvantaged neighborhoods, the police disproportionately use force when attempting to control and/or apprehend suspects (Kane, 2002; Smith, 1986; Terrill and Reisig, 2003). Officers' disparate use of force in high-crime, minority neighborhoods may unknowingly diminish their moral authority in the eyes of community residents. Poor blacks disproportionately experience over-policing, and research demonstrates that people are less likely to cooperate with officers' directives if they are not treated with respect (Tyler, 2006). Hence, aggressive policing strategies set the stage for increased acrimony between the police and disadvantaged blacks.

Brunson and Miller (2006) found that young black men reported being routinely stopped by police and "...believed that despite their best efforts, they were not able to convincingly present themselves as law-abiding, even when they were, due to the confounding influences of race and place in the creation of symbolic assailants" (p. 636). An abundant body of research reveals that officers' preconceived notions about race, place and crime can lead to patterns of behavior that leave urban black males believing they are perpetual targets for the police (for a summary, see Brunson and Gau, 2014). Fairness and impartiality are fundamental to police legitimacy (Tyler, 2006). Heavy-handed policing tactics underway in far too many black neighborhoods, coupled with some officers' predetermined view regarding criminal involvement of young black men, seriously challenge efforts to improve police legitimacy in minority neighborhoods.

Although recent scholarship has devoted considerable attention to the harmful consequences of over-policing, in economically disadvantaged, black neighborhoods residents' concerns about local crime control efforts may equally center on under-policing (see Kennedy, 1997; Smith, 1986). Specifically, urban blacks frequently express dissatisfaction regarding delayed response times, uncertain prioritization of calls for service, and the overall perception that police are not committed to solving crimes that have been reported (Brunson, 2007). Brunson and Weitzer (2009) examined disadvantaged urban males' experiences with police across three neighborhoods that varied by racial composition: one was lower class and black, the second was lower class and predominantly white, and the third was lower class and racially mixed. They noted that "perceived police under-protection or poor service in poor, minority neighborhoods has been complained about for generations, and some of [their] respondents made the same complaint" (p. 876). Poor service and a lack of empathy can certainly occur at the same time police officers are saturating neighborhoods with resources to control outbreaks of violence.

Citizens complain of under-policing when officers appear to dismiss certain calls for service or fail to make arrests in poor neighborhoods for offenses that individuals living there unequivocally believe would be severely punished in wealthier communities (Klinger, 1997). Residents of distressed, high-crime neighborhoods consistently report higher levels of dissatisfaction with the police and often blame the police for persistent crime and disorder problems (Weitzer and Tuch, 2006; Weitzer, 2010).

Residents of crime-plagued neighborhoods often call for *greater* police presence. In fact, Weitzer (2010: 121) "... found that 85 percent of Hispanics and 88 percent of African Americans favored more police surveillance of high crime areas." Much like their white counterparts, minority citizens understand the need for improved police effectiveness. However, routine eruptions of neighborhood violence often cause poor minorities to doubt that they are receiving equal protection, reducing their overall confidence in and satisfaction with police.

CONCLUSION

Police executives, politicians and political commentators need to refrain from using overly simplistic descriptions — such as "black-on-black" violence — when describing outbreaks of serious criminal violence in black neighborhoods. Because the police represent the most visible face of government and have primary responsibility for maintaining public safety in all neighborhoods, police executives in particular should avoid framing urban violence problems in this way. Inappropriate use of such phrases can inadvertently promote inappropriate policing activities in black neighborhoods, which in turn erode the community's trust and confidence in the police and inhibit cooperation with them. Disadvantaged neighborhoods that suffer from serious violence need and benefit from focused police attention. Black residents clearly want police in their neighborhoods. However, they want the police to know the community, treat residents with respect and dignity, prevent future outbreaks of violence rather than merely respond to incidents, and engage with them in appropriately focused rather than indiscriminate policing strategies.

Careful analysis can lead to clarity in describing urban violence patterns and can thus improve police-minority community relations in at least two important ways. First, police executives can better frame and communicate to constituents the true nature of serious violent crime problems. Second, careful analysis can lead to the development and implementation of effective and appropriately focused crime reduction strategies. The type of analysis conducted in Boston, described above, is well within the reach of most urban police departments.

Inappropriate framing of urban criminal violence problems, and the policies and practices that result, constitute substantial obstacles for police departments and for minority communities struggling to solve these critical issues. We believe the key to progress lies with careful analysis of the specific dynamics that generate patterns of violence and a broader appreciation of the value of carefully tailored police interventions.

Acknowledgments

The authors would like to thank Charles Ramsey, Malcolm Sparrow, Darrel Stephens, Christine Cole, and members of the Harvard Executive Session on Policing and Public Safety for their helpful comments on earlier versions of this paper. They also would like to thank Anthony Bator for his excellent research assistance.

References

Bass, Sandra. 2001. "Policing Space, Policing Race: Social Control Imperatives and Police Discretionary Decisions." *Social Justice* 28: 156-176.

Block, Carolyn R., and Richard Block. 1993. *Street Gang Crime in Chicago*. Research in Brief. Washington, D.C.: U.S. Department of Justice, National Institute of Justice.

Blumstein, Alfred. 1995. "Youth Violence, Guns, and the Illicit-Drug Industry." *Journal of Criminal Law and Criminology* 86: 10-36.

Braga, Anthony A. 2003. "Serious Youth Gun Offenders and the Epidemic of Youth Violence in Boston." *Journal of Quantitative Criminology* 19(1): 33-54.

Braga, Anthony A. 2008. *Problem-Oriented Policing and Crime Prevention,* 2nd ed. Boulder, Colorado: Lynne Rienner Publishers.

Braga, Anthony A., David Hureau and Christopher Winship. 2008. "Losing Faith? Police, Black Churches, and the Resurgence of Youth Violence in Boston." *Ohio State Journal of Criminal Law* 6(1): 141-172.

Braga, Anthony A., Andrew V. Papachristos and David M. Hureau. 2010. "The Concentration and Stability of Gun Violence at Micro Places in Boston, 1980-2008." *Journal of Quantitative Criminology* 26(1): 33-53.

Braga, Anthony A., Anne M. Piehl and David M. Kennedy. 1999. "Youth Homicide in Boston: An Assessment of Supplementary Homicide Reports." *Homicide Studies* 3(4): 277-299.

Braga, Anthony A., and David L. Weisburd. 2010. *Policing Problem Places: Crime Hot Spots and Effective Prevention.* New York: Oxford University Press.

Braga, Anthony A., and David L. Weisburd. 2012. "The Effects of Focused Deterrence Strategies on Crime: A Systematic Review and Meta-Analysis of the Empirical Evidence." *Journal of Research in Crime and Delinquency* 49(3): 323-358.

Brunson, Rod K. 2007. "'Police Don't Like Black People': African American Young Men's Accumulated Police Experiences." *Criminology & Public Policy* 6: 71-102.

Brunson, Rod K., and Jacinta M. Gau. 2014. "Race, Place, and Policing the Inner-City." In *The Oxford Handbook on Police and Policing,* edited by Michael D. Reisig and Robert J. Kane. New York: Oxford University Press.

Brunson, Rod K., and Jody Miller. 2006. "Young Black Men and Urban Policing in the United States." *British Journal of Criminology* 46: 613-640.

Brunson, Rod K., and Ronald Weitzer. 2009. "Police Relations with Black and White Youths in Different Urban Neighborhoods." *Urban Affairs Review* 44: 858-885.

Carr, Patrick, Laura Napolitano and Jessica Keating. 2007. "We Never Call the Cops and Here is Why: A Qualitative Examination of Legal Cynicism in Three Philadelphia Neighborhoods." *Criminology* 45: 445-480.

Cook, Philip J., and John Laub. 2002. "After the Epidemic: Recent Trends in Youth Violence in the United States." In *Crime and Justice: A Review of Research,* Vol. 29, edited by Michael Tonry. Chicago: University of Chicago Press.

Cooper, Alexia, and Erica Smith. 2011. *Homicide Trends in the United States, 1980-2008.* Washington, D.C.: U.S. Department of Justice, Bureau of Justice Statistics.

Cork, Daniel. 1999. "Examining Space-Time Interaction in City-Level Homicide Data: Crack Markets and the Diffusion of Guns Among Youth." *Journal of Quantitative Criminology* 15: 379-406.

Crayton, Anna, and Paul Glickman. 2007. *Crime and Public Policy.* Center on Media, Crime and Justice, Report 1. New York: John Jay College of Criminal Justice.

Donziger, S. (ed.). 1996. *The Real War on Crime: The Report of the National Criminal Justice Commission.* New York: Harper Collins.

Federal Bureau of Investigation. 2013. *Crime in the United States, 2012.* Washington, D.C.: U.S. Department of Justice, Federal Bureau of Investigation.

Goldstein, Herman. 1990. *Problem-Oriented Policing.* Philadelphia: Temple University Press.

Hawkins, Darnell. 1999. "What Can We Learn From Data Disaggregation? The Case of Homicide and African Americans." In *Homicide: A Sourcebook of Social Research,* edited by M. Dwayne Smith and Margaret A. Zahn. Thousand Oaks, California: Sage Publications.

Hickman, Matthew J., and Brian Reaves. 2001. *Community Policing in Local Police Departments, 1997 and 1999.* Washington, D.C.: U.S. Department of Justice, Bureau of Justice Statistics.

Holcomb, Jefferson, Marian Williams and Stephen Demuth. 2004. "White Female Victims and Death Penalty Disparity Research." *Justice Quarterly* 21: 877- 902.

Kane, Robert J. 2002. "The Social Ecology of Police Misconduct." *Criminology* 40: 867-896.

Kennedy, David M., Anne M. Piehl, and Anthony A. Braga. 1996. "Youth Violence in Boston: Gun Markets, Serious Youth Offenders, and a Use-Reduction Strategy." *Law and Contemporary Problems* 59(1): 147-196.

Kennedy, Randall. 1997. *Race, Crime, and the Law.* New York: Vintage.

Klinger, David. 1997. "Negotiating Order in Police Work: An Ecological Theory of Police Response to Deviance." *Criminology* 35: 277-306.

Langton, Lynn, Michael Planty and Jennifer Truman. 2013. *Criminal Victimization, 2012.* Washington, D.C.: U.S. Department of Justice, Bureau of Justice Statistics.

Lauritsen, Janet, and Robert Sampson. 1998. "Minorities, Crime, and Criminal Justice." In *The Handbook of Crime and Punishment,* edited by Michael Tonry. New York: Oxford University Press.

Lee, Catherine. 2005. "The Value of Life in Death: Multiple Regression and Event History Analyses of Homicide Clearance in Los Angeles County." *Journal of Criminal Justice* 33: 527-534.

Lehr, Dick, and Gerard O'Neill. 2000. *Black Mass: The Irish Mob, the FBI, and a Devil's Deal.* New York: Public Affairs Press.

Litwin, Kenneth. 2004. "A Multilevel Multivariate Analysis of Factors Affecting Homicide Clearances." *Journal of Research in Crime and Delinquency* 41: 327-351.

Lundman, Richard, and Meghan Myers. 2012. "Explanations of Homicide Clearances: Do Results Vary Dependent Upon Operationalization and Initial (Time 1) and Updated (Time 2) Data?" *Homicide Studies* 16: 23-40.

MacDonald, Michael Patrick. 1999. *All Souls: A Family Story from Southie.* Boston: Beacon Press.

Maxfield, Michael. 1989. "Circumstances in Supplementary Homicide Reports: Variety and Validity." *Criminology* 27: 671-695.

O'Neill, Gerard, and Dick Lehr. 1989. *The Underboss: The Rise and Fall of a Mafia Family.* New York: Public Affairs Press.

Papachristos, Andrew V. 2009. "Murder by Structure: Dominance Relations and the Social Structure of Gang Homicide." *American Journal of Sociology* 115: 74-128.

Papachristos, Andrew V., Anthony A. Braga, and David M. Hureau. 2012. "Social Networks and the Risk of Gunshot Injury." *Journal of Urban Health* 89(6): 992-1003.

Puckett, Janice, and Richard J. Lundman. 2003. "Factors Affecting Homicide Clearances: Multivariate Analysis of a More Complete Conceptual Framework." *Journal of Research in Crime and Delinquency* 40: 171-193.

Riedel, Marc, Margaret A. Zahn and Lois Felton Mock. 1985. *The Nature and Patterns of American Homicide.* Washington, D.C.: U.S. Department of Justice, National Institute of Justice.

Roberts, Aki, and Christopher J. Lyons. 2011. "Hispanic Victims and Homicide Clearance by Arrest." *Homicide Studies* 15: 48-73.

Sampson, Robert J. 2012. *Great American City: Chicago and the Enduring Neighborhood Effect.* Chicago: University of Chicago Press.

Sampson, Robert J., Stephen W. Raudenbush, and Felton Earls. 1997. "Neighborhoods and Violent Crime: A Multilevel Study of Collective Efficacy." *Science* 277: 918-924.

Sampson, Robert J., and William Julius Wilson. 1995. "Toward a Theory of Race, Crime, and Urban Inequality." In *Crime and Inequality,* edited by John Hagan and Ruth Peterson. Stanford, California: Stanford University Press.

Skogan, Wesley. 2006. "The Promise of Community Policing." In *Police Innovation: Contrasting Perspectives,* edited by David Weisburd and Anthony A. Braga. New York: Cambridge University Press.

Skogan, Wesley, and Kathleen Frydl (eds.). 2004. *Fairness and Effectiveness in Policing: The Evidence.* Committee to Review Research on Police Policy and Practices. Committee on Law and Justice, Division of Behavioral and Social Sciences and Education. Washington, D.C.: The National Academies Press.

Smith, Douglas. 1986. "The Neighborhood Context of Police Behavior." In *Communities and Crime,* Crime and Justice, Vol. 8, edited by Albert J. Reiss Jr. and Michael Tonry. Chicago: University of Chicago Press.

Surette, Ray. 1998. *Media, Crime, and Criminal Justice: Images and Realities,* 2d ed. Belmont, California: Wadsworth.

Terrill, William, and Michael D. Reisig. 2003. "Neighborhood Context and Police Use of Force." *Journal of Research in Crime and Delinquency* 40: 291-321.

Tita, George K., Jack Riley, Greg Ridgeway, Clifford Grammich, Allan F. Abrahamse and Peter W. Greenwood. 2004. *Reducing Gun Violence: Results from an Intervention in East Los Angeles.* Santa Monica, California: Rand Corporation.

Tonry, Michael. 1995. *Malign Neglect: Race, Crime, and Punishment in America.* New York: Oxford University Press.

Tyler, Tom. 2006. *Why People Obey the Law,* 2nd ed. Princeton, New Jersey: Princeton University Press.

Websdale, Neil. 2001. *Policing the Poor: From Slave Plantation to Public Housing.* Boston: Northeastern University Press.

Weisburd, David, and John Eck. 2004. "What Can Police Do to Reduce Crime, Disorder, and Fear?" *Annals of the American Academy of Political and Social Science* 593: 42-65.

Weisburd, David, Cody Telep, Joshua Hinkle, and John Eck. 2010. "Is Problem-Oriented Policing Effective in Reducing Crime and Disorder? Findings from a Campbell Systematic Review. *Criminology & Public Policy* 9: 139-172.

Weitzer, Ronald. 2010. "Race and Policing in Different Ecological Contexts." In *Race, Ethnicity and Policing: New and Essential Readings,* edited by Stephen K. Rice and Michael D. White. New York: New York University Press.

Weitzer, Ronald, and Steven Tuch. 2006. *Race and Policing in America: Conflict and Reform.* New York: Cambridge University Press.

Wellford, Charles, and James Cronin. 2000. "Clearing Up Homicide Clearance Rates." *National Institute of Justice Journal* 243 (April): 2-7.

Wilson, James Q. and Richard Herrnstein. 1985. *Crime and Human Nature.* New York: Simon and Schuster.

AUTHOR NOTE

Anthony Braga is the Don M. Gottfredson Professor of Evidence-Based Criminology, School of Criminal Justice, Rutgers University, and Senior Research Fellow, Program in Criminal Justice Policy and Management, John F. Kennedy School of Government, Harvard University. Rod K. Brunson is Vice Dean for Academic Affairs, Ph.D. Program Director, and Associate Professor, School of Criminal Justice, Rutgers University.

End Notes

[1] http://dailycaller.com/2014/08/18/wsjs-jason-riley-unloads-on-obama-black-leadership-and-the-media-over-ferguson-video/#ixzz3BQiu2G00.

[2] https://www.youtube.com/watch?v = tApI4YqeKck.

[3] http://www.msnbc.com/msnbc/chicagoviolence-rahm-emanuel-calls-toug.

[4] http://www.washingtonpost.com/opinions/ michael-bloomberg-stop-and-frisk-keeps-newyork-safe/2013/08/18/8d4cd8c4-06cf-11e3-9259- e2aafe5a5f84_story.html.

[5] http://www.nydailynews.com/new-york/ commissioner-kelly-defends -stop -andfrisk-ta rget ing-a frica n-americans-a r t icle1.1332840#ixzz3BPPs3Dzo.

[6] http://wuwm.com/post/chief-flynn-sayspolicing-not-cause-high-rate-black-ma le-incarceration.

[7] http://dictionary.reference.com/browse/ random (accessed May 8, 2014).

[8] According to the National Crime Victimization Survey, in 2012, blacks had a serious violent victimization (rape, robbery, aggravated assault) rate of 11.3 per 1,000 people ages 12 and older, whereas whites had a serious violent victimization rate of 6.8 per 1,000 people ages 12 and older (Langton, Planty and Truman, 2013).

[9] According to the Federal Bureau of Investigation, whites accounted for 58.7 percent of persons arrested for violent crimes, and blacks represented 38.5 percent of persons arrested for violent crimes in 2012. However, in 2012, blacks represented 49.4 percent of persons arrested for murder and non-negligent manslaughter while whites represented 48.2 percent of persons arrested for murder and non-negligent manslaughter (Federal Bureau of Investigation, 2013). In 2012, the U.S. Census Bureau estimated that blacks represented only 13.1 percent of the U.S. population. http://quickfacts.census.gov/qfd/ states/00000.html (accessed Apr. 27, 2014).

In: Perspectives on Policing
Editor: Holly Wheeler
ISBN: 978-1-63484-555-7

Chapter 7

CHILDHOOD TRAUMA AND ITS EFFECTS: IMPLICATIONS FOR POLICE*

Richard G. Dudley, Jr.

Repeated exposure to traumatic events during childhood can have dramatic and long-lasting effects. During the past 20 years, there has been an enormous increase in our understanding of how being repeatedly traumatized by violence affects the growth and development of preadolescent children, especially when such traumatized children lack a nurturing and protective parental figure that might mitigate the impact of the trauma. In this paper, I summarize the current understanding of the effects of ongoing trauma on young children, how these effects impair adolescent and young adult functioning, and the possible implications of this for policing.

To demonstrate this, I describe the case of a 17-year-old African American male who was charged with attempted murder. I was asked to perform a psychiatric evaluation because (1) everyone who knew him was shocked about what happened because, before the crime, he had never been in trouble and he had always appeared to be functioning well; and (2) he appeared to be extremely unemotional about what happened, which his attorney viewed as either a lack of remorse or a failure to appreciate how much trouble he was in.

Although this young man had always lived in an extremely violent and drug-infested neighborhood, he was neither a drug dealer nor a gang member. Instead, he had shown such promise that his single mother had gotten him a scholarship to a private school. He was performing well in school despite the problems in his neighborhood and his home, including his mother's involvement in a series of relationships in which she had been physically abused. When I asked him about the multiple homemade tattoos on his body, he told me that each represented a family member or friend who had been killed. He cried as he described the first in this series of deaths, including the death of his best friend, which occurred when they were 8 years old and walking home from school. He also noted that the most recent death, that of his brother, occurred about a year ago. As he spoke of these deaths, that first one, which

---

* This is an edited, reformatted and augmented version of a paper, NCJ 248686, in the New Perspectives in Policing series, issued by the U.S. Department of Justice, National Institute of Justice, July 2015.

occurred about 9 years ago, seemed just as fresh to him as the recent death of his brother. In addition, I was struck by the fact that this young man had never been given any parental support that might have helped him begin to cope with these losses. When he was only 8 years old, instead of helping her young son cope with his trauma, his mother yelled at him for being on a street that she had told him not to go on.

During his psychiatric evaluation, it became clear that the young man's initial unemotional presentation was a psychological defense against his enormous fear that he would be killed. He had been carrying a gun since his brother was killed; the shooting incident for which he was charged was the first time he had used the gun. Furthermore, the fear for his life, coupled with his almost taking another's life, made the incident yet another traumatic experience for him.

It also became clear that his history of trauma influenced his interaction with the police at the time of his arrest. The police had shown no sensitivity to him when he was 8 years old, found holding and crying over his dead friend's body. Instead, they simply pulled him away from his friend, pushed him into the background, and never attempted to assess his physical or emotional status or make sure that someone else did so. During his early adolescent years, he had seen police officers mistreat others, which made it harder for him to trust or feel comfortable with police officers. His interaction with the police was further complicated by their initial presumption that he, like the victim, was a gang member and that the attempted murder was gang-related, which influenced not only perceptions of him but also how they treated him, even though he presented no physical threat to them. As a result, the police were physically aggressive with him. Being roughed up made him fearful of the police, and his attempts to manage that high level of anxiety and fear with an unemotional and cold presentation caused the police to be suspicious that he would suddenly act out, which in turn caused them to be even more confrontational and physical with him.

Police officers may also suffer from trauma-related difficulties that impair their ability to do their work. These may be long-standing difficulties stemming from their own childhood that were never identified or adequately addressed, or they may stem from traumatic experiences that occurred while working as a police officer. However, a fuller discussion of that is beyond the scope of this paper.

Stress, Trauma and Parental Protection

Understanding the stress response in children requires consideration of both the persistence and the severity of the stressor — which can range from those experienced by all children to the most severe traumatic events — and the availability of parental nurture, support and protection.

All children have stressful experiences, such as the anxiety associated with the first day of school, being frustrated by a friend's behavior, or being frightened by a big dog. Stresses such as these can be positive experiences when a nurturing adult helps the child learn healthy ways to manage anxiety, frustration and fear (Briere and Lanktree, 2008; Gunnar and Quevedo, 2008; Tarullo and Gunnar, 2006). Some children are also exposed to far more stressful experiences, such as the death of a parent or other close family member, their own childhood illness, or exposure to an isolated incident of violence. Here, too, a nurturing, protective adult can help the child overcome the distress associated with the event and thereby help the child not only tolerate the stressor but also grow from the event (Goslin et al., 2013; Maschi, 2006).

Some children are exposed to events that are exceptionally stressful. The impact of such traumatic events is more severe when they occur repeatedly (Breslau et al., 1999). Various types of violence can traumatize children, including sexual abuse and nonsexual physical abuse (Beitchman et al., 1992; Saywitz et al., 2000). Trauma can also result if a child witnesses acts of violence, including domestic violence and street violence (Berton and Stabb, 1996; Fitzpatrick and Boldizar, 1993). Additionally, psychological abuse that threatens violence, especially when the child has seen the perpetrator become violent, can traumatize children (Levendosky et al., 2002).

Although parental support can attenuate the effects of repeated exposure to extremely traumatic events, this support tends not to be available to these children, who need it the most (Green et al., 1991; Terr, 1991). In the vast majority of these cases, the parents of these children are either abusive (i.e., perpetrators of the abuse) or neglectful (i.e., they have failed to protect the child from exposure to the violence) or both, instead of nurturing and protecting the child. This repeated violent traumatization in the absence of parental nurture and protection is toxic to developing children. The group of children who suffer from this harmful combination are the focus of this paper. The resulting psychiatric impairments and associated dysfunction they exhibit as children and adolescents significantly increase their risk of coming into contact with police officers and present a significant challenge to police officers when such contact occurs.

Parents who fail to adequately nurture and protect their children usually have problems of their own (Green et al., 1991), including their own history of abuse or neglect; serious mental health problems, including intellectual deficits and substance abuse; and situational difficulties that have so overwhelmed them that they cannot parent, such as poverty or their own victimization by a partner (Gewirtz and Edleson, 2007; Lieberman, Van Horn and Ippen, 2005). Therefore, in addition to having to cope with repeated trauma without parental nurture and support, often these children also have to cope with a range of other problems related to the difficulties that their parents might be having. For example, in addition to not adequately protecting his or her child, a parent might be so depressed, drug addicted or cognitively impaired that he or she fails to meet the child's most basic needs.

For example, I was involved in a case where a woman had became involved with a man who seemed to be a "good man" until he moved in with her, when he began to psychologically control and severely physically abuse her and her 6-year-old son. Due to her own history and associated psychiatric difficulties, she was so overwhelmed by the psychological domination and physical abuse that she could not protect herself or extricate herself from the situation. She was also repeatedly abused in front of her son, thereby repeatedly exposing him to violence. She was so overwhelmed by her predicament that she could not protect her son from the abuse that he was enduring. As a result, her son felt constantly at risk of harm, constantly feared that his mother would be harmed or killed, felt there was no place where he would be safe, and saw no reason why things would or even might soon be better. Not surprisingly, the boy developed multiple trauma-related symptoms, such as extreme hypervigilance and overreactivity, that were never identified and treated (these symptoms are described in more detail later). Therefore, as he got older, he repeatedly overreacted violently to perceived threats of harm in all sorts of interactions, including his interactions with police officers.

THE CHILD'S RESPONSE TO REPEATED TRAUMA AND ITS IMPLICATIONS IN LATER LIFE

The combination of repeated childhood trauma and the absence of parental nurture, support and protection can result in the development of multiple psychiatric and neuropsychiatric disorders. For the purposes of this paper, it is more meaningful to talk in terms of symptoms instead of psychiatric disorders because discussing symptoms will help readers better appreciate the severity of the distress and the magnitude of the dysfunction seen in persons with such a childhood history.

I will discuss four categories of symptoms:

1) trauma-related neurological symptoms,
2) trauma-related psychological symptoms,
3) developmental difficulties brought on by poor parenting, and
4) other associated difficulties. Each of these categories or clusters of symptoms cause children considerable emotional distress and impair their ability to function, and the distress and dysfunction are even more severe when they are combined. Although these four sets of difficulties are hard to "cure," appropriate mental health treatment can act as a buffer against them and their effects, especially when such treatment is initiated during childhood (Cicchetti and Toth, 1995; Toth and Cicchetti, 1993). In the absence of treatment, however, trauma-related difficulties and their effects tend to persist into adolescence and adulthood and become difficult to reverse (Perry et al., 1995; Schore, 2001).

Trauma-Related Neurological Symptoms

In the past two decades, a greater understanding of the effects of stress on the human brain has bolstered our understanding of the dynamics of childhood exposure to traumatic stress. Research has demonstrated that repeated violent traumatization of children in the absence of parental protection can permanently rewire their brains, which do not become fully developed until early adulthood. This influences the structure and the functioning of the brain so as to create symptoms that were previously thought to be purely psychological (Van der Kolk, 1994).

The human body's physiological response to stress is well-documented. When one encounters a stressor and becomes frightened, the body produces stress hormones; this has been called the "fight or flight response" (Kearney et al., 2010; Van der Kolk, 2005). This is a transient hormonal response, which healthy individuals experience and manage with little long-term effect on their functional capacities (Gunnar and Quevedo, 2008; Tarullo and Gunnar, 2006). However, in children, excessive stimulation of this hormonal response for prolonged periods of time — due to the combination of repeated trauma and the absence of parental intervention that helps the child manage or calm the response — eventually impairs regulation of the response (Handwerger, 2009; Van Voorhees and Scarpa, 2004). That is when the "fight or flight response" ceases to become a useful transient response to danger that the individual can regulate; instead, it becomes a constant, uncontrollable physiological warning of danger that persists even when no danger is present. Over the past 20 years, research has shown that this impaired regulation results from the effects of the toxic stress-hormonal load on the structure and functioning of the still-developing child brain (Lupien et al., 2009; Teicher et al., 2003).

Studies have shown that, when children are repeatedly exposed to trauma, the amygdala — the area of the brain known to activate the physiological stress response — overdevelops. This overdevelopment increases the fear and anxiety these children experience and causes them to be hyperresponsive to frightening situations in both their physiology and their observable behavior (Pollak, 2008; Shin, Rauch and Pitman, 2006). At the same time, the development of the hippocampus — the area of the brain known to turn off the stress response — is inhibited, decreasing its capacity to control the response (Bremner et al., 2003). Impairment of the hippocampus also results in difficulties in memory, mood regulation and contextual learning, which includes learning to differentiate dangerous situations from safe ones (Pugh et al., 1997; Rudy, Kuwagama and Pugh, 1999). In addition, high levels of stress hormones impair the development of the connections to and within the prefrontal cortex of the brain (Elzinga and Bremner, 2002; Richert et al., 2006). The prefrontal cortex plays a role in modulating the physiological stress response and is responsible for decision-making, which includes assessing a perceived threat and responding appropriately (Lee and Seo, 2007; Morgan and LeDoux, 1995; Morgan, Romanski and LeDoux, 1993; Robbins, 2000).

Trauma-Related Psychological Symptoms

In addition to neurological impairments, many trauma-exposed children also develop psychological trauma-related symptoms similar to those seen in adults with posttraumatic stress disorder (PTSD). These children tend to be anxious (Copeland et al., 2007). They are hypervigilant, meaning that they are always expecting something bad to happen to them and they often perceive danger where none exists (Briere and Lanktree, 2008; Terr, 1991; Van Zomeren-Dohm et al., 2013). They also tend to be hyperreactive to perceived threats of danger (Terr, 1991). These children try not to think about their traumatic experiences and they become distressed when those experiences come to mind (Terr, 1991). New experiences that remind them of their past traumatic experiences, or symbolize those experiences, exacerbate these and other trauma-related symptoms that they may have acquired (Ehlers and Clark, 2000; Terr, 1991). Children also have difficulty calming down once hyperreactivity has been triggered (Van der Kolk, 1994). Although these difficulties might be apparent to others who know them, the author believes such affected children are far too young to appreciate the fact that they are suffering from psychiatric difficulties. Trauma-related neurological and psychological difficulties interact so as to exacerbate each other.

I evaluated a young man who was born when his mother was still a young adolescent. For some years, he and his mother lived with his maternal grandmother. His grandmother repeatedly physically abused both him and his mother, which so overwhelmed his young mother that she was of little help to him. As a result of the combined effect of his psychological and physiological response to the trauma, he was always extremely nervous and fearful. Although, finally, the young man's mother took him and ran away from his grandmother's home, the neighborhood that she ended up in was extremely dangerous and he was constantly exposed to violence that neither he nor his mother knew how to cope with.

This new danger only served to exacerbate the difficulties he had already developed. The young man became even more hypervigilant: He was in constant fear for his life and, by the time he was a pre-adolescent, he carried a gun with him all of the time. He never shot or even brandished the gun. However, as part of a police initiative to stop and search adolescents in his neighborhood for drugs and weapons, he was repeatedly stopped by the police. When stopped, he was always found to have a gun; as a result, he developed a juvenile record of repeated arrests for gun possession. I present this case because it demonstrates the effects of trauma and because no one ever seemed to wonder why this young man was being repeatedly arrested for the same thing. Regrettably, he was never evaluated by a mental health professional and never received the treatment he so desperately needed.

Other Developmental Difficulties Resulting from Trauma and Lack of Parental Nurture

Individuals whose childhood traumatization is left unchecked may also experience developmental symptoms such as instability in their sense of self (Van der Kolk, 2005). Without parental nurture and support, this shifting sense of self can be so extreme that sometimes the individual feels empty. These feelings of emptiness can be associated with cutting (i.e., repeatedly cutting oneself to feel pain and see the bleeding) or similar behavior in an attempt to feel something and know that one is alive (Briere and Gil, 1998; Landecker, 1992; Van der Kolk, 2005). These individuals also experience relational difficulties characterized by intense but unstable relationships. These relational difficulties are due, at least in part, to a frantic need for attachments to feel whole, accompanied by fears of abandonment. Such difficulties are also due to rapidly alternating perceptions of important others, which shift from idealizing them to devaluing them because of feelings that the other person does not care about the traumatized individual (Gunderson and Sabo, 1993; Herman, 1992). Afflicted individuals also experience difficulty in regulating mood because of intense depressive, irritable or anxious reactions to nontraumatic situations. This mood instability can result in suicidal behavior, inappropriate and intense outbursts of anger, or difficulty in controlling anger. In addition, traumatized individuals may exhibit impulsive, potentially self-damaging behavior such as reckless sex and substance abuse (Van der Kolk, 2005). When under extreme stress, such individuals can briefly become paranoid and they may experience dissociative symptoms such as not feeling in control of their own body or actions (Steiner, Garcia and Matthews, 1997; Van Der Kolk et al., 2009).

Such broad-based instability in so many important areas results in considerable emotional distress and dysfunction. "Trust issues" are a part of this constellation of developmental difficulties that result from inadequate parenting; these trust issues exacerbate the anxiety, fear and hypervigilance that are part of the trauma response. Many adolescents will attempt to block out or mask that intense anxiety and fear with a tough, "I don't care about anything" façade. When this façade is coupled with the difficulty in managing anger and impulsivity that are part of this constellation of developmental difficulties, these adolescents can appear hostile and threatening. When police officers come upon such adolescents, they have to instill safety and order quickly. However, when the officers' use of increasingly more forceful language and more aggressive behavior starts to result in increasingly paranoid and defiant behavior on the part of the adolescent, this might indicate that the adolescent is suffering from trauma-related difficulties and that de-escalating the situation will require a more calming intervention on the officers' part.

Other Associated Difficulties

Most children who develop the above three types of disorders eventually also suffer from one or more commonly associated difficulties: depression, aggressive acting out (in an effort to "never be a victim again"), substance abuse, which often starts as an attempt to self-medicate overwhelming anxiety (Heffernan et al., 2000; Van der Kolk, 2005). Each of these associated difficulties can, by itself, impair judgment and decision-making. When superimposed upon the psychiatric and neuropsychiatric difficulties that result from early exposure to repeated trauma in the absence of parental nurture and support, they can render someone extremely dysfunctional.

Some severely physically abused children sustain serious injuries to their developing brain that result in cognitive deficits. For example, serious injury to the front of the brain might result in severely impaired decision-making capacity. In addition, in a home where domestic violence occurs, a child with existing intellectual or other cognitive deficits is often at greatest risk of being physically abused, at least in part because the abusive parent views that child as more difficult to manage. Therefore, intellectual or other cognitive deficits should be included in the list of other associated difficulties that might be seen in these children. Such neuropsychiatric difficulties further impair functioning on their own, but they also interact with and exacerbate many of the other psychiatric and neuropsychiatric difficulties. They may also impair insight and judgment so as to severely compromise the individual's capacity to recognize a need for mental health treatment, access treatment, and benefit from treatment.

Although these four discrete sets of disorders — neurological, psychological, developmental and other associated difficulties — can be described separately, they often occur simultaneously in the same person. When they occur together, these disorders tend to exacerbate one another, in part because their symptoms, such as hypervigilance and hyperresponsiveness, overlap. Therefore, instead of being simply cumulative in contributing to the expression of these symptoms, each disorder increases the intensity of the symptoms exponentially.

For example, both depression and substance abuse further impair the decision-making mechanisms that exposure to trauma has already compromised. The slowed thinking associated with depression impairs decision-making. Certain drugs can exacerbate depression, making its impact on decision-making more severe (Cornelius et al., 1998; Kelly, Daley and Douaihy, 2012). In addition, some drugs impair one's ability to monitor one's environment, which can increase feelings of fear in an already fearful individual. Additionally, the hypervigilance or heightened sense of danger, among the cluster of trauma-related symptoms such individuals may experience, can exacerbate their existing relational difficulties (Ehlers and Clark, 2000; Rich and Grey, 2005).

We now understand that children who are repeatedly exposed to violent, traumatic events in the absence of parental nurture and support develop a number of discrete difficulties that are already challenging to cope with on their own but then interact with and intensify one another in a way that renders normal functioning still more difficult. Even during childhood, traumatized individuals may exhibit clinically significant symptoms that impair their ability to function. Left untreated, their problems persist and intensify into their adolescence and adulthood and become irreversible (Perry et al., 1995; Schore, 2001).

PREVALENCE OF TRAUMA-RELATED DIFFICULTIES AMONG PERSONS EXPOSED TO VIOLENCE

The number of individuals who, as children, were repeatedly exposed to violent trauma in the absence of parental protection, and then went on to develop the cluster of psychiatric and neuropsychiatric difficulties, is difficult to determine. This is because there are no studies that have attempted to determine the overall prevalence of children exposed to one or more of the various types of violent trauma known to cause such psychiatric or neuropsychiatric difficulties. Nor are there any studies that followed the traumatized children to see what percentage actually develop such psychiatric or neuropsychiatric difficulties. However, studies that have tried to look at prevalence in subsets of these children suggest that the rate is alarmingly high.

For example, it is estimated that 35 percent of children exposed to domestic violence will develop trauma-related difficulties (Moretti et al., 2006). A recent estimate puts the number of children exposed to domestic violence during 2012 at 266,110 (U.S. Department of Health and Human Services, 2013) — meaning that approximately 93,139 children will develop trauma-related difficulties as a result of exposure to domestic violence during that year.

Similarly, it is estimated that between 42 percent and 90 percent of child victims of sexual abuse will develop trauma-related difficulties (De Bellis, Spratt and Hooper, 2011). During 2012, an estimated 62,936 children were victims of sexual abuse (U.S. Department of Health and Human Services, 2013) — meaning that between 26,433 and 56,642 of those children will likely develop trauma-related difficulties as a result of being sexually abused.

Although these data give some indication of the scope of exposure to domestic violence and childhood sexual abuse, statistics related to both these issues are thought to be underestimates (Leventhal, 1998; Wilt and Olson, 1996). It is therefore likely that the actual prevalence of PTSD stemming from both childhood sexual abuse and exposure to domestic violence is greater than stated above.

More difficult to estimate is the number of children repeatedly exposed to or even directly threatened by various forms of neighborhood violence. We know that, although domestic violence and child sexual abuse occur in all neighborhoods, children who are raised in poor, drug-infested, violent neighborhoods are at increased risk of exposure to street violence, increasing their risk of developing trauma-related difficulties (Buka et al., 2001; Stein et al., 2003). In addition, because these children are much less likely to be identified as needing treatment and have less access to medical care, their difficulties are more likely to continue unabated into adolescence and adulthood (Cooper, Masi and Vick, 2009).

IMPLICATIONS FOR POLICING

In the course of their duties, police officers often encounter individuals who have suffered repeated exposure to traumatic events during their childhood. Understanding the effects of such childhood trauma, and the behaviors that these individuals are likely to exhibit as a result, has practical implications for police operations in three areas: first, where police deal with violence and children are victims or witnesses; second, where police encounter individuals already affected by childhood trauma who exhibit behaviors often attributed to aggressiveness and callousness; and, third, when a suspect in police custody or under interrogation manifests behaviors symptomatic of a history of trauma, case officers need to recognize those symptoms and make appropriate referrals, as they would for any other mental disorder.

Police Challenges in Encounters with Traumatized Individuals

Because of their tendency to violent and erratic behavior, these sizable numbers of individuals who experience trauma-related difficulties are at an increased risk of coming into contact with police officers. The likelihood of police contact is even greater if these traumatized individuals live in violent neighborhoods. This is for two reasons. First, violent neighborhoods tend to have a large police presence, meaning that all residents of these neighborhoods come into contact with police more frequently (Hangartner, 1994). Second, if an individual already suffers from trauma-related difficulties, a new traumatic experience will exacerbate those difficulties. This combination of past trauma and subsequent exposure to violence increases the likelihood that an individual will have violent reactions of the type that would bring them into contact with police officers and complicate that contact (Donley et al., 2012).

Without training focused on issues related to childhood trauma, it is unlikely that police officers will recognize that individuals may be acting out due to difficulties stemming from past traumatic experiences. Although anxiety, fear and impaired regulation of the brain's stress response drive the behavior of traumatized individuals, their visible symptoms are more obvious. Attention to these visible symptoms at the expense of their underlying causes results in police misperceiving these children, adolescents and young adults. Traumatized individuals tend to be hypervigilant and hypersensitive to perceived threats, and they tend to overreact to such threats, often violently. This extreme reaction becomes the focus of police attention. For example, a traumatized person may mask anxiety with an extreme bravado, which police view as arrogance or a lack of caring instead of the psychological defense mechanism that it is (Arroyo, 2001). Also, the brain's impaired regulation of the stress response makes it difficult, if not impossible, for traumatized individuals to calm themselves down, even when it would be in their best interest to do so, which makes them seem more aggressive (Van der Kolk et al., 2009). In addition, associated difficulties such as substance abuse can also become a focus of police attention, with no thought about whether underlying psychiatric difficulties might have contributed to such substance abuse.

Factors other than the absence of police training on childhood trauma contribute to a misunderstanding of individuals with a history of such trauma, especially when the individual is a young man of color. Many believe that children and adolescents who have been exposed to violence — a sizable portion of whom are African American children — have become immune to violence (Gottlieb, 2004). In my experience, this notion is readily expanded into a belief that such children and adolescents have become hardened to violence and its effects and that they virtually embrace violence instead of being frightened by it. However, for most children repeatedly exposed to violence, this is not the case (Thomas et al., 2012; Cooley-Strickland et al., 2011). Furthermore, recent studies have begun to confirm the common anecdotal observation that African American boys are viewed as older, less childlike and less innocent than white same-age peers (Goff et al., 2014). Because they are viewed as more like adults, African American boys are seen as more responsible for their behavior and, as a result, they are at risk of being treated more harshly than their white counterparts by police and other components of the criminal justice system (Goff et al., 2014). Therefore, any training on childhood trauma and its effects must address how race frames one's understanding of behavior and how, for many, such race-based beliefs overshadow other well-established factors in their perception of the behavior of young men of color. In other words, if a goal of this training is to influence the thinking and alter the behavior of police officers toward traumatized young men of color, the training must first undo the false belief that such young men may have never been that traumatized and instead became immune to violence.

An increased awareness of the high prevalence of severe childhood trauma and an increased appreciation of its effects on both the developing child and later adolescent and adult functioning might impact the thinking and behavior of police officers in several ways as they go about the work of policing.

Considerations for Dealing with Traumatized Individuals

First, with regard to prevention, or at least early intervention, in the development of trauma-related disorders, police officers can learn more about traumatized children when regularly called to investigate alleged cases of domestic violence (Butzer, Bronfman and Stipak, 1996). An increased appreciation for the impact of exposure to domestic violence on developing children might lead police to develop better mechanisms for reporting domestic violence to their local child protective services and to better advocate for the development of mental health services to address the needs of children so exposed. Furthermore, because a significant subset of children living in homes where there is domestic violence are victims of child abuse and neglect, those children will also need services to address these issues.

Police officers already recognize that one of their roles is to enhance a sense of safety in the communities they serve (Plant and Scott, 2009). However, recognizing that this effort also helps decrease the prevalence of childhood trauma-related difficulties — and guard against the exacerbation of symptoms in those who already suffer from such difficulties — might help police understand how important this aspect of their work is, and how central it is to decreasing crime. Ideally, this would also prompt police to explore whether certain police practices that seem to undercut this goal might be altered without impeding police work.

One police chief, with whom I spoke in connection with writing this article and who wished to be unnamed, noticed that many violent crime scenes were left undisturbed far longer than was required for officers to do their work. In his view, having to constantly see these crime scenes — with blood and police tape or evidence markers and medical refuse —

made citizens more fearful and caused them to be all the more traumatized by the crimes that had occurred. The police chief instituted an effort to clean up crime scenes as quickly as possible, which significantly reduced citizens' exposure to reminders of neighborhood violence. Recognizing that this decreased exposure was particularly critical to the well-being of children, this chief also began a practice where his department notified local schools when there were violent crimes in the neighborhood. Such notifications allowed school personnel to keep an eye out for students with any trauma-related difficulties.

In addition, the list of possible causes of any behavior that the police are called upon to investigate and address could be broadened to include the cluster of psychiatric and neuropsychiatric difficulties that result from childhood trauma. This might change how police officers view and treat alleged perpetrators.

Armed with such knowledge, possibly from internal databases and made available at dispatch or, in smaller departments, common knowledge about an individual, police officers would come to understand that, when managing individuals with a childhood trauma history, certain interventions may escalate rather than control difficulties. For example, interventions involving displays of aggression such as yelling, rough physical contact and intense eye contact ("the stare"), though meant to curb aggressive behavior, may provoke aggression. This understanding reinforces the notion that police need not behave in an overly aggressive manner, except when officers deem it necessary to ensure the safety of themselves or those around them. It may also prompt police organizations to develop new interventions that might help manage individuals whom the police already know to suffer from trauma-related difficulties.

Recommendations for Dealing with Traumatized Individuals

With regard to developing trauma-specific interventions, much can be learned from many police organizations' efforts to develop alternative interventions to manage individuals who suffer from a range of psychiatric and neuropsychiatric issues. For example, many police organizations have developed units of officers who understand and appreciate the impact of paranoid delusions. They also learned

a) how to respond to individuals suffering from such delusions in a way that helps calm them instead of making them more paranoid, and
b) what to do if attempts to calm individuals suffering from delusions fail. Although the fears of traumatized individuals are not delusional, neither are they rational — their fears are greater than the situation merits. Furthermore, as with persons suffering from paranoid delusions, the fears of persons suffering from trauma-related difficulties can be exacerbated by the behavior of those they come in contact with. Therefore, it is reasonable for police organizations to develop a protocol for trauma-specific interventions, with goals and objectives similar to those developed to manage other mentally ill individuals.

Moving beyond on-street dealings with traumatized individuals, once a suspect is taken into custody and is being questioned and a full investigation is under way, understanding childhood trauma and its effects might inform next steps. At this point, trained officers can recognize, better than they can during on-street encounters, that they are dealing with a person with a trauma history, and they can use the knowledge, understanding and associated skills that they have developed to deal with such a person. This knowledge and these skills may help officers obtain the cooperation of a suspect instead of making the suspect so much more fearful that he or she shuts down and refuses to cooperate or even speak. This knowledge may also help officers better understand the suspect's responses to questioning and determine the best approach to further questioning. In addition, this new awareness may help officers understand more accurately what happened during the course of the alleged crime.

When individuals suffering from the psychiatric and neuropsychiatric effects of childhood trauma are victimized again as adolescents or young adults, or when someone close to them is victimized, this can significantly exacerbate their symptoms. Unfortunately, this problem is far too common in poor communities of color, and there are virtually no victim services, mental health treatment or social services programs specifically designed for young men of color who are revictimized (Bell and Jenkins, 1991; Edwards and Foley, 1997; Snowden, 2001). Because leaving their difficulties unaddressed causes them additional pain, suffering and dysfunction and further increases their risk of coming into contact with the police, an awareness of these issues might help police become important advocates for the development of treatment and service programs for these victims.

As police and police organizations increase their understanding of childhood trauma and its effects, they will be more invested in and better able to develop and institute police practices that take this serious mental health problem into consideration. In addition, if this training is integrated with training on how race frames our understanding of human behavior, then the relationships that the police have with communities of color could be significantly enhanced.

Child Development — Community Policing

In Child Development — Community Policing (CD-CP) service areas, mental health professionals are on call 24 hours a day, seven days a week, to respond immediately to police calls involving child victims or witnesses to violence or other trauma. Working together, police, mental health professionals, child protective services and other providers coordinate multisystem interventions that re-establish safety, security and well-being in the immediate wake of violent events. CD-CP has served as a model for law enforcement–mental health partnerships around the country.

The goals of the CD-CP program are to:

- Increase officer awareness and identification of children exposed to violence and other trauma.
- Increase clinical assessment and coordinated services to targeted children and families.

The Office of Juvenile Justice and Delinquency Prevention recognizes the program as a successful model and has designated the Childhood Violent Trauma Center, a component of the Yale Child Study Center at Yale University School of Medicine, as the National Center for Children Exposed to Violence (NCCEV), with Charlotte-Mecklenburg as the

NCCEV Southeast Regional Training Center. The Charlotte-Mecklenburg CD-CP replicates the parent program between the Yale Child Study Center and the New Haven Department of Police Service. For more information about the program at Yale, see http://www.nccev.org. For more information about the program in Charlotte-Mecklenburg, see http://charmeck. org/Mecklenburg/county/PSO/CJS/Pages/CD-CP.aspx.

See also the International Association of Chiefs of Police website, www.theiacp.org, for additional resources about the program, including an article from *Police Chief Magazine,* http://www.policechiefmagazine.org/magazine/index.cfm?fuseaction=display_archandarticle_id=2882andissue_id=32013.

Summary and Conclusion

For children, repeated exposure to violent trauma, particularly in the absence of parental nurture, support and protection that might mitigate the impact of such trauma, can have devastating effects on their psychiatric and neuropsychiatric development. These include the development of mutually exacerbating disorders: neurological difficulties, trauma-specific psychological difficulties, developmental difficulties and other associated functional difficulties.

These psychiatric and neuropsychiatric difficulties become evident when traumatized children are still children, long before they understand what is happening to them or can assume responsibility for addressing what is happening to them. Early therapeutic intervention can help enormously. However, when such early therapeutic intervention does not occur, many of these difficulties become irreversible. Individuals continue to suffer from these difficulties during their adolescent and adult years, and they are vulnerable to exacerbation of their symptoms by subsequent traumatic events as well as events that remind them of or symbolize the childhood traumas that they endured.

Although children from any neighborhood can be exposed to the type of trauma described here, children from poor communities of color are particularly at risk for such exposure. Because these communities are often the focus of police attention, it is important that police be aware of the high prevalence of severe childhood trauma in such communities, appreciate its effects on the developing child, and understand its impact on adolescent and adult functioning. With this knowledge, police officers will have a greater capacity to help decrease the prevalence of this major public mental health problem and will be able to better manage those they come in contact with who suffer from trauma-related psychiatric and neuropsychiatric difficulties.

Acknowledgments

Dr. Dudley would like to especially thank Anthony Bator for his research assistance, without which the completion of this paper wouldn't have been possible. Dr. Dudley would also like to thank the members of the Harvard Executive Session on Policing and Public Safety for their helpful comments on earlier versions of this paper, especially those from police organizations who suggested the ways in which the information summarized in this paper could be utilized by individual police officers and police organizations.

REFERENCES

Arroyo, W. 2001. PTSD in children and adolescents in the juvenile justice system. *PTSD in Children and Adolescents* 20: 59-86.

Beitchman, J.H., K.D. Zucker, J.E. Hood, G.A. DaCosta, D. Akman and E. Cossavia. 1992. A review of the long-term effects of child sexual abuse. *Child Abuse & Neglect* 16: 101-118.

Bell, C.C., and E.J. Jenkins. 1991. Traumatic stress and children. *Journal of Health Care for the Poor and Underserved* 2: 175-188.

Berton, M.W., and S.D. Stabb. 1996. Exposure to violence and post-traumatic stress disorder in urban adolescents. *Adolescence* 31(122): 489-498.

Bremner, J.D., M. Vythilingam, E. Vermetten, S.M. Southwick, T. McGlashan, L.H. Staib, R. Soufer and D.S. Charney. 2003. Neural correlates of declarative memory for emotionally valenced words in women with posttraumatic stress disorder related to early childhood sexual abuse. *Biological Psychiatry* 53(10): 879-889.

Breslau, N., H.D. Chilcoat, R.C. Kessler and G.C. Davis. 1999. Previous exposure to trauma and PTSD effects of subsequent trauma: Results from the Detroit Area Survey of Trauma. *American Journal of Psychiatry* 156(6): 902-907.

Briere, J., and E. Gil. 1998. Self-mutilation in clinical and general population samples: Prevalence, correlates, and functions. *American Journal of Orthopsychiatry* 68(4): 609-620.

Briere, J., and C. Lanktree. 2008. *Integrative Treatment of Complex Trauma for Adolescents (ITCT-A): A Guide for the Treatment of Multiply-Traumatized Youth.* Long Beach, Calif.: U.S. Department of Health and Human Services, Substance Abuse and Mental Health Services Administration, National Child Traumatic Stress Network, and University of Southern California, Miller Children's Abuse and Violence Intervention Center.

Buka, S.L., T.L. Stichick, I. Birdthistle and F.J. Earls. 2001. Youth exposure to violence: Prevalence, risks, and consequences. *American Journal of Orthopsychiatry* 71(3): 298-310.

Butzer, D., L.M. Bronfman and B. Stipak. 1996. The role of police in combating domestic violence in the United States: A case study of the Domestic Violence Reduction Unit, Portland Police Bureau. In *Policing in Central and Eastern Europe: Comparing Firsthand Knowledge With Experience From the West,* ed. M. Pagon. Ljubljana, Slovenia: College of Police and Security Studies: 161-172.

Cicchetti, D., and S.L. Toth. 1995. A developmental psychopathology perspective on child abuse and neglect. *Journal of the American Academy of Child and Adolescent Psychiatry* 34(5): 541-565.

Cooley-Strickland, M.R., R.S. Griffin, D. Darney, K. Otte and J. Ko. 2011. Urban African American youth exposed to community violence: A school-based anxiety preventive intervention efficacy study. *Journal of Prevention & Intervention Community* 39(2):149-166.

Cooper, J.L., R. Masi and J. Vick. 2009. *Social-Emotional Development in Early Childhood: What Every Policymaker Should Know.* New York: Columbia University, Mailman School of Public Health, National Center for Children in Poverty.

Copeland, W.E., G. Keeler, A. Angold and E.J. Costello. 2007. Traumatic events and posttraumatic stress in childhood. *Archives of General Psychiatry* 64(5): 577-584.

Cornelius, J.R., I.M. Salloum, M.E. Thase, R.F. Haskett, D.C. Daley, A. Jones-Barlock, C. Upsher and J.M. Perel. 1998. Fluoxetine versus placebo in depressed alcoholic cocaine abusers. *Psychopharmacology Bulletin* 34: 17-21.

De Bellis, M.D., E.G. Spratt and S.R. Hooper. 2011. Neurodevelopmental biology associated with childhood sexual abuse. *Journal of Child Sexual Abuse* 20(5): 548-587.

Donley, S., L. Habib, T. Jovanovic, A. Kamkwalala, M. Evces, G. Egan, B. Bradley and K.J. Ressler. 2012. Civilian PTSD symptoms and risk for involvement in the criminal justice system. *Journal of the American Academy of Psychiatry and the Law* 40(4): 522-529.

Edwards, Bob, and M.W. Foley. 1997. Social capital and the political economy of our discontent. *American Behavioral Scientist* 40(5): 668-677.

Ehlers, A., and D.M. Clark. 2000. A cognitive model of posttraumatic stress disorder. *Behaviour Research and Therapy* 38(4): 319-345.

Elzinga, B.M., and J.D. Bremner. 2002. Are the neural substrates of memory the final common pathway in posttraumatic stress disorder (PTSD)? *Journal of Affective Disorders* 70(1): 1-17.

Fitzpatrick, K.M., and J.P. Boldizar. 1993. The prevalence and consequences of exposure to violence among African-American youth. *Journal of the American Academy of Child and Adolescent Psychiatry* 32(2): 424-430.

Gewirtz, A.H., and J.L. Edleson. 2007. Young children's exposure to intimate partner violence: Towards a developmental risk and resilience framework for research and intervention. *Journal of Family Violence* 22(3): 151-163.

Goff, P.A., M.C. Jackson, B.A.L. Di Leone, C.M. Culotta and N.A. DiTomasso. 2014. The essence of innocence: Consequences of dehumanizing Black children. *Journal of Personality and Social Psychology* 106(4): 526-545.

Goslin, M.C., C.S. Stover, S. Berkowitz and S. Marans. 2013. Identifying youth at risk for difficulties following a traumatic event: Pre-event factors are associated with acute symptomatology. *Journal of Traumatic Stress* 26(4): 475-482.

Gottlieb, R. 2004. Fighting for an education. *The Hartford Courant,* June 13: 1, 6.

Green, B.L., M. Korol, M.C. Grace, M.G. Vary, A.C. Leonard, G.C. Gleser and S. Smitson-Cohen. 1991. Children and disaster: Age, gender, and parental effects on PTSD symptoms. *Journal of the American Academy of Child and Adolescent Psychiatry* 30(6): 945-951.

Gunderson, J.G., and A.N. Sabo. 1993. The phenomenological and conceptual interface between borderline personality disorder and PTSD. *American Journal of Psychiatry* 150: 19-27.

Gunnar, M.R., and K.M. Quevedo. 2008. Early care experiences and HPA axis regulation in children: A mechanism for later trauma vulnerability. *Progress in Brain Research* 167: 137-147.

Handwerger, K. 2009. Differential patterns of HPA activity and reactivity in adult posttraumatic stress disorder and major depressive disorder. *Harvard Review of Psychiatry* 17: 184-205.

Hangartner, J. 1994. The constitutionality of large scale police tactics: Implications for the right of intrastate travel. *Pace Law Review* 14: 203-233.

Heffernan, K., M. Cloitre, K. Tardiff, P.M. Marzuk, L. Portera and A.C. Leon. 2000. Childhood trauma as a correlate of lifetime opiate use in psychiatric patients. *Addictive Behaviors* 25(5): 797-803.

Herman, J.L. 1992. Complex PTSD: A syndrome in survivors of prolonged and repeated trauma. *Journal of Traumatic Stress* 5(3): 377-391.

Kearney, C.A., A. Wechsler, H. Kaur and A. LemosMiller. 2010. Posttraumatic stress disorder in maltreated youth: A review of contemporary research and thought. *Clinical Child and Family Psychology Review* 13(1): 46-76.

Kelly, T.M., D.C. Daley and A.B. Douaihy. 2012. Treatment of substance abusing patients with comorbid psychiatric disorders. *Addictive Behaviors* 37(1): 11-24.

Kemmis, L., J.K. Hall, R. Kingston and M.J. Morgan. 2007. Impaired fear recognition in regular recreational cocaine users. *Psychopharmacology* 194(2): 151-159.

Landecker, H. 1992. The role of childhood sexual trauma in the etiology of borderline personality disorder: Considerations for diagnosis and treatment. *Psychotherapy: Theory, Research, Practice, Training* 29(2): 234-242.

Lee, D., and H. Seo. 2007. Mechanisms of reinforcement learning and decision making in the primate dorsolateral prefrontal cortex. *Annals of the New York Academy of Sciences* 1104: 108-122.

Levendosky, A.A., A.C. Huth-Bocks, M.A. Semel and D.L. Shapiro. 2002. Trauma symptoms in preschool-age children exposed to domestic violence. *Journal of Interpersonal Violence* 17(2): 150-164.

Leventhal, J.M. 1998. Epidemiology of sexual abuse of children: Old problems, new directions. *Child Abuse & Neglect* 22(6): 481-491.

Lieberman, A.F., P. Van Horn and C.G. Ippen. 2005. Toward evidence-based treatment: Child-parent psychotherapy with preschoolers exposed to marital violence. *Journal of the American Academy of Child and Adolescent Psychiatry* 44(12): 1241-1248.

Lupien, S.J., B.S. McEwen, M.R. Gunnar and C. Heim. 2009. Effects of stress throughout the lifespan on the brain, behaviour and cognition. *Nature Reviews Neuroscience* 10(6): 434-445.

Maschi, T. 2006. Trauma and violent delinquent behavior among males: The moderating role of social support. *Stress, Trauma, and Crisis* 9(1): 45-72.

Moretti, M.M., I. Obsuth, C.L. Odgers and P. Reebye. 2006. Exposure to maternal vs. paternal partner violence, PTSD, and aggression in adolescent girls and boys. *Aggressive Behavior* 32(4): 385-395.

Morgan, M.A., and J.E. LeDoux. 1995. Differential contribution of dorsal and ventral medial prefrontal cortex to the acquisition and extinction of conditioned fear in rats. *Behavioral Neuroscience* 109(4): 681-688.

Morgan, M.A., L.M. Romanski and J.E. LeDoux. 1993. Extinction of emotional learning: Contribution of medial prefrontal cortex. *Neuroscience Letters* 163(1): 109-113.

Perry, B.D., R.A. Pollard, T.L. Blakley, W.L. Baker and D. Vigilante. 1995. Childhood trauma, the neurobiology of adaptation, and use-dependent development of the brain: How states become traits. *Infant Mental Health Journal* 16(4): 271-291.

Plant, J.B., and M.S. Scott. 2009. *Effective Policing and Crime Prevention: A Problem-Oriented Guide for Mayors, City Managers, and County Executives.* Washington, D.C.: U.S. Department of Justice, Office of Community Oriented Policing Services.

Pollak, S.D. 2008. Mechanisms linking early experience and the emergence of emotions: Illustrations from the study of maltreated children. *Current Directions in Psychological Science* 17(6): 370-375.

Pugh, C.R., D. Tremblay, M. Fleshner and J.W. Rudy. 1997. A selective role for corticosterone in contextual-fear conditioning. *Behavioral Neuroscience* 111: 503-511.

Rich, J.A., and C.M. Grey. 2005. Pathways to recurrent trauma among young Black men: Traumatic stress, substance use, and the "code of the street." *American Journal of Public Health* 95(5): 816-824.

Richert, K.A., V.G. Carrion, A. Karchemskiy and A.L. Reiss. 2006. Regional differences of the prefrontal cortex in pediatric PTSD: An MRI study. *Depression and Anxiety* 23(1): 17-25.

Robbins, T.W. 2000. From arousal to cognition: The integrative position of the prefrontal cortex. *Progress in Brain Research* 126: 469-483.

Rudy, J.W., K. Kuwagama and C.R. Pugh. 1999. Isolation reduces contextual but not auditory-cue fear conditioning: A role for endogenous opioids. *Behavioral Neuroscience* 113: 316-323.

Saywitz, K.J., A.P. Mannarino, L. Berliner and J.A. Cohen. 2000. Treatment for sexually abused children and adolescents. *American Psychologist* 55: 1040-1049.

Schore, A.N. 2001. The effects of early relational trauma on right brain development, affect regulation, and infant mental health. *Infant Mental Health Journal* 22(12): 201-269.

Shin, L.M., S.L. Rauch and R.K. Pitman. 2006. Amygdala, medial prefrontal cortex, and hippocampal function in PTSD. *Annals of the New York Academy of Sciences* 1071(1): 67-79.

Snowden, L.R. 2001. Barriers to effective mental health services for African Americans. *Mental Health Services Research* 3: 181-188.

Stein, B.D., L.H. Jaycox, S. Kataoka, H.J. Rhodes and K.D. Vestal. 2003. Prevalence of child and adolescent exposure to community violence. *Clinical Child and Family Psychology Review* 6(4): 247-264.

Steiner, H., I.G. Garcia and Z. Matthews. 1997. Posttraumatic stress disorder in incarcerated juvenile delinquents. *Journal of the American Academy of Child and Adolescent Psychiatry* 36(3): 357-365.

Tarullo, A.R., and M.R. Gunnar. 2006. Child maltreatment and the developing HPA axis. *Hormones and Behavior* 50: 632-639.

Teicher, M.H., S.L. Andersen, A. Polcari, C.M. Anderson, C.P. Navalta and D.M. Kim. 2003. The neurobiological consequences of early stress and childhood maltreatment. *Neuroscience and Biobehavioral Reviews* 27(1): 33-44.

Terr, L.C. 1991. Childhood traumas: An outline and overview. *American Journal of Psychiatry* 148(1): 10-20.

Thomas, A. J., D. Carey, K.-R. Prewitt, E. Romero, M. Richards and B. Velsor-Friedrich. 2012. African-American youth and exposure to community violence: Supporting change from the inside. *Journal for Social Action in Counseling and Psychology* 4(1): 54-68.

Toth, S.L., and D. Cicchetti. 1993. Child maltreatment: Where do we go from here in our treatment of victims? *Child Abuse, Child Development, and Social Policy* 8: 399-437.

U.S. Department of Health and Human Services, Administration for Children and Families, Administration on Children, Youth and Families, Children's Bureau. 2013. *Child Maltreatment 2012.* Washington, D.C.: U.S. Department of Health and Human Services,

Administration for Children and Families, Administration on Children, Youth and Families, Children's Bureau. Available from http://www.acf.hhs.gov/programs/cb/research-data-technology/statistics-research/ child-maltreatment.

Van der Kolk, B.A. 1994. The body keeps the score: Memory and the evolving psychobiology of posttraumatic stress. *Harvard Review of Psychiatry* 1(5): 253-265.

Van der Kolk, B.A. 2005. Developmental trauma disorder. *Psychiatric Annals* 35(5): 401-408.

Van der Kolk, B.A., R.S. Pynoos, D. Cicchetti, M. Cloitre, W. D'Andrea, J.D. Ford, A.F. Lieberman, F.W. Putnam, G. Saxe, J. Spinazzola, B.C. Stolbach and M. Sand Teicher. 2009. Proposal to include a developmental trauma disorder diagnosis for children and adolescents in DSM-V. Unpublished manuscript. Verfügbar unter: http://www.cathymalchiodi.com/dtd_nctsn.pdf (accessed May 20, 2011).

Van Voorhees, E., and A. Scarpa. 2004. The effects of child maltreatment on the hypothalamic-pituitary-adrenal axis. *Trauma, Violence, and Abuse* 5: 333-352.

VanZomeren-Dohm, A., R. Ng, K. Howard, M. Kenney, L. Ritchmeier Cyr, J. Gourneau and C. Michaels. 2013. *How Trauma "Gets Under the Skin": Biological and Cognitive Processes of Child Maltreatment.* St. Paul, Minn.: University of Minnesota Extension, Children, Youth & Family Consortium.

Wilt, S., and Olson, S. 1996. Prevalence of domestic violence in the United States. *JAMWA* 51(3): 77-82.

OTHER RESOURCES

Fernández-Serrano, M.J., M. Pérez-García and A. Verdejo-García. 2011. What are the specific vs. generalized effects of drugs of abuse on neuropsychological performance? *Neuroscience and Biobehavioral Reviews* 35(3): 377-406.

Sharkey, P.T., N. Tirado-Strayer, A.V. Papachristos and C.C. Raver. 2012. The effect of local violence on children's attention and impulse control. *American Journal of Public Health* 102(12): 2287-2293.

Sullivan, E.V. 2012. War-related PTSD, blast injury, and anosognosia. *Neuropsychology Review* 22(1): 1-2.

In: Perspectives on Policing
Editor: Holly Wheeler
ISBN: 978-1-63484-555-7

Chapter 8

MEASURING PERFORMANCE IN A MODERN POLICE ORGANIZATION*

Malcolm K. Sparrow

INTRODUCTION

Perhaps everything the modern police executive needs to know about performance measurement has already been written. But much of the best work on the subject is both voluminous and now more than a decade old, so there is no guarantee that today's police executives have read it. Indeed, it appears that many police organizations have not yet taken some of its most important lessons to heart.

I hope, in this paper, to offer police executives some broad frameworks for recognizing the value of police work, to point out some common mistakes regarding performance measurement, and to draw police executives' attention to key pieces of literature that they might not have explored and may find useful. I also hope to bring to the police profession some of the general lessons learned in other security and regulatory professions about the special challenges of performance measurement in a risk-control or harm-reduction setting.

A research project entitled "Measuring What Matters," funded jointly by the National Institute of Justice (NIJ) and the Office of Community Oriented Policing Services (COPS Office), led to the publication in July 1999 of a substantial collection of essays on the subject of measuring performance.[1] The 15 essays that make up that collection are fascinating, not least for the divergence of opinion they reveal among the experts of the day. The sharpest disagreements pit the champions of the New York Police Department's (NYPD's) early CompStat model (with its rigorous and almost single-minded focus on reductions in reported crime as the "bottom line" of policing) against a broad range of scholars who mostly espoused more expansive conceptions of the policing mission and pressed the case for more inclusive and more nuanced approaches to performance measurement.

---

* This is an edited, reformatted and augmented version of a paper, NCJ 248476, in the New Perspectives in Policing series, issued by the U.S. Department of Justice, National Institute of Justice, March 2015.

Three years later, in 2002, the Police Executive Research Forum (PERF) published another major report on performance measurement, *Recognizing Value in Policing: The Challenge of Recognizing Police Performance,* authored principally by Mark H. Moore.[2] PERF followed that up in 2003 with a condensed document, *The "Bottom Line" of Policing: What Citizens Should Value (and Measure!) in Police Performance,*[3] authored by Moore and Anthony Braga.

Despite the richness of the frameworks presented in these and other materials, a significant proportion of today's police organizations seem to remain narrowly focused on the same categories of indicators that have dominated the field for decades:

a) Reductions in the number of serious crimes reported, most commonly presented as local comparisons against an immediately preceding time period.
b) Clearance rates.
c) Response times.
d) Measures of enforcement productivity (e.g., numbers of arrests, citations or stop-and-frisk searches).

A few departments now use citizen satisfaction surveys on a regular basis, but most do not. Clearance rates are generally difficult to measure in a standardized and objective fashion, so category (b) tends to receive less emphasis than the other three. Categories (c) and (d) — response times and enforcement productivity metrics — are useful in showing that police are getting to calls fast and working hard but reveal nothing about whether they are working intelligently, using appropriate methods or having a positive impact.

Therefore, category (a) — reductions in the number of serious crime reports — tends to dominate many departments' internal and external claims of success, being the closest thing available to a genuine crime-control outcome measure. These measures have retained their prominence despite everything the field is supposed to have learned in the last 20 years about the limitations of reported crime statistics. Those limitations (which this paper will explore in greater detail later) include the following:

1) The focus is narrow because crime control is just one of several components of the police mission.
2) The focus on serious crimes is narrower still, as community concerns often revolve around other problems and patterns of behavior.
3) Relentless pressure to lower the numbers, without equivalent pressure to preserve the integrity of the recording and reporting systems, invites manipulation of crime statistics — suppression of reports and misclassification of crimes — and other forms of corruption.
4) Focusing on reported crime overlooks unreported crimes. Overall levels of victimization are generally two to three times higher than reported crime rates.[4] Particularly low reporting rates apply to household thefts, rape, other sexual assaults, crimes against youths ages 12 to 17, violent crimes committed at schools, and crimes committed by someone the victim knows well.[5]
5) Pressure to reduce the numbers is counterproductive when dealing with invisible crimes (classically unreported or underreported crimes, such as crimes within the

family, white collar crimes, consensual crimes such as drug dealing or bribery, and crimes involving intimidation). Successful campaigns against these types of crime often involve deliberate attempts to expose the problem by first driving reporting rates up, not down.[6]

6) A focus on crime rate reductions does not consider the costs or side effects of the strategies used to achieve them.
7) Emphasizing comparisons with prior time periods affords a short-term and very local perspective. It may give a department the chance to boast, even while its crime rates remain abysmal compared with other jurisdictions. Conversely, best performers (with low crime rates overall) might look bad when random fluctuations on a quarterly or annual basis raise their numbers. Genuine longer term trends may be masked by temporary changes, such as those caused by weather patterns or special events. More important than local short-term fluctuations are sustained longer term trends and comparisons with crime rates in similar communities. Pressure to beat one's own performance, year after year, can produce bizarre and perverse incentives.
8) Even if crime levels were once out of control, the reductions achievable will inevitably run out eventually, when rates plateau at more acceptable levels. At this point, the department's normal crime-control success story — assuming that reductions in reported crime rates had been its heart and soul — evaporates. Some executives fail to recognize the point at which legitimate reductions have been exhausted. Continuing to demand reductions at that point is like failing to set the torque control on a power screwdriver: first you drive the screw, which is useful work; but then you rip everything to shreds and even undo the value of your initial tightening. The same performance focus that initially produced legitimate gains becomes a destructive force if pressed too hard or for too long.
9) A number is just a number, and reliance on it reduces all the complexity of real life to a zero or a one. One special crime, or one particular crime unsolved, may have a disproportionate impact on a community's sense of safety and security. Aggregate numbers fail to capture the significance of special cases.

Reported crime rates will always belong among the suite of indicators relevant for managing a complex police department, as will response times, clearance rates, enforcement productivity, community satisfaction and indicators of morale. But what will happen if police executives stress one or another of these to the virtual exclusion of all else? What will happen if relentless pressure is applied to lower the reported crime rate, but no counterbalancing controls are imposed on methods, the use of force, or the integrity of the recording and reporting systems? From the public's perspective, the resulting organizational behaviors can be ineffective, inappropriate and even disastrous.

If we acknowledged the limitations of reported crime rates and managed to lessen our dependence on them, then how would we recognize true success in crime control? And how might we better capture and describe it?

I believe the answer is the same across the full range of government's risk-control responsibilities, whether the harms to be controlled are criminal victimization, pollution, corruption, fraud, tax evasion, terrorism or other potential and actual harms. The definition of success in risk control or harm reduction is to spot emerging problems early and suppress them before they do much harm.[7] This is a very different idea from "allow problems to grow so hopelessly out of control that we can then get serious, all of a sudden, and produce substantial reductions year after year after year."

What do citizens expect of government agencies entrusted with crime control, risk control, or other harm-reduction duties? The public does not expect that governments will be able to prevent all crimes or contain all harms. But they do expect government agencies to provide the best protection possible, and at a reasonable price, by being:

1) Vigilant, so they can spot emerging threats early, pick up on precursors and warning signs, use their imaginations to work out what could happen, use their intelligence systems to discover what others are planning, and do all this before much harm is done.
2) Nimble, flexible enough to organize themselves quickly and appropriately around each emerging crime pattern rather than being locked into routines and processes designed for traditional issues.
3) Skillful, masters of the entire intervention toolkit, experienced (as craftsmen) in picking the best tools for each task, and adept at inventing new approaches when existing methods turn out to be irrelevant or insufficient to suppress an emerging threat.[8]

Real success in crime control — spotting emerging crime problems early and suppressing them before they do much harm — would not produce substantial year-to-year reductions in crime figures because genuine and substantial reductions are available only when crime problems have first grown out of control. Neither would best practices produce enormous numbers of arrests, coercive interventions or any other specific activity because skill demands economy in the use of force and financial resources and rests on artful and well-tailored responses rather than extensive and costly campaigns.

Ironically, therefore, the two classes of metrics that still seem to wield the most influence in many departments — crime reduction and enforcement productivity — would utterly fail to reflect the very best performance in crime control.

Furthermore, we must take seriously the fact that other important duties of the police will never be captured through crime statistics or in measures of enforcement output. As NYPD Assistant Commissioner Ronald J. Wilhelmy wrote in a November 2013 internal NYPD strategy document:

> [W]e cannot continue to evaluate personnel on the simple measure of whether crime is up or down relative to a prior period. Most importantly, CompStat has ignored measurement of other core functions. Chiefly, we fail to measure what may be our highest priority: public satisfaction. We also fail to measure quality of life, integrity, community relations, administrative efficiency, and employee satisfaction, to name just a few other important areas.[9]

WHO IS FLYING THIS AIRPLANE, AND WHAT KIND OF TRAINING HAVE THEY HAD?

At the most recent meeting of the Executive Session, we asked the police chiefs present, "Do you think your police department is more or less complicated than a Boeing 737?" They all concluded fairly quickly that they considered their departments more complicated and put forward various reasons.

First, their departments were made up mostly of people, whom they regarded as more complex and difficult to manage than the electrical, mechanical, hydraulic and software systems that make up a modern commercial jetliner.

Second, they felt their departments' missions were multiple and ambiguous, rather than single and clear. Picking Denver as a prototypical flight destination, they wondered aloud, "What's the equivalent of Denver for my police department?" Given a destination, flight paths can be mapped out in advance and scheduled within a minute, even across the globe. Unless something strange or unusual happens along the way, the airline pilot (and most likely an autopilot) follows the plan. For police agencies, "strange and unusual" is normal. Unexpected events happen all the time, often shifting a department's priorities and course. As a routine matter, different constituencies have different priorities, obliging police executives to juggle conflicting and sometimes irreconcilable demands.

Assuming that for these or other reasons, the answer is "more complicated," then we might want to know how the training and practices of police executives compare with those of commercial pilots when it comes to using information in managing their enterprise.

The pilot of a Boeing 737 has access to at least 50 types of information on a continuing basis. Not all of them require constant monitoring, as some of the instruments in the cockpit beep or squeak or flash when they need attention. At least 10 to 12 types of information are monitored constantly. What do we expect of pilots? That they know, through their training, how to combine different types of information and interpret them in context, so they can quickly recognize important conditions of the plane and of the environment and know how they should respond.

A simple question like, "Am I in danger of stalling?" (i.e., flying too slowly to retain control of the aircraft) requires at least seven types of information to resolve: altitude, air temperature, windspeed, engine power, flap deployment, weight and weight distribution, together with knowledge of the technical parameters that determine the edge of the flight envelope. Some of these factors relate to the plane, and some relate to external conditions. All these indicators must be combined to identify a potential stall.

Thanks to the availability of simulators, commercial airline pilots are now trained to recognize and deal with an amazing array of possible scenarios, many of which they will never encounter in real life.[10] They learn how various scenarios would manifest themselves through a variety of indicators, so they can recognize them quickly, diagnose them accurately and respond appropriately.

With so many forms of information available to the pilot, we might wonder how many of the dials in the cockpit are designated key performance indicators or, for that matter, how many of them are regarded as performance indicators at all. The answer is none. No single dial in the cockpit tells the pilot how well he or she is doing or is used to judge performance. Airline pilots appreciate and use an extensive array of different types of information, habitually use them in combination and in relation to one another, but are very slow to label any of them performance indicators.

By contrast, many public sector agencies (and this problem is by no means confined to police departments) pay close attention to a comparatively small number of indicators and seem all too keen to select one or two of them (usually no more than five) as key performance indicators. Designating a measure as a performance indicator usually means we determine in advance whether we expect it to move up or down, and we may even set a particular level as a target. Public sector executives then often seem surprised when the narrow range of information monitored produces partial or inadequate interpretations of what is really happening and when the narrow performance focus drives behaviors that turn out to be perverse and contrary to the public interest.

Executive Session participants were quick to point out the lack of "simulator training" currently available for senior police managers. Simulations in the form of practical exercises are frequently used in entry-level training for recruits and in training courses for specialty functions (e.g., hostage negotiations, SWAT). For executives, simulator-style training is occasionally available in crisis leadership courses, where trainees are invited to take their turn at the helm in a crisis response exercise. But absent a crisis, most executive teams operate without any special training to help them interpret the myriad signals available or recognize important conditions quickly and pick the best response to different scenarios.

In the absence of such training, many executive teams muddle through, having learned most of what they know through their own experience on the way up through the managerial ranks rather than through formal training. As one chief noted, the closest equivalent to executive-level simulator training is when one department has the opportunity to learn from the misery of another. A collegial network of police executives, ready to share both their successes and failures, is a valuable asset to the profession.

Any "numbers game" is, of course, a simplification. Carl Klockars expresses this beautifully (and with a nod to Arthur "Dooley" Wilson) in *Measuring What Matters:*

SCENARIOS FOR POLICE EXECUTIVES

Imagining a simulator for police executives might be interesting. Here are three scenarios:

(1) You notice the following:

a) The conviction rate for cases prosecuted is unusually low and falling.
b) The proportion of complaints against officers that are internally generated is rising.
c) The number of internal requests for transfers is unusually high, as is the use of sick days.
d) Based on community surveys, public confidence in the agency is rising, but the response rate on surveys is falling.
e) The reported crime rate is dropping fast.
f) What is happening? What else would you want to know? What might you do?

(2) You notice the following:

a) Drug-related arrests are up 30 percent over last year.

b) The department has just (proudly) announced "record drug seizures" for the last quarter.
c) The proportion of drug-related prosecutions that result in jail terms has fallen to record low levels.
d) (d)Street-level drug prices are at record lows.
e) What is happening? What else would you want to know? What might you do?

(3) You notice the following:

a) The number of domestic violence calls received by the department has risen sharply over the last 6 months.
b) The number of homicides determined to be domestic violence-related has dropped by one-third in the same period.
c) The proportion of domestic violence arrests that result in charges has just dropped below 40 percent for the first time.
d) The proportion of domestic violence cases prosecuted that result in convictions has also fallen below 70 percent for the first time.

What is happening? What else would you want to know? What might you do?

These three scenarios were presented to the Executive Session in the context of our discussions on performance measurement. Given the time limitations, we did not have the chance to explore them at length, and none of the police leaders present ventured an opinion as to what he or she thought might be happening in each case. But they did agree that they would quite likely reach very different conclusions from one another, given their varied experiences and biases.

These scenarios are relatively simple ones involving only four or five indicators. Even so, using these indicators in combination and treating them as important management information might lead one to very different conclusions than treating one or another of them as a performance metric and specifying whether it should move up or down or reach some target level.

Scenario 1 might reveal an agency in crisis with plummeting morale. The community may be giving up on the police, no longer bothering to report crimes. Only "friends of the department" bother to respond to surveys; everyone else has given up on them. Corruption problems may be surfacing, evidenced by a higher rate of internally generated complaints and loss of cases in court, perhaps due to tainted evidence or community distrust.

Scenario 2 might suggest a failing drug-control strategy, with numerous arrests exhausting the capacity of the justice system but no positive or structural impact on the drug problem.

Scenario 3 might reveal the early stages of an energetic and successful campaign against domestic violence, which is helping to expose the problem more effectively while using arrests and prosecutions aggressively as deterrence tactics (even if prosecutions are not taken all the way through the system).

Notice that the two scenarios suggesting various forms of failure and trouble (1 and 2) show a reduction in reported crime rates (traditionally regarded as a sign of success). One of them (scenario 2) shows high levels of enforcement productivity.

The only story here that suggests an effective crime-control strategy (scenario 3) shows an increase in reported crime rates and a decrease in the conviction rate (traditionally signals of poor performance).

Even these relatively straightforward examples show how too close a focus on one or two classes of metric could blind an organization to meaning and context and possibly mislead everyone about what is really happening.

In every instance of measurement, the conversion of a thing, event, or occasion to a number requires ignoring or discarding all other meaning that thing, event, or occasion might have. The easy way to appreciate this very hard point in all its paradox and irony is to remember this: a kiss is just a kiss, a sigh is just a sigh, and a crime is just a crime, as time goes by. (Which, of course, anyone who has kissed, sighed, or committed, investigated, or been the victim of a crime knows is not true.)[11]

Filmmakers and writers of police television dramas seem to have picked up on the collision that happens, somewhere in the middle ranks of a police department, between high-level general strategies (often numbers driven) and the rich texture of real life. It does not really matter whether one is watching Detective McNulty in "The Wire," Detective Chief Superintendent Foyle in "Foyle's War," or any other fictional midrank police officer.

At some point or another, in most episodes, an assistant commissioner or some other senior officer is going to show up unexpectedly at the local police station. Never is his visit good news! The senior officers are invariably portrayed as interfering nitwits, ignorant and dismissive of what is happening at the street level. Often, they appear with their own new pet initiatives, requiring this many cases to be made or that many arrests of a particular type. Their agendas seem motivated by political, personal or career-enhancing imperatives or are blatantly corrupt. The senior officers never listen and never help, but walk in with their general solutions that are not well thought out and demand a campaign of arrests or prosecutions that they claim will serve as a visible public demonstration of how seriously the department takes such-and-such an issue. Such visits interrupt valuable work and create imperatives for frontline officers that seem unhelpful, absurd or not in the public interest. Morale suffers, and the star of the show is left to fend off the ridiculous pressures from above so that his or her subordinates can carry on with "real police work," knowing full well it will never be recognized by the department.

Of course, incompetent and corrupt senior management always makes for good theater. But the creators of police dramas do seem to have picked up on a specific organizational dynamic relevant to policing. The episode is about a specific scenario, which has all the quirky peculiarities of real life. That is what makes each episode unique, interesting and worth watching. The senior officers are unflatteringly portrayed as besotted with a general strategy and a narrow performance focus, neither of which does justice to the complex and varied nature of police work.

If a department appreciates that complexity; does well on vigilance, nimbleness, and skill; and therefore excels at spotting emerging problems early and suppressing them before they do much harm, what will success look like? How will such a department demonstrate its crime-control expertise?

The answer is that its performance account will consist largely of problem-specific project accounts describing emerging crime patterns and what happened to each one. Each project account will describe how the department spotted the problem in the first place, how it analyzed and subsequently understood the problem, what the department and its partners did about the problem, and what happened as a result. Some in policing call that the scanning, analysis, response and assessment (SARA) model. It is a straightforward, problem-oriented account that has little to do with aggregate numbers of any particular kind.

BROADER FRAMEWORKS FOR MONITORING AND MEASUREMENT

If the analogy of the cockpit turns out to be useful, then the following sections may help senior managers develop a broader sense of the banks of instruments they might want to have available in their cockpits and a clearer sense of how to use them for different purposes. To understand the diversity of indicators that could be relevant and useful in a police department's cockpit, we should remember (1) the breadth of the policing mission, (2) the multiple dimensions of performance that are therefore relevant, (3) the different managerial purposes that measurement can serve, and (4) the different types of work that occur within an agency, each of which naturally generates different types of information.

Much literature is available on all of these subjects, but for the sake of efficiency here I will refer readers to one principal author for each:

Herman Goldstein, for breadth of mission;[12] Mark Moore, for multiple dimensions of performance;[13] Robert Behn, for different managerial purposes;[14] and my own work on operational risk control for different types of work.[15]

Broadening the Frame: The Mission of Policing

In his 1977 book, *Policing a Free Society,* Herman Goldstein summarized the functions of the police[16]

1) To prevent and control conduct widely recognized as threatening to life and property (serious crime).
2) To aid individuals who are in danger of physical harm, such as the victims of criminal attacks.
3) To protect constitutional guarantees such as the right of free speech and assembly.
4) To facilitate the movement of people and vehicles.
5) To assist those who cannot care for themselves: the intoxicated, the addicted, the mentally ill, the physically disabled, the old and the young.
6) To resolve conflict, whether between individuals, groups of individuals, or individuals and their government.
7) To identify problems that have the potential to become more serious for the individual citizen, the police or the government.
8) To create and maintain a feeling of security in the community.

This template, now 37 years old, seems a solid place to start and perfectly usable today as a frame for describing the multiple components of the police mission. Each of the eight areas Goldstein mentions might constitute one chapter in a police department's annual report. Perhaps, at the outset, the first chapter (crime control) might be more thickly populated than some of the others, but with some effort a better balance might be achieved.

Goldstein's framework pushes police to view their role more broadly than as part of the criminal justice system. The community policing movement and the evolution of CompStat systems into broader CitiStat systems[17] have pushed police departments farther in recognizing their role as a part of municipal government. As Moore and Poethig point out in their *Measuring What Matters* essay:

> If we conceive of the police as nothing more than "the first step in the criminal justice system," then we might easily miss the contributions that they make "outside the box" of crime control, law enforcement, and arresting people. On the other hand, if we conceive of the police as an agency of municipal government that shares with other agencies the broad responsibility for strengthening the quality of urban life, then we are in a better position to notice that the police contribute much more to those goals than is captured by the simple idea of reducing crime. We also notice that the police have capabilities that go far beyond their ability to make arrests and that these capabilities are valuable to the enterprise of city government. In short, the police are a more valuable asset when viewed from the vantage point of trying to strengthen urban life than they are when viewed from the narrower perspective of reducing crime through making arrests.[18]

An obvious example of this broader role, as Moore and Poethig point out, is emergency response:

> [P]artly because the police department is the only agency that works 24 hours a day, 7 days a week, and makes house calls, police will continue to be the "first responders" to a wide variety of emergencies. These emergencies can be medical (although ambulance services increasingly take care of these) or they can be social, such as deranged people threatening themselves or others, homeless children found wandering the streets with no parents to care for them, or drunks at risk of freezing to death after falling asleep on a park bench.[19]

The terrorist attacks of September 11, 2001, brought another kind of multiagency network to the fore. Police departments, especially those in major cities, were now required (and with no diminution of their other responsibilities) to participate in a range of counterterrorism, domestic security and intelligence collaborations at regional, national and international levels. Reporting systems that focused too heavily on local crime statistics would likely overlook their contributions on this front. Of course, much of the work conducted in the security domain cannot be discussed in public as readily as routine crime-control activities. Nevertheless, it would be a shame not to include this aspect of the modern police mission in a department's performance account, even if parts of the story could be presented only to those stakeholders authorized to hear it.

Broadening the Frame: Dimensions of Performance

Working from Goldstein's (and other commentators') broader sense of the policing mission, Mark Moore develops a framework for holding police departments accountable. In *Recognizing Value in Policing: The Challenge of Measuring Police Performance,* he and his coauthors explore the range of data types and methods of observation that could provide a basis for assessing police performance in each of the following seven dimensions:[20]

1) Reducing criminal victimization.
2) Calling offenders to account.
3) Reducing fear and enhancing personal security.
4) Guaranteeing safety in public spaces (including traffic safety).
5) Using financial resources fairly, efficiently and effectively.
6) Using force and authority fairly, efficiently and effectively.
7) Satisfying customer demands/achieving legitimacy with those policed.

Moore notes that reported crime statistics only partially capture levels of criminal victimization and that criminal victimization is only one of the seven dimensions of performance that matter to the public. In particular, he takes issue with the notion that crime statistics should be treated as the "bottom line" of policing. William J. Bratton had stated this view in an essay he contributed to NIJ's *Measuring What Matters*: "Crime statistics have become the department's bottom line, the best indicator of how the police are doing, precinct by precinct and citywide."[21]

Moore says the analogy with a commercial firm's bottom line is flawed because the crime statistics themselves do not capture the costs of the methods used to achieve them. Reductions in crime levels ought, he says, to be treated as part of gross revenues (not net revenues), and the use by police of financial resources and especially the use of force or authority should be regarded as costs and therefore counted against the revenues.[22] The "bottom line" is therefore served if police manage to bring down crime rates and are economical with their uses of force and money.

> [C]rime reduction is closer to the idea of the *gross revenues* a private company earns by producing and selling particular products and services, not its *profit.* [...]
>
> Managers ought to be interested in trying to widen the difference between the valuable results the police produce (reduced crime), and the costs incurred in producing those results.[23]

In the early days of CompStat in New York City, with widespread use of aggressive street order maintenance tactics, it did not appear that huge numbers of arrests were regarded as a cost. In fact, the number of arrests seems to have been a source of pride for the department. George Kelling, in the essay he contributed to *Measuring What Matters,* commented:

> Even by more widely touted measurements, New York police do relatively well; so many people have been arrested that neither jails nor prisons can hold them. If the number of cells was expanded, few doubt that New York City police could fill almost any added capacity as well.[24]

Carl Klockars, in his essay for *Measuring What Matters,* stressed the importance of the skill of minimizing the use of force.[25] He points out how much officers vary in this regard and in their predisposition to resort to violent or nonviolent means to exercise control in their encounters with civilians:

> In any police agency there are officers who are well known for their ability to walk into an out-of-control situation and stabilize it peacefully. (There are others, of course, who can turn any situation into a riot.) The skill of such officers is [in] knowing how to work in ways that minimize the use of force.[26]

Stuart Scheingold, in his essay for *Measuring What Matters,* warned that "... the kinds of police practices associated with zero-tolerance and hyper law enforcement seem likely to increase the mistrust of the police that robs crime control of its consensus building capacity."[27] Scheingold also recalls the warnings about the effects of zero tolerance and hyper law enforcement that Wesley Skogan provided in his 1990 book, *Disorder and Decline: Crime and the Spiral of Decay in American Neighborhoods:*

> Even if they are conducted in a strictly legal fashion, aggressive tactics such as saturating areas with police, stopping cars frequently, conducting extensive field interrogations and searches, and bursting into apartments suspected of harboring gambling or drugs can undermine police-community relations in black and Hispanic neighborhoods.[28]

The underlying tensions between police and predominantly minority communities may amplify these costs, according to Skogan:

> [R]esidents of poor and minority neighborhoods with serious disorder problems often have antagonistic relations with the police. They regard the police as another of their problems, frequently perceiving them to be arrogant, brutal, racist, and corrupt.[29]

Moore, along with these and many other commentators, has urged police to recognize coercive power as a precious commodity to be used sparingly and invites them to search for artful interventions that use authority efficiently rather than defaulting to massive enforcement campaigns of one kind or another.[30] The point is not to rule out enforcement campaigns where these are required. Rather, the point is that a full accounting of police performance demands serious attention to the costs as well as the gross revenues of such campaigns.

Moore also proposes an expansive view of client satisfaction that includes an assessment of the experience of those arrested or cited. Not that we would expect them to be "pleased" that they were caught! But we would hope to hear that their rights were respected, that excessive force was not used against them, and that they were treated with dignity and courtesy even while being brought to book.[31]

Broadening the Frame: Purposes of Measuring Performance

Robert Behn's 2003 article, "Why Measure Performance? Different Purposes Require Different Measures,"[32] has recently been celebrated as one of the most influential articles in the history of the journal in which it was published, *Public Administration Review.* I often recommend this as foundational reading for practitioners wanting to rethink their department's use of metrics and indicators.

In this article, Behn lays out eight different managerial purposes that may be served by various types of performance measurement and monitoring. He summarizes these in a table,[33] reproduced here as table 1.

Table 1. Eight Purposes That Public Managers Have for Measuring Performance

Purpose : The public manager's question that the performance measure can help asswer	
Evaluate	How well is my public agency performing?
Control	How can I ensure that my subordinates are doing the right thing?
Budget	On what programs, people or projects should my agency spend the public's money?
Motivation	How can I motivate line staff, middle managers, nonprofit and for-profit collaborators, stakeholders and citizens to do the things necessary to improve performance?
Promote	Hoe can I convince political superiors, legislations, stakeholders, journalists and citizens that my agency is doing a good job?
Celebrate	Ehat accomplishments are worthy of the important organizational ritual of celebrating success?
Learn	Why is what working or not working?
Improve	Ehat exactly should who do differently to improve performance?

Source: Robert D. Behn, "Why Measure Performance? Different Purposes Require Different Measures," Public Administration Review 63 (5) (Sept./Oct. 2003): 586-606, table 1.

Behn also explores the different types of indicators that will serve these eight managerial purposes.[34]

For example, evaluation of agency performance at the aggregate level (purpose 1) will involve attempts to link agency outputs with societal outcomes and will need to consider the effects of exogenous factors.

Motivating teams internally (purpose 4) may use real-time, functionally specific activity and productivity metrics disaggregated to the team level. These might be compared with production targets or even pitted against one another in an internal competition.

Organizational learning (purpose 7) may rest more on disaggregated data that can reveal anomalies and deviations from norms, revealing problems to be understood and resolved.

Improvement of departmental processes (purpose 8) will require linking internal process design changes with their effects on agency outputs, efficiency and outcomes.

Broadening the Frame: Recognizing Different Types of Work

The fourth way to broaden the frame is to recognize the characteristics of different classes of work that coexist within a complex organization.

First, and most familiar, is functional work, which groups workers with other similarly skilled workers. Investigators work together within a detective bureau, auditors in the audit bureau, educators in the training department, and lawyers in the general counsel's office. Functional professionalism requires staying current, skilled and state-of-the-art.

For any specialist functional unit, the most readily available metrics cover quantity and quality. Quantity is easiest to measure: how many cases opened and closed, how many audits completed, how many hours of training delivered. But each function should also have and emphasize its own quality metrics lest concerns over quantity drown out concerns over quality.

Ideas about quality may include indications of significance or relevance (of a case or an audit) as well as assessments of whether the activities are conducted more or less professionally. A functional unit, if it divides its output quantity by its inputs, may also furnish indications of productivity or efficiency (e.g., the number of cases closed per investigator, the number of audits completed per auditor or the number of training hours delivered per instructor).

Second, and also familiar, is process-based work. By this I mean any kind of transactional work that is repeated hundreds or thousands of times. Obvious examples include tax agencies processing tax returns, environmental agencies issuing or renewing environmental permits for industry, and a licensing authority processing applications, as well as police departments responding to emergency calls or to complaints from the public about officer conduct. Given the repetitive nature and volume of such work, organizations invest in process design (involving procedures, protocols, automation and flow patterns) to handle the loads in expeditious, smooth and predictable ways.

Five categories of management information are associated with every process:

1) *Volume*: Measures of transaction volume (and trends in volume over time). This is important management information, as it affects resource allocation decisions even though the incoming volume may not be under the organization's control.
2) *Timeliness*: How long it takes to process transactions. Many processes have mandatory timelines. Measures used may include average processing times, worst-case times, or percentage of the transaction load that is handled within mandated or specified time periods.
3) *Accuracy*: The proportion of the determinations or judgments made that turn out to be "correct." Metrics on accuracy usually come from case reviews or audits of samples conducted after the fact. Getting a decision right early is preferable to getting it right eventually (after review or on appeal), as it is quicker, cheaper and generally more satisfactory for all the stakeholders.
4) *Cost-efficiency*: Indicators of the cost of running the process divided by the transaction volume. (Processing costs per transaction can be driven down through process improvement, process redesign and automation.)
5) *Client satisfaction*: Almost every process transaction involves a client (a caller, a complainant, an applicant). Clients can be sampled and surveyed retrospectively to determine the nature of their experience with the process. Even if the client did not get the decision he or she wanted, he or she can still legitimately comment on whether the process seemed fair and efficient and whether he or she was treated properly.

The third type of work, risk-based work, differs from functional work and process work. In the vocabulary of the police profession, the most familiar phrase for this would be problem-oriented work. It is not about one particular method (functional), and it is not about quality management in the context of an established process; rather, it is about a specific risk concentration, issue or problem. For risk-based work, professionalism begins with spotting the problems early and discerning their character and dynamics, long before anyone decides which tactics might be relevant or whether any of the organization's routine processes touch the problem at all.

The following extract from *The Character of Harms* describes some of the frustrations that arise when agencies depend too heavily on functional and process-based metrics and fail to recognize problem-oriented or risk-based work as different:

> Even the combination of [the functional and process-based] performance stories falls short with respect to demonstrating effective harm-control. It might show the agency worked hard to apply the functional tools it has, and that it operated its established processes with alacrity and precision. But it leaves open the question of whether tool selection is effective, and whether the processes established touch the pressing issues of the day. The audience can see agencies working hard, which they like. But they would like to be convinced they are also working effectively on the problems they choose to address, and that they are identifying and selecting the most important issues to address. Neither the function-based performance story (e.g., "we completed this many high-quality investigations") nor the process-based version ("we cleared our backlogs and streamlined our system") provide such assurance.[35]

The risk-based or problem-oriented performance story is quite different from the other two. It consists of a collection of project-based accounts, each comprising five elements.[36]

(a) A description of the data or intelligence that alerted the department to the problem and showed it to be of sufficient scope and significance to warrant special attention.
(b) A description of the metrics selected (which are project-specific) to be used in determining whether the condition "got better"; in other words, outcome or impact metrics through which project success or failure might be judged.
(c) A description of the action plan adopted and maybe a second or third one used if and when it was determined that the first one failed.
(d) A description of what happened to the project metrics over time and how the project team interpreted those changes.
(e) A decision about project closure, hopefully with the problem sufficiently abated that resources could be withdrawn so the department could move on to the next pressing issue. Continuing attention to the problem would enter a longer term (and less resource-intensive) monitoring and maintenance phase.

If a department succeeds in its crime-control mission, the heart of its success story will be the collection of project-based accounts, each describing an emerging crime pattern spotted early and dealt with skillfully. The more vigilant the department becomes in spotting emerging problems early, the less available significant crime reductions will be. Aggregate levels of crime may remain low but relatively steady, even as the department works hard to spot new threats before they have a chance to grow out of control.

Criminologists and other evaluators of police performance — who tend to use changes in the aggregate reported crime rate as the outcome variable in their analysis — may not recognize best practice, as the crime reductions visible at the aggregate level may not be statistically significant or may not be present at all.[37]

However, the risk-based performance account — which describes how the department kept the aggregate rates low — is always available. That account relies much less on aggregate crime numbers and instead describes the collection of problem-specific interventions. Relevant metrics are tailored to each project and derive from disaggregated data filtered to fit the problem being addressed.

On Setting Goals Using Performance Metrics

With the distinctions between functional, process-based and risk-based work clarified, it might be worth observing which types of metrics associated with each type of work could or should be used for goal-setting — that is, as performance metrics.

Some departments set targets for functional outputs, including enforcement activities such as arrests, stops, searches and traffic citations. This only makes sense in particular circumstances and should never be the default position or become normal practice. If you want quality work from a carpenter, it makes no sense to demand that he or she drill a certain number of holes or hammer a quota of nails. The essence of craftsmanship involves mastery of all the tools and the ability to select among them based on a clear understanding of the specific task in hand. Functional quotas make little sense in this context.

The use of quotas for enforcement activity is always contentious, subject to officer whistleblowing and media scrutiny.[38] The danger is that setting enforcement goals may bias the judgment of police officers in potentially dangerous ways and may contribute to aggressive or oppressive police conduct. Some jurisdictions have banned the use of quotas for traffic tickets.[39] Mandating a certain level of enforcement activity drives up the costs of policing for society and therefore reduces the "bottom line." There may be smarter ways, more economical with respect to the use of force or authority, to procure the compliance or behavioral changes sought.

Some departments deny setting quotas but admit to using enforcement productivity as a measure of patrol officers' effort — in other words, as a performance metric. In terms of the effect on police operations, the two ideas are virtually indistinguishable. Measures of overall productivity spanning the full range of patrol tasks (including but not limited to enforcement) can reveal over time who is working hard and who is not. That, of course, is important management information.

The danger of setting goals specifically for enforcement actions is that it may incline officers to stretch the limits of legality and fairness for the sake of another arrest or ticket. It is liable to produce quantity without regard to quality, relevance or side effects. It undermines the importance of discretion and judgment exercised at the frontline.

Despite these general cautions, the use of some kind of enforcement campaign might still be appropriate in specific circumstances, but the need would arise only when a specific type of enforcement focus has been selected as the solution to address a specific crime problem. All of the following conditions would need to be satisfied:

1) A specific pattern of crime is being addressed.
2) The problem has been properly analyzed.
3) A specific pattern of crime is being addressed.
4) The problem has been properly analyzed.
5) All the intervention options have been given full and open-minded consideration.
6) An action plan has been chosen that requires a period of intensive enforcement attention to specific violations (which we might call an enforcement campaign).
7) Instructions to frontline officers make it clear that, despite the context, every enforcement action must, given the circumstances of the case, be legally justifiable and appropriate.
8) During the implementation of the plan, management constantly and carefully monitors the legality, reasonableness, relevance, impact and side effects of the enforcement activities so that operations can wind down or change course as soon as is appropriate.

In this context, the use of functional focus fits Behn's managerial purposes of control (to make sure employees are carrying out the plan) and motivation (to increase intensity of effort). But the plan being carried out is one thoughtfully designed in response to a specific crime problem. The campaign is appropriate, therefore, because it constitutes an intervention for a specific problem. This differs from setting enforcement quotas just because "that's what we do to show we're serious" or because particular executives have an ideological preference for certain types of activity. A wise craftsman does not "believe in" any one tool any more than any other. Enforcement campaigns should be seldom used and their occasional use should be thoughtful, carefully monitored and temporary.

If unrelenting pressure is applied to police officers to meet activity quotas of any kind (enforcement-related or not), they will surely find ways to produce quantity, even at the expense of quality, relevance, appropriateness or their own better judgment. If the goals set are unreasonable or not achievable through legitimate means, then illegitimate means may well be employed, producing behaviors not in the public interest.

As Andrew P. Scipione, Commissioner of Police in New South Wales, Australia, wrote in 2012:

> There is a delicate balance. A preoccupation with numbers is unhealthy if it distracts from the primary need to apprehend the most serious criminals and care for the most traumatized victims; it is unhealthier still if it causes police on the streets to set aside sound judgment and the public good in the pursuit of arrest quotas, lest they attract management criticism or compromise their chances of promotion.[40]

What about setting process-based goals? For core processes, it rarely makes sense to set goals for the incoming volume of transactions, as that is not usually under the organization's control. It is appropriate to set goals for timeliness in processing, accuracy in determinations and client satisfaction. All three of these are candidates for close-to-real-time monitoring and target-setting. But managers should be careful to adjust the balance between them, as too great an emphasis on timeliness can end up damaging accuracy and client satisfaction.

Cost-efficiency is more often improved by periodically rethinking or redesigning the underlying processes (using technology and business process improvement methods) than by exerting constant pressure on operational staff.

What about setting goals for risk-based work? Executives should demand vigilance from their crime analysis and intelligence staff so that their department spots emerging problems earlier rather than later. Executives should demand nimbleness and fluidity from those responsible for allocating resources within the system so that the right set of players can be formed into the right kind of team, at the right level, to tackle each unique pattern of crime or harm that appears. In addition, executives can emphasize their expectations for creativity and skill from those to whom problem-solving projects are entrusted.

Those involved in risk-based (problem-oriented) work should retain a strong methodological focus on achieving relevant outcomes rather than churning out enormous volumes of familiar outputs. It is tempting, once a plausible plan has been selected that involves activities, to allow the monitoring systems to focus on the production of those activities rather than achievement of the desired outcomes. What starts as thoughtful risk-based work can morph over time into functional quotas — not least because functional quotas are much easier to monitor.

A Closer Look at Crime Reduction as the Bottom Line of Policing

Holding these broader frameworks in mind, let us return for a moment to the dangers of relying too heavily on reported crime rates as the bottom line for policing. More needs to be said about the ways in which a relentless focus on reductions in reported crime rates (a) produces too narrow a focus and (b) invites manipulation of statistics and other forms of corruption.

The Dangers of Narrowness

The focus is narrow because crime control is just one of several components of the police mission. The focus on serious crimes is narrower still, as community concerns often revolve around other problems. The focus on aggregate numbers is misleading, as some crimes have a disproportionate impact on community life or levels of fear.

Focusing on reported crime overlooks unreported crimes, which are generally more numerous than reported crimes. Particular types of crime — sexual assaults, domestic violence and other crimes within the family, white-collar crimes, crimes involving intimidation or where victims have a reason not to want to go to the authorities — are all notoriously underreported. Klockars[41] points out that even homicide rates may be unreliable to a degree. Apparent suicides, deaths reported as accidental, and unresolved cases of missing persons may all act as masks for some murders. "Particularly vulnerable to having their murders misclassified this way are transients, street people, illegal aliens, and others who, if missed at all, are not missed for long."[42]

Consensual crimes (such as bribery or drug dealing), with no immediate victim to complain, go essentially unreported and therefore appear in police statistics only if they are uncovered through police operations.

Most commentators recognize the difficulty and expense of carrying out victimization surveys in order to get better estimates. But most find no available alternative and recommend police departments consider the option seriously. As Moore and colleagues put it:

> Determining the level of *unreported crime* is important not only to get a more accurate measure of the real rate of criminal victimization, but also to determine how much confidence citizens have in asking the police for help.
>
> The only way to measure the underlying rate of victimization is to conduct a general survey of citizens asking about their victimization, and their reasons for failing to report crime to the police.
>
> ... [I]f one wants to get close to the real level of victimization, and to learn about the extent to which the police have earned citizens' confidence in responding to criminal offenses, then there is little choice but to complement information on reported crime with information gained from general surveys of local populations.[43]

Moore and his coauthors also note the efficiencies available once a system for conducting victimization surveys has been set up:

> [W]e can use that system to *answer many other important questions about policing*. Specifically, we can learn a great deal about citizens' fears and their self-defense efforts, as well as their criminal victimization. We can learn about their general attitudes toward the police and how those attitudes are formed.[44]

Moore and Braga[45] also point out the value of using other data sources as a way of cross-checking or validating trends suggested by police statistics. Particularly useful would be public health data from hospital emergency rooms that might reveal "the physical attacks that happen behind closed doors, or which are otherwise not reported to the police."[46] Langton and colleagues estimate that, nationwide, 31 percent of victimizations from 2006 to 2010 involving a weapon and injury to the victim went unreported to police.[47] Even when assaults involved the use of a firearm, roughly 4 in 10 cases went unreported to police.[48] Many such cases are visible to public health systems.

As noted earlier, pressure to reduce the numbers is counterproductive when dealing with the whole class of invisible crimes (classically unreported or underreported crimes). Successful campaigns against these types of crime often involve deliberate attempts to expose the problem by first driving reporting rates up, not down.[49]

Corruption in Reporting Crime Statistics

Relentless pressure to reduce the number of crimes reported, without equivalent pressure to preserve the integrity of the recording and reporting systems, invites manipulation of statistics. The most obvious forms of manipulation involve suppression of reports (failing to take reports of crime from victims) and misclassification of crimes to lower categories in order to make the serious crime statistics look better.

This ought not to surprise anyone. It is an obvious danger naturally produced by too narrow a focus on one numerical metric. John A. Eterno and Eli B. Silverman, in their 2012 book, *The Crime Numbers Game: Management by Manipulation*,[50] have compiled an extensive history of corruption scandals involving manipulation of crime statistics that spans decades and many countries. England and Wales, France, and the Australian states of New South Wales and Victoria have all experienced major scandals.[51] In the 1980s, the Chicago Police Department suffered a major scandal, accused of "killing crime" on a massive scale by refusing to write up official reports of offenses reported to them.[52] Detectives were caught "unfounding" (determining a case was unverifiable) complaints of rape, robbery and assault without investigation.[53] Other major U.S. cities have had similar scandals, including Baltimore, Washington, D.C., New York City, Atlanta, Boca Raton, Fla., and Chicago.[54]

Cheating on crime statistics, as a formidable temptation for police departments, goes with the territory. It remains a current problem, with a continuing stream of allegations and inquiries in various jurisdictions. In the United Kingdom, Chief Inspector of Constabulary Tom Winsor testified to a Commons Committee in December 2013 that British police forces were undoubtedly manipulating crime statistics, and the question was only "where, how much, how severe?"[55] According to the *Guardian* newspaper, he later hinted that he thought the cheating might be on an "industrial" scale.[56]

Two investigative reports published by *Chicago Magazine* in April and May 2014 raised new questions about manipulation of crime statistics by the Chicago Police Department, including the downgrading of homicide cases.[57] In Scotland, the U.K. Statistics Authority rejected the government's claims to have achieved record low crime rates in August 2014 amid claims from retired police officers that crime figures had been manipulated "to present a more rosy picture of law and order to the public."[58]

Eterno and Silverman also show, through their survey of relevant public management literature, that such dangers are well understood in other fields and by now ought to be broadly recognized throughout the public sector.[59]

In 1976, social psychologist Donald Campbell wrote:

> The more any quantitative social indicator is used for social decision-making, the more subject it will be to corruption pressures and the more apt it will be to distort or corrupt the social processes it is intended to monitor.[60]

Addressing the phenomenon of crime statistics in particular, Campbell notes:

> Crime rates are in general very corruptible indicators. For many crimes, changes in rates are a reflection of changes in the activity of the police rather than changes in the number of criminal acts [references deleted]. It seems to be well documented that a well-publicized, deliberate effort at social change — Nixon's crackdown on crime — had as its main effect the corruption of crime-rate indicators ... achieved through under-recording and by downgrading the crimes to less serious classifications.[61]

Diane Vaughan, who has studied many forms of organizational misconduct, says that trouble arises when the social context puts greater emphasis on achieving the ends than on restricting the means:

> When the achievement of the desired goals received strong cultural emphasis, while much less emphasis is placed on the norms regulating the means, these norms tend to lose their power to regulate behavior.[62]

What I have elsewhere termed "performance-enhancing risk-taking" turns out to be one of the most common sources of public-sector corruption. Officials take actions that are illegal, unethical or excessively risky, and they do so not because they are inherently bad people or motivated by personal gain but because they want to help their agency do better or look better and they are often placed under intense pressure from a narrow set of quantitative performance metrics.[63] As a consequence of the pressures, an internal culture emerges that celebrates those who "know what's required and are prepared to step up" — whether that means torturing terror suspects to extract information, "testilying" to procure convictions, or cooking the books to achieve the crime reductions that executives demand.

Few in the police profession will need to be told how one might "cook the books." Robert Zink, the Recording Secretary of NYPD's Patrolmen's Benevolent Association, put it plainly in 2004:

> [S]o how do you fake a crime decrease? It's pretty simple. Don't file reports, misclassify crimes from felonies to misdemeanors, under-value the property lost to crime so it's not a felony, and report a series of crimes as a single event. A particularly insidious way to fudge the numbers is to make it difficult or impossible for people to report crimes — in other words, make the victims feel like criminals so they walk away just to spare themselves further pain and suffering.[64]

INTEGRITY ISSUES RELATED TO COMPSTAT AND CRIME REPORTING AT THE NYPD

There is good reason to pay special attention to the NYPD's early experience with CompStat. A great many other departments have copied it and now run similar systems or variants of it. The use of CompStat-style systems has therefore substantially affected how many police departments view performance measurement, both in the ways they describe their performance at the agency level and in the ways they hold subunits accountable. So the effects of such systems — both positive and negative — need to be broadly understood.

The original form of CompStat as implemented by the NYPD in 1994 had a set of very particular features.

The system focused almost exclusively on reported rates for Part I Index crimes.[65] The principal data source was "reported crime," and the performance focus was unambiguously and always to "drive the numbers down." Crime analysis was principally based on place and time so that hot spots could be identified and dealt with. Accountability for performance was organized geographically and by precinct and was therefore intensely focused on precinct commanders. The precinct commanders were required to stand and deliver their results, or explain the lack of them, at the "podium" in the CompStat meetings — a famously stressful experience.

The managerial style employed seemed combative and adversarial. Garry McCarthy, who experienced the system in New York and replicated it in Chicago, recalled the New York experience of CompStat meetings in an interview with *Chicago Magazine:* "When I was a commander in New York, it was full contact," he said in 2012. "And if you weren't careful, you could lose an eye."[66]

The early days of CompStat also focused on a particular class of offenders and offenses and promoted a somewhat standardized response. As Bratton wrote in 1999, "Intensive quality-of-life enforcement has become the order of the day in the NYPD."[67] The targets were disorganized street criminals, as Bratton noted: "In fact, the criminal element responsible for most street crime is nothing but a bunch of disorganized individuals, many of whom are not very good at what they do. The police have all the advantages in training, equipment, organization, and strategy."[68] The primary intervention strategy solution was aggressive street-order maintenance: "We can turn the tables on the criminal element. Instead of reacting to them, we can create a sense of police presence and police effectiveness that makes criminals react to us."[69]

The CompStat system was also used to drive enforcement quotas throughout the city for arrests, citations and stops/searches as well as to press senior management's demands for reductions in reported crime rates.

There is no doubt that the system was effective in driving performance of the type chosen. As Bratton wrote: "Goals, it turns out, are an extremely important part of lifting a low-performing organization to higher levels of accomplishment and revitalizing an organizational culture."[70]

In 2002, Moore described the early implementation of CompStat in the NYPD thus:

> It was close to a strict liability system focused on outcomes. As a result, it is not surprising that the system ran a strong current through the department. Given that the system was consciously constructed to be behaviorally powerful, it becomes particularly important to know what it was motivating managers to do.[71]

Eterno and Silverman surveyed retired NYPD managers at or above the rank of captain to try to understand the effects of the CompStat system on the nature and extent of crime statistics manipulation. One of their survey findings was that respondents reported a diminished sense of pressure for integrity in reporting, even as CompStat imposed enormous pressure for crime reductions.[72]

Public concerns about what CompStat was motivating managers to do were heightened when the *Village Voice* published transcripts of Officer Adrian Schoolcraft's secretly recorded audiotapes of roll calls and other police meetings. Journalist Graham Rayman authored five articles, published in *The Village Voice* from May 4 to August 25, 2010, exploring the manipulation of crime statistics and the use of arrest and stop-and-frisk quotas in Brooklyn's Bedford-Stuyvesant's 81st Precinct, as well as a 2012 follow-up article confirming the results of the investigation into Schoolcraft's allegations.[73]

In addition, 2010 saw the first wave of internal investigations within the NYPD for crime statistics manipulation. A department spokesman told the *New York Times* in February 2010 that Commissioner Raymond Kelly had disciplined four precinct commanders and seven other senior managers for downgrading crime reports.[74] In October 2010, the department disciplined the former commander of the 81st Precinct and four others for downgrading or refusing to take crime reports.[75]

In January 2011, Commissioner Kelly appointed a panel of three former federal prosecutors to examine NYPD's crime statistics recording and reporting practices, giving them 3 to 6 months to report.[76] Sadly, one of the three died while the panel was conducting its investigation, but the remaining two published the final report on April 8, 2013.[77]

The Crime Reporting Review (CRR) Committee acknowledged the danger of senior managers exerting pressure on subordinates to manipulate crime statistics and noted that there had been substantiated reports of manipulation in the past.[78] They reported that the NYPD's own investigation of the 81st Precinct had "largely substantiated" Officer Schoolcraft's allegations regarding precinct supervisors exerting significant pressure on patrol officers not only to meet quotas on activities such as issuing traffic tickets but also to manipulate or not take crime reports.[79]

The CRR Committee had not been asked to determine the extent to which the NYPD had manipulated or was manipulating crime statistics. Rather, their task was to examine the control systems in place to see if they were robust enough to guarantee integrity in the face of the obvious and substantial pressures of the CompStat environment.

First, the committee examined the process-level controls and protocols governing the taking and classifying of crime reports. They determined that these were insufficient to counteract the danger of intentional manipulation.[80]

They then examined the audit systems that the NYPD used to review crime reports and crime classification decisions after the fact. They found, not surprisingly, that "the risk of suppression (as measured by its effect on reported crime) may be more substantial than the risk of downgrading."[81]

With downgrading, there is at least a trail of records that can be reviewed, from the initial "scratch report" to the final system entry, and a set of policy criteria are available to test the determinations made. The system of audits conducted by the Quality Assurance Division (QAD) that the department used to test crime classifications uncovered patterns of downgrading with respect to robberies, burglaries and larcenies. QAD audits identified patterns of larcenies downgraded to lost property when complainants did not see their property being stolen, robberies being downgraded to larcenies, burglaries being downgraded to larcenies by omitting a complaint of an unlawful entry, and attempted burglaries evidenced by broken locks or attempted breakdown of a door being classified as criminal mischief.[82]

With crime suppression — failing to take a complaint, discouraging or intimidating a complainant, or otherwise making it awkward or unpleasant to report crime — there is often no written record to review, except in the case of 911 "radio runs" when the central call system retains a note of the original call.

The most plausible way to detect patterns of suppression is to audit the radio runs and revisit the callers, comparing what happened within the department with what should have happened as a result of the call. The NYPD implemented such audits (called SPRINT audits) in 2010. The CRR Committee noted that before 2010 no mechanisms were in place to determine the level of crime suppression, and hence there was no way of estimating the effect that any patterns of crime suppression may have had on NYPD's recorded crime rates.[83] The committee also noted that implementation of the SPRINT audits had resulted in a relatively high rate of disciplinary actions, with investigations of 71 commands in 2011 and 57 commands in 2012, and administrative sanctions being sought against 173 officers as a result of those investigations.[84] The committee recommended a substantial increase in the breadth, depth and volume of SPRINT audits in the future as, at the time of the committee's report (2013), these had been applied only to limited categories of calls (robbery and burglary).[85]

Wesley Skogan points out that this type of audit, even if used extensively, can still only provide a partial view of crime suppression practices.[86] Sampling the transactions that pass through a centralized 911 system misses all the other attempts by citizens to report crimes through the panoply of alternate channels now available — beepers, cell phones, voice mail and face-to-face reporting.[87]

Almost nobody denies that the relentless pressure to reduce reported (or, to be more precise, recorded) crime rates produced patterns of misclassification and crime report suppression. The question of the extent to which manipulation of crime statistics became institutionalized at NYPD, or whether the cases of manipulation that have come to light were isolated, remains unresolved. This paper cannot and does not attempt to resolve that question. Nobody doubts that crime has fallen dramatically in New York City in the last 20 years and that the city is now much safer than it was before. The CRR Committee was keen to make that clear, noting in its conclusion that declines in overall crime rates in NYC over the previous 10 or 20 years were indeed "historic."[88]

The purpose here is not to undermine the achievements of the NYPD. CompStat was a major innovation when it was introduced and no doubt contributed substantially to the crime rate reductions achieved, even though criminologists still disagree about how much.[89]

There is evidence that the NYPD has recognized some of the dangers of its original CompStat model. The NYPD has disciplined a substantial number of officers over issues of crime suppression and misclassification and increased the number and types of audits designed to help guarantee integrity in reporting. Precinct-level officers interviewed by the CRR Committee during the review period, 2011-2013, indicated that "the culture surrounding complaint-reporting had changed [improved] from 'what it had been.'"[90] The NYPD has also backed off its use of enforcement quotas to some degree. These are signs that the NYPD is rebalancing the pressures acting on its officers and paying more attention to the means as well as to the ends of reducing reported crime rates.

Looking forward, and with a focus on best practice, I stress that intense pressure for a reduction in crime numbers is liable — for many reasons well understood throughout private industry and in public management — to produce corruption, manipulation of statistics, and other patterns of behavior not in the public interest, unless an equivalent and counterbalancing level of attention is paid to the integrity of recording and reporting systems, the governance of means and careful monitoring of side effects.

Departments that do great work, but leave themselves open to integrity risks, may face public cynicism about their self-reported results and have an ugly cloud over their successes.

Implications for CompStat-Like Systems

There has been much debate as to whether the early focus of CompStat and the methods that the system drove were ever right, even for New York City. The 1999 collection of essays,

Measuring What Matters,[91] reflects much of that debate. But this narrow form is certainly not appropriate now and certainly is not appropriate in general or in other jurisdictions.

In the past 20 years, the police profession has had the opportunity to learn a great deal about the strengths and weaknesses of the original CompStat model and to figure out what types of modifications to the original model can improve it or better adapt it for use in other jurisdictions. Many variations can now be found. Some of them still reflect particular and narrow aspects of the original form. Other versions are much broader, more mature, and seem both more versatile and, in some ways, more humane. Which version a department uses is likely to have a significant effect on its approach to performance measurement and reporting.

Table 2 shows six dimensions in which CompStatlike systems for crime analysis and accountability might be either narrower or broader. These six dimensions provide an opportunity for police executives to examine their own system and determine where, along each spectrum, their current CompStat implementation lies. Any dimension in which a system sits close to the narrow end represents an opportunity for improvement and might enable a department to replace its current model with a more versatile and less restrictive version.

Table 2. CompStat Implementation Options

	Narrow forms	Broader (mature) forms
Data sources	Reported crime rates	Multiple sources, Data sources including victimization surveys
Forms of analysis	Geographic (by precinct and cluster) and temporal	Versatile, considering full range of relevant dimensions
Perfornance focus	Drive the numbers down	Emphasize increased reporting to expose and deal with hiden problem
Lotus of responsibility	Precinct commanders	Tailored to each problem
Managerial style	Adversarial	Cooperative/coaching
Preferred tactics	Direted patrol, street order maintenance	Full range of interventions

Many of the issues discussed so far in this paper would naturally push toward the broader end of each spectrum. Recognizing Goldstein's more inclusive view of the police mission, Moore's multiple dimensions of performance, and the need for organizational nimbleness and skill in addressing many different types of problems that police face should all help to shake police departments out of too narrow a focus.

Data sources: As this paper has already made clear, Part I index crimes remain important, but community concerns frequently center on other issues. Many crimes are not reported, and therefore police would need to use a broader range of data sources — including public health information and victimization surveys — even to be able to see the full range of problems that matter.

Forms of analysis: Crime analysis should no longer revolve solely or mainly around hot spot analysis. Goldstein repeatedly pressed police to recognize that crime problems were often not concentrated geographically but were concentrated in other dimensions (e.g., repeat offenders who roamed the city, repeat victims, methods of commission, patterns of behavior and types of victims).[92] Therefore, adding forms of analysis that focus on dimensions other than time and place is important for broadening the range of problems that crime analysis can reveal.

Performance focus: The performance focus should be carefully chosen, depending on the character of the problem being addressed. "Driving numbers down" is an appropriate focus only for crimes where discovery rates are high and the frequency of the crime is currently far greater than normal levels (i.e., there is slack to be taken up). It is not appropriate for the many types of invisible problems that need to be better exposed before they can be dealt with. And "reducing the numbers" will not be possible in perpetuity as crime rates will inevitably level off once they have reached reasonable levels. For jurisdictions that are relatively safe to begin with, reductions may not be possible, even in the short term.

Locus of responsibility: It makes sense to make precinct commanders unambiguously responsible for problems that are tightly concentrated within one precinct. But many issues are citywide or fit awkwardly into the precinct organization. A mature problem-oriented organization will use more fluid systems that allow for the formation of problem-solving teams at many different levels of an organization to match the breadth and distribution of various problems.

Managerial style: In terms of managerial style, pressure to perform is one thing. But a modern police department has no place for tyrannical management, deliberate humiliation of officers in front of their peers, or attempts to catch them out with analytic findings not previously shared. Mature forms of CompStat should embody congenial and cooperative managerial relationships, even as they remain ruthlessly analytical and outcome oriented. Adversarial managerial styles exercised at high levels within a department tend to trickle all the way down, resulting in intolerable pressure on frontline officers and, ultimately, inappropriate forms of police action on the streets.

Preferred tactics: Aggressive zero-tolerance style policing is relevant only to specific classes of street crime and, as many commentators have observed, can destroy community relationships and cooperation. Persistent use of aggressive policing tactics, particularly in disadvantaged and minority neighborhoods, may be a recipe for anti-police riots in the end, given some appropriate spark. A mature CompStat system should bring no underlying preference for any particular set of tactics. Teams working on problems should be required and expected to consider the full range of interventions available to them and to invent new methods where necessary.

Table 2 offers a simple tool for diagnosing whether and in which particular ways an existing CompStat implementation might still be narrow or immature, highlighting opportunities to develop more sophisticated ideas about performance and more nuanced organizational responses to a broader range of issues across the six dimensions presented.

CONCLUSION

The principal purpose of this paper has been to highlight some of the narrower traditions into which police organizations fall when describing their value and reporting their performance. A modern police organization needs a broader view of its mission (per Goldstein),[93] a broader view of the dimensions of performance (per Moore),[94] and a clear understanding of the metrics that go with different types of work. Overall, police departments need more complex cockpits. Police executives need a more sophisticated understanding of how to use different types of information to understand the condition of their organizations and what is happening in the communities they serve.

Another purpose was to point police executives toward existing resources on this subject that they might find useful. For those interested in developing a more comprehensive suite of instruments for their "cockpit" and a clearer sense of how to use them all, I would particularly recommend the selections referenced in the "Recommended Further Readings" as relevant, practical and accessible.

In discussing this subject with police executives in the classroom, two questions invariably come up. First, someone will object, "So what's new? Haven't you just invented the balanced scorecard for public agencies?"

Not exactly. The cockpit I imagine is not really a "balanced scorecard"; it is hardly a "scorecard" at all. It is a richer information environment with much more sophisticated users. Police executives need a more comprehensive suite of managerial information but — like the airline pilot — should be slow to label any specific dial a performance indicator. As soon as you designate an indicator as a performance indicator, you need to think carefully about the currents that will run through the organization and make sure that you anticipate and can control perverse behaviors that may arise.

The second question that students raise is this: "So, to get the public and the politicians to pay attention to this broader, more complex performance story, should we withhold the traditional statistics (reported Part I crime figures) so we are not held hostage by them?"

My normal advice is basically this: "No, it's a democracy, and transparency is the default setting. You cannot and would not want to hide that information. It remains important managerial information. Your job is not to withhold the traditional performance account but to dethrone it. You have to provide a richer story that better reflects the breadth of your mission and the contributions your agency makes. You have to provide that story even if the press, the politicians and the public do not seem to be asking for it just yet. Educate them about what matters, by giving it to them whether they ask for it or not. In the end, you can reshape their expectations."

Recommended Further Readings

- In *Measuring What Matters,* pages 43 to 47, Wesley Skogan provides a practical discussion of methods for assessing levels of disorder in neighborhoods.[95]
- In *Measuring What Matters,* pages 47 to 50, Skogan also offers advice on measuring the fear of crime and its impact on community behavior and the use of public spaces.[96]
- In *Measuring What Matters,* pages 58 to 59, Darrel Stephens offers ideas about measuring disorder and describes work by volunteer groups in St. Petersburg to survey residents and record physical conditions in neighborhoods.[97]
- In *Measuring What Matters,* pages 202 to 204, Carl Klockars provides examples of simple-to-administer crime victim surveys, asking for feedback on the nature and quality of services delivered to them by police departments.[98]
- In *Measuring What Matters,* pages 208 to 212, Klockars also stresses the importance of assessing levels of integrity within a police department (as a matter of

organizational culture, rather than trying to measure actual levels of corruption) and describes some practical ways of doing what many might claim cannot be done.[99]

- In *The "Bottom Line" of Policing,* pages 30 to 75,[100] in a section entitled "Measuring Performance on the Seven Dimensions," Mark Moore and Anthony Braga provide a rich collection of practical ways to gather data, use existing data, and generate indicators relevant to each of the seven dimensions of performance. These are summarized in note form in table 3, pages 80 to 82,[101] with suggestions for immediate investments prioritized in table 4, pages 83 to 85.[102]
- Chapter 8 of *The Character of Harms* explores the special challenges that go with the class of invisible risks (those with low discovery rates). Much of that discussion revolves around issues of measurement, in particular the methods required to resolve the inherent ambiguity of readily available metrics.[103]
- The 2012 Bureau of Justice Statistics Special Report, *Victimizations Not Reported to the Police, 2006-2010,* by Lynn Langton and colleagues, provides an interesting and data-rich analysis of the frequency with which various forms of victimization are not reported to the police.[104]
- Chapter 12 of *The Character of Harms* provides a more rigorous analysis of performance-enhancing risks, describing the special threats to integrity that commonly arise when too much emphasis is placed on too narrow a set of quantitative metrics.[105]

End Notes

[1] Measuring What Matters: Proceedings From the Policing Research Institute Meetings, edited by Robert H. Langworthy. Research Report. Washington, D.C.: U.S. Department of Justice, National Institute of Justice, July 1999. NCJ 170610, https://www.ncjrs.gov/pdffiles1/nij/170610.pdf.

[2] Moore, Mark H., with David Thacher, Andrea Dodge and Tobias Moore, Recognizing Value in Policing: The Challenge of Measuring Police Performance. Washington, D.C.: Police Executive Research Forum, 2002.

[3] Moore, Mark H., and Anthony Braga, The "Bottom Line" of Policing: What Citizens Should Value (and Measure!) in Police Performance. Washington, D.C.: Police Executive Research Forum, 2003. http://www.policeforum.org/assets/docs/Free_Online_Documents/Police_Evaluation/the%20bottom% 20line %20of%20 policing%202003.pdf.

[4] Skogan, Wesley G., "Measuring What Matters: Crime, Disorder, and Fear," in Measuring What Matters: Proceedings From the Policing Research Institute Meetings, edited by Robert H. Langworthy. Research Report. Washington, D.C.: U.S. Department of Justice, National Institute of Justice, July 1999. NCJ 170610, https://www.ncjrs. gov/pdffiles1/nij/170610.pdf, pp. 36-53, at 38.

[5] For a detailed study of the frequency with which various forms of victimization are not reported to the police, see Langton, Lynn, Marcus Berzofsky, Christopher Krebs and Hope Smiley-McDonald, Victimizations Not Reported to the Police, 2006-2010. Special Report. Washington, D.C.: U.S. Department of Justice, Bureau of Justice Statistics, August 2012. NCJ 238536, http://www. bjs.gov/content/pub/pdf/vnrp0610.pdf.

[6] For a detailed discussion of invisible harms and the special challenges involved in controlling them, see Chapter 8, "Invisible Harms," in Sparrow, Malcolm K., The Character of Harms: Operational Challenges in Control. Cambridge, England: Cambridge University Press, 2008.

[7] Sparrow, The Character of Harms, pp. 143-144.

[8] Adapted from Sparrow, Malcolm K., "Foreword," in Financial Supervision in the 21st Century, edited by A. Joanne Kellerman, Jakob de Haan, and Femke de Vries. New York, New York: Springer-Verlag, 2013. This framework was first described in Sparrow, Malcolm K., "The Sabotage of Harms: An Emerging Art Form for Public Managers," ESADE Institute of Public Governance & Management, E-newsletter, March 2012 (published in English, Spanish and Catalan).

[9] The report, which is not public, was provided to the author by Assistant Commissioner Wilhelmy.

[10] The advent of the six-axis or "full-flight" simulators for pilot training in the 1990s is regarded as one of the most significant recent contributors to enhanced safety in commercial aviation.

[11] Klockars, Carl B., "Some Really Cheap Ways of Measuring What Really Matters," in Measuring What Matters: Proceedings From the Policing Research Institute Meetings, edited by Robert H. Langworthy. Research Report. Washington, D.C.: U.S. Department of Justice, National Institute of Justice, July 1999. NCJ 170610, https://www.ncjrs. gov/pdffiles1/nij/170610.pdf, pp. 195-214, at 197.

[12] See, e.g., Goldstein, Herman, Policing a Free Society. Cambridge, Massachusetts: Ballinger, 1977.

[13] See, e.g., Moore and Braga, The "Bottom Line" of Policing; Moore et al., Recognizing Value in Policing.

[14] See, e.g., Behn, Robert D., "Why Measure Performance? Different Purposes Require Different Measures," Public Administration Review 63 (5) (Sept./Oct. 2003): 586-606.

[15] See, e.g., Sparrow, The Character of Harms.

[16] Goldstein, Policing a Free Society, p. 35.

[17] Behn, Robert D., "On the Core Drivers of: CitiStat." Bob Behn's Public Management Report 2 (3) (November 2004).

[18] Moore, Mark H., and Margaret Poethig, "The Police as an Agency of Municipal Government: Implications for Measuring Police Effectiveness," in Measuring What Matters: Proceedings From the Policing Research Institute Meetings, edited by Robert H. Langworthy. Research Report. Washington, D.C.: U.S. Department of Justice, National Institute of Justice, July 1999. NCJ 170610, https://www.ncjrs.gov/pdffiles1/nij/170610.pdf, pp. 151-167, at 153.

[19] bid., p. 157.

[20] Moore et al., Recognizing Value in Policing, p. 76, table 2.

[21] Bratton, William J., "Great Expectations: How Higher Expectations for Police Departments Can Lead to a Decrease in Crime," in Measuring What Matters: Proceedings From the Policing Research Institute Meetings, edited by Robert H. Langworthy. Research Report. Washington, D.C.: U.S. Department of Justice, National Institute of Justice, July 1999. NCJ 170610, https://www.ncjrs. gov/pdffiles1/nij/170610.pdf, pp. 11-26, at 15.

[22] Moore et al., Recognizing Value in Policing, pp. 24-25.

[23] Ibid., p. 25.

[24] Kelling, George, "Measuring What Matters: A New Way of Thinking About Crime and Public Order," in Measuring What Matters: Proceedings From the Policing Research Institute Meetings, edited by Robert H. Langworthy. Research Report. Washington, D.C.: U.S. Department of Justice, National Institute of Justice, July 1999. NCJ 170610, https://www.ncjrs.gov/pdffiles1/nij/170610.pdf, pp. 27-35, at 27.

[25] Klockars, "Some Really Cheap Ways of Measuring What Really Matters," pp. 205-208.

[26] Ibid., p. 206.

[27] Scheingold, Stuart A. "Constituent Expectations of the Police and Police Expectations of Constituents," in Measuring What Matters: Proceedings From the Policing Research Institute Meetings, edited by Robert H. Langworthy. Research Report. Washington, D.C.: U.S. Department of Justice, National Institute of Justice, July 1999. NCJ 170610, https://www.ncjrs. gov/pdffiles1/nij/170610.pdf, pp. 183-192, at 186.

[28] Skogan, Wesley G., Disorder and Decline: Crime and the Spiral of Decay in American Neighborhoods. New York, New York: The Free Press, 1990, p. 166.

[29] Ibid., p. 172.

[30] Moore et al., Recognizing Value in Policing.

[31] Ibid., p. 79.

[32] Behn, "Why Measure Performance?"

[33] Ibid., p. 588, table 1.

[34] For a summary of this analysis, see ibid., p. 593, table 2.

[35] Sparrow, The Character of Harms, pp. 123-124. See Chapter 6, "Puzzles of Measurement," for a discussion of the unique characteristics of a risk-control performance account.

[36] The formal structure and essential rigors of the problem-oriented approach are described in detail in ibid., chapter 7. The associated performance measurement challenges are explored in chapters 5 and 6.

[37] For a detailed discussion of the potential tensions between problem-oriented policing and "evidence-based" program evaluation techniques, see Sparrow, Malcolm K., Governing Science. New Perspectives in Policing Bulletin. Washington, D.C.: U.S. Department of Justice, National Institute of Justice, 2011.

[38] See, e.g., Hipolit, Melissa, "Former Police Officer Exposes Chesterfield's Ticket Quota Goals," CBS 6 News at Noon, July 14, 2014. http://wtvr. com/2014/07/14/chesterfield-quota-investigation.

[39] "Whew! No More Traffic Ticket Quotas in Illinois," CNBC News, Law Section, June 16, 2014. http://www.cnbc.com/id/101762636#.

[40] Scipione, Andrew P., "Foreword," in Eterno, John A., and Eli B. Silverman, The Crime Numbers Game: Management by Manipulation. Boca Raton, Florida: CRC Press, 2012, p. xviii.
[41] Klockars, "Some Really Cheap Ways of Measuring What Really Matters," p. 196.
[42] Ibid.
[43] Moore et al., Recognizing Value in Policing, pp. 42-43.
[44] Ibid., p. 38.
[45] Moore and Braga, The "Bottom Line" of Policing.
[46] Ibid., p. 37.
[47] Langton et al., Victimizations Not Reported to the Police, 2006-2010, p. 5.
[48] Ibid.
[49] See note 6.
[50] Eterno and Silverman, The Crime Numbers Game.
[51] Ibid., pp. 85-104.
[52] Skogan, Wesley G., Police and Community in Chicago: A Tale of Three Cities. New York, New York: Oxford University Press, 2006. Chapter 3 describes crime-recording practices used by Chicago police during the 1980s.
[53] Skogan, "Measuring What Matters: Crime, Disorder, and Fear," p. 38.
[54] Eterno and Silverman, The Crime Numbers Game, pp. 11-12. See also the discussion of alleged manipulation of crime statistics by the NYPD, p. 23, under "Integrity Issues Related to CompStat and Crime Reporting at the NYPD."
[55] Rawlinson, Kevin, "Police Crime Figures Being Manipulated, Admits Chief Inspector," The Guardian, Dec. 18, 2013. http://www.theguardian. com/uk-news/2013/dec/18/police-crime-figuresmanipulation-chief-inspector.
[56] Ibid.
[57] Bernstein, David, and Noah Isackson, "The Truth About Chicago's Crime Rates," Chicago Magazine, Special Report, Part 1: Apr. 7, 2014. Part 2: May 19, 2014. http://www. chicagomag.com/Chicago-Magazine/May-2014/ Chicago-crime-rates.
[58]. Hutcheon, Paul, "Independent Watchdog Refuses to Endorse Police Statistics That Claim Crime Is at a Near 40-Year Low," Sunday Herald, Aug. 17, 2014. http://www.heraldscotland.com/ news/home-news/independent-watchdog-refuses-to-endorse-police-statistics-that-claim-crime-is-at-a-ne.25062572.
[59] Eterno and Silverman, The Crime Numbers Game, pp. 9-12.
[60]. Campbell, Donald T., Assessing the Impact of Planned Social Change. Occasional Paper Series, #8. Hanover, New Hampshire: Dartmouth College, The Public Affairs Center, Dec. 1976, p. 49, cited in Eterno and Silverman, The Crime Numbers Game, p. 10.
[61] Campbell, Assessing the Impact of Planned Social Change, pp. 50-51.
[62] Vaughan, Diane, Controlling Unlawful Organizational Behavior: Social Structure and Corporate Misconduct. Chicago, Illinois: University of Chicago Press, 1983, p. 55, summarizing Merton, Robert K., "Social Structure and Anomie," in Robert K. Merton, Social Theory and Social Structure, enlarged ed., New York: New York: The Free Press, 1968, pp. 185-214.
[63] For a detailed discussion of this phenomenon, see Chapter 12, "Performance-Enhancing Risks," in Sparrow, The Character of Harms.
[64] Zink, Robert, "The Trouble with Compstat," PBA Magazine, Summer 2004, cited in Eterno and Silverman, The Crime Numbers Game, p. 27.
[65] Part I Index crimes, as defined under the Uniform Crime Reporting system, are aggravated assault, forcible rape, murder, robbery, arson, burglary, larceny-theft and motor vehicle theft.
[66] Bernstein and Isackson, "The Truth About Chicago's Crime Rates," Part 1.
[67] Bratton, "Great Expectations," p. 15.
[68] Ibid., p. 17.
[69] Ibid., p. 17.
[70] Ibid., p. 11.
[71] Moore et al., Recognizing Value in Policing, p. 150.
[72] Eterno and Silverman, The Crime Numbers Game, pp. 28-34.
[73] Rayman, Graham, "The NYPD Tapes: Inside Bed-Stuy's 81st Precinct," The Village Voice, May 4, 2010; Rayman, Graham, "The NYPD Tapes, Part 2: Ghost Town," The Village Voice, May 11, 2010; Rayman, Graham, "The NYPD Tapes, Part 3: A Detective Comes Forward About Downgraded Sexual Assaults," The Village Voice, June 8, 2010; Rayman, Graham, "The NYPD Tapes, Part 4: The Whistle Blower, Adrian Schoolcraft," The Village Voice, June 15, 2010; Rayman, Graham, "The NYPD Tapes, Part 5: The Corroboration," The Village Voice, Aug. 25, 2010; Rayman, Graham, "The NYPD Tapes Confirmed," The

Village Voice, Mar. 7, 2012. The entire series of articles is available online at http://www.villagevoice.com/specialReports/ the-nypd-tapes-the-village-voices-series-onadrian-schoolcraft-by-graham-rayman-4393217/.

[74] Rashbaum, William K., "Retired Officers Raise Questions on Crime Data," The New York Times, Feb. 6, 2010. http://www.nytimes.com/2010/02/07/ nyregion/07crime.html?pagewanted=all&_r=0.

[75] Baker, Al, and Ray Rivera, "5 Officers Face Charges in Fudging of Statistics," The New York Times, Oct. 15, 2010. http://www.nytimes. com/2010/10/16/nyregion/16statistics.html.

[76] Baker, Al, and William K. Rashbaum, "New York City to Examine Reliability of Its Crime Reports," The New York Times, Jan. 5, 2011. http://www.nytimes.com/2011/01/06/ nyregion/06crime.html?pagewanted=all.

[77] Kelley, David N., and Sharon L. McCarthy, "The Report of the Crime Reporting Review Committee to Commissioner Raymond W. Kelly Concerning CompStat Auditing," Apr. 8, 2013. http://www.nyc.gov/html/nypd/downloads/pdf/public_information/crime_reporting_review_committee_final_report_2013.pdf.

[78] Ibid., p. 18.

[79] Ibid., p. 17, note 43.

[80] Ibid., p. 21.

[81] Ibid., p. 52.

[82] Ibid., pp. 41-42.

[83] Ibid., p. 52.

[84] Ibid., p. 53.

[85] Ibid., p. 58.

[86] Skogan, "Measuring What Matters: Crime, Disorder, and Fear."

[87] Ibid., p. 38.

[88] Kelley and McCarthy, "The Report of the Crime Reporting Review Committee to Commissioner Raymond W. Kelly Concerning CompStat Auditing," p. 54.

[89] For a thorough analysis of this issue, see Chapter 4, "Distinguishing CompStat's Effects," in Behn, Robert D., The PerformanceStat Potential: A Leadership Strategy for Producing Results. Washington, D.C.: Brookings Institution Press, 2014. Behn, who is a great admirer of PerformanceStat systems in general, surveys the literature on the subject, considers the 10 other explanations most commonly put forward as alternative explanations, and concludes that due to the limitations of the methods of social science, we will probably never know for sure what proportion of the crime reductions seen from 1994 onward was due to CompStat and what proportion is attributable to other factors.

[90] Kelley and McCarthy, "The Report of the Crime Reporting Review Committee to Commissioner Raymond W. Kelly Concerning CompStat Auditing," p. 21.

[91] See note 1.

[92] See, e.g., Goldstein, Herman, "Improving Policing: A Problem-Oriented Approach," Crime & Delinquency 25 (April 1979): 236-258.

[93] See, e.g., Goldstein, "Improving Policing: A Problem-Oriented Approach"; Goldstein, Policing a Free Society.

[94] See, e.g., Moore and Braga, The "Bottom Line" of Policing; Moore et al., Recognizing Value in Policing.

[95] Skogan, "Measuring What Matters: Crime, Disorder, and Fear," pp. 43-47.

[96] Ibid., pp. 47-50.

[97] Stephens, Darrel W. "Measuring What Matters," in Measuring What Matters: Proceedings From the Policing Research Institute Meetings, edited by Robert H. Langworthy. Research Report. Washington, D.C.: U.S. Department of Justice, National Institute of Justice, July 1999. NCJ 170610, https://www.ncjrs.gov/pdffiles1/nij/170610.pdf, pp. 55-64, at 58-59.

[98] Klockars, "Some Really Cheap Ways of Measuring What Really Matters," pp. 202-204.

[99] Ibid., pp. 208-212.

[100] Moore and Braga, The "Bottom Line" of Policing, pp. 30-75.

[101] Ibid., pp. 80-82, table 3.

[102] Ibid., pp. 83-85, table 4.

[103] Sparrow, The Character of Harms, Chapter 8, "Invisible Risks."

[104] Langton et al., Victimizations Not Reported to the Police, 2006-2010.

[105] Sparrow, The Character of Harms, Chapter 12, "Performance Enhancing Risks."

Author Note

Malcolm K. Sparrow is professor of the practice of public management at the John F. Kennedy School of Government at Harvard University. This bulletin was written for the Executive Session on Policing and Public Safety at the school.

INDEX

#

20th century, 73
9/11, 14

A

Abraham, 66
abuse, 60, 103, 108, 109, 118
access, 87, 107, 108, 123
accountability, 17, 30, 38, 45, 53, 54, 61, 143
accounting, 130
activity theory, 72
adaptation, 28, 116
adjustment, 11
Administration for Children and Families, 117
administrative efficiency, 122
administrators, 4
adolescents, 103, 106, 109, 110, 112, 114, 117, 118
adulthood, 104, 108
adults, 105, 110
advancement, 31, 33, 71
African-American(s), 70, 76, 83, 94, 96, 115, 117
age, 41, 74, 85, 88, 89, 110, 116
agencies, 3, 5, 6, 10, 11, 15, 16, 27, 31, 32, 34, 36, 39, 46, 49, 59, 61, 62, 64, 66, 74, 75, 76, 92, 122, 123, 124, 128, 132, 133, 145
aggregation, 11
aggression, 111, 116
aggressive behavior, 87, 106, 111
aggressiveness, 109
air temperature, 123
amygdala, 105
anger, 70, 106
anxiety, 102, 105, 106, 107, 109, 114
appetite, 36
appraisals, 93
arousal, 117
arrest(s), 2, 3, 4, 8, 16, 17, 18, 26, 43, 47, 48, 62, 78, 85, 90, 91, 93, 94, 102, 106, 120, 122, 124, 125, 126, 128, 129, 134, 135, 140
arson, 148
aspiration, 30
assault, 4, 83, 99, 138, 148
assessment, 9, 11, 17, 33, 39, 44, 76, 126, 130
assets, 146
attachment, 40
attitudes, 49, 52, 65, 77, 82, 87, 91, 137
Attorney General, 59
audit(s), 131, 132, 141, 142
authorit(ies), 5, 29, 30, 32, 35, 36, 38, 44, 47, 50, 53, 59, 60, 61, 62, 73, 74, 75, 93, 129, 130, 132, 134, 136
automation, 132
autonomy, 45, 53
awareness, 110, 112

B

baggage, 36
banks, 127
base, 8
basic needs, 103
behavioral change, 134
behaviors, 9, 13, 16, 44, 51, 59, 82, 109, 124, 135, 145
benefits, 30, 39, 44, 52
bias, 47, 51, 59, 134
Blacks, 84, 85
blame, 36, 94
bleeding, 106
blood, 110
borderline personality disorder, 115, 116
brain, 104, 105, 107, 109, 116, 117
breakdown, 141

Bureau of Justice Assistance, 64
Bureau of Justice Statistics, 41, 96, 97, 145, 146
businesses, 3, 6, 15, 27, 73

C

caliber, 32
campaigns, 121, 122, 130, 135, 137
cancer, 71
candidates, 135
case stud(ies), 11, 18, 31, 49, 114
catalyst, 66
categorization, 84
causal relationship, 17
causality, 70
CBS, 147
cell phones, 142
Census, 41, 88, 99
chain of command, 32
challenges, 14, 27, 35, 37, 66, 74, 75, 119, 145, 146, 147
checks and balances, 57
Chicago, 8, 10, 13, 21, 23, 24, 26, 48, 49, 50, 52, 54, 55, 67, 75, 80, 83, 95, 96, 97, 98, 138, 140, 148
chicken, 30
child abuse, 110, 114
child maltreatment, 118
child protective services, 110, 112
childhood, 101, 102, 104, 106, 107, 108, 109, 110, 111, 112, 113, 114, 115, 116, 117
childhood history, 104
childhood sexual abuse, 108, 114, 115
children, vii, 6, 76, 81, 83, 87, 101, 102, 103, 104, 105, 107, 108, 109, 110, 111, 112, 113, 114, 115, 116, 117, 118, 128
cities, 2, 5, 8, 13, 45, 48, 52, 62, 75, 82, 87, 88, 90, 91, 128, 138
citizens, 2, 4, 6, 45, 48, 50, 51, 53, 59, 60, 73, 82, 83, 85, 93, 94, 111, 122, 131, 137, 142
citizenship, 92
civil law, 44
civil rights, 4, 64, 74, 75
civil servants, 4
civil society, 47
clarity, 95
classes, 32, 33, 63, 122, 126, 131, 144
classification, 92, 141
classroom, 33, 34, 35, 37, 63, 145
climate, 27, 31, 38
clinical assessment, 112
close relationships, 15
closure, 133
clusters, 12, 104
coal, 72
cocaine, 5, 87, 115, 116
cocaine abuse, 115
coercion, 50
cognition, 116, 117
cognitive deficit(s), 107
cognitive flexibility, 39
cognitive science, 60
coherence, 30, 54
collaboration, 28, 38
collateral, 61
collateral damage, 61
colleges, 58
collisions, 50
color, 70, 78, 83, 110, 112, 113
combined effect, 105
commercial, 123, 129, 147
commodity, 35, 130
communication, 4, 49, 60, 61, 63
communication skills, 61, 63
communit(ies), 1, 2, 3, 4, 5, 7, 9, 10, 11, 12, 13, 14, 15, 16, 17, 18, 27, 34, 39, 44, 45, 46, 48, 49, 50, 51, 52, 53, 54, 58, 59, 60, 61, 62, 65, 66, 69, 70, 71, 72, 73, 76, 77, 78, 81, 82, 83, 84, 87, 90, 92, 93, 94, 95, 110, 112, 113, 114, 117, 120, 121, 122, 124, 125, 127, 130, 136, 143, 144, 145
community relations, 16, 53, 95, 122, 130, 144
competition, 131
complement, 9, 12, 137
complexity, 27, 31, 33, 40, 41, 121, 126
compliance, 44, 47, 50, 51, 52, 61, 64, 134
composition, 16, 94
compounds, 34
conception, 43, 47
conditioning, 117
conflict, 10, 32, 59, 61, 64, 127
conflict resolution, 10
consensus, 3, 5, 14, 16, 130
consent, 73, 74, 75, 78
constituents, 95
Constitution, 31, 53, 57, 64, 65, 66, 74
constitutional law, 44, 45
consulting, 73
controversial, 70, 74, 75, 78
conversations, vii, 2, 14, 34
conviction, 124, 125
cooking, 139
cooperation, 12, 16, 51, 85, 90, 91, 95, 112, 144
coordination, 28
correlations, 26
corruption, 120, 121, 136, 138, 139, 142, 145
cortex, 105
cost, 3, 54, 129, 132

counsel, 131
counseling, 78
counterterrorism, 128
creativity, 17, 136
crimes, 2, 3, 4, 5, 6, 8, 13, 15, 16, 27, 70, 74, 81, 83, 84, 91, 94, 99, 111, 120, 122, 125, 136, 137, 138, 139, 142, 143, 144, 148
criminal activity, 91
criminal acts, 138
criminal behavior, 3, 44, 62, 81, 84
criminal investigations, 4
criminal justice system, 3, 53, 54, 62, 82, 89, 110, 115, 127, 128
criminal violence, 94, 95
criminality, 69, 70, 71, 72
criminals, 2, 5, 69, 75, 78, 91, 92, 135, 139, 140
critical analysis, 40
critical thinking, 60, 61
criticism, 45, 135
crowd control, 28
crowns, 29
CRR, 141, 142
cues, 64
cultural transformation, 65
culture, 31, 32, 35, 36, 37, 51, 57, 59, 61, 62, 76, 78, 83, 139, 142, 145
cure, 104
curriculum, 53, 63, 64, 65
customers, 30

D

danger, 67, 104, 105, 106, 107, 123, 127, 134, 138, 141
data collection, 17
deaths, 50, 101, 136
decentralization, 10
declarative memory, 114
deficiencies, 15
delinquency, 87
delinquent behavior, 116
delusions, 111
democracy, 53, 57, 62, 63, 64, 145
Department of Health and Human Services, 108, 114, 117
Department of Justice, 1, 18, 19, 21, 22, 23, 24, 25, 27, 41, 43, 57, 59, 66, 67, 69, 78, 79, 81, 95, 96, 97, 101, 116, 119, 146, 147, 149
depression, 107
deprivation, 87
depth, 35, 92, 142
detachment, 60
deterrence, 2, 7, 9, 12, 13, 14, 15, 16, 46, 47, 49, 52, 63, 70, 74, 92, 125
developing brain, 107
developmental psychopathology, 114
differential treatment, 77
dignity, 46, 47, 51, 59, 60, 95, 130
directives, 44, 93
disaster, 115
discrimination, 84
disorder, 5, 6, 7, 9, 10, 11, 12, 13, 15, 16, 18, 26, 70, 71, 84, 89, 92, 93, 94, 105, 107, 114, 115, 116, 117, 118, 130, 145
dissatisfaction, 4, 93, 94
distortions, 82
distress, 103, 104
distribution, 69, 123, 144
divergence, 119
diversity, 1, 17, 36, 127
dogs, 5
domestic violence, 31, 89, 103, 107, 108, 110, 114, 116, 118, 125, 136
dorsolateral prefrontal cortex, 116
drawing, 76
drug addict, 103
drugs, 106, 107, 118, 130

E

early warning, 77
Eastern Europe, 114
economic disadvantage, 90
education, 57, 71, 78, 115
educators, 37, 131
egg, 30
emergency, 128, 132, 137
emergency response, 128
emotional distress, 104, 106
empathy, 59, 94
empirical studies, 13
employees, 31, 34, 75, 135
empowerment, 54
encouragement, 73
enforcement, vii, 12, 14, 16, 45, 49, 50, 53, 62, 71, 73, 78, 81, 93, 120, 121, 122, 125, 130, 134, 135, 140, 142
England, 20, 39, 40, 52, 138, 146
environment(s), 4, 5, 15, 27, 28, 29, 31, 33, 34, 35, 38, 59, 65, 67, 87, 107, 123, 141, 145
epidemic, 5
equipment, 5, 58, 61, 140
equity, 59
erratic behavior, 109
ethics, 57

ethnicity, 70
etiology, 116
Europe, 66
evidence, vii, 1, 2, 4, 5, 6, 7, 8, 9, 11, 12, 13, 14, 15, 16, 17, 18, 26, 30, 39, 47, 50, 51, 61, 83, 84, 86, 87, 92, 110, 116, 125, 142, 147
evil, 45, 60, 71
evolution, 92, 127
examinations, 51
exclusion, 81, 121
execution, 37
exercise(s), 32, 38, 43, 45, 59, 74, 124, 129
expertise, 29, 30, 126
exposure, 53, 101, 102, 103, 104, 107, 108, 109, 110, 111, 113, 114, 115, 117
extinction, 116

F

fairness, 44, 45, 47, 51, 58, 134
false belief, 110
families, 77, 78, 82, 112
fear(s), 4, 5, 6, 10, 11, 45, 47, 52, 57, 61, 62, 63, 64, 69, 75, 84, 90, 92, 102, 105, 106, 107, 109, 111, 116, 117, 129, 136, 137, 145
Federal Bureau of Investigation (FBI), 26, 29, 33, 88, 96, 97, 99
feelings, 47, 106, 107
fidelity, 15
financial, 122, 129
financial resources, 122, 129
fingerprints, 4
firearms, 65
first responders, 28, 128
flavor, 67, 76
flaws, 2
flexibility, 17
flight, 6, 104, 123, 147
fluctuations, 121
fluid, 35, 144
force, 4, 8, 29, 30, 31, 49, 52, 59, 61, 77, 93, 121, 122, 129, 130, 134
Ford, 118
formation, 32, 144
formula, 67
Fourteenth Amendment, 46
Fourth Amendment, 59
framing, 12, 13, 94, 95
France, 138
fraud, 121
freedom, 38, 45, 46, 70, 72
freezing, 128
friendship, 74, 92
fruits, 36
funding, 7, 32, 64
funds, 14, 49

G

gambling, 130
gangs, 14, 31, 74, 88, 90, 91
Gates, Henry Louis, 43, 45
geography, 11, 49, 73
goal-setting, 134
google, 42
governance, 44, 142
governments, 71, 122
graffiti, 5
Great Britain, 75
growth, vii, 2, 8, 31, 40, 101
guardian, 57, 58, 59, 61, 65
guidelines, 77

H

hate crime, 83
health, 40, 64, 71, 112, 137
Health and Human Services, 117
health care, 40, 71
higher education, 3
hippocampus, 105
hiring, 17, 69
Hispanics, 84, 94
historical overview, 2
history, 36, 40, 52, 53, 76, 81, 92, 102, 103, 109, 111, 112, 130, 138
homeland security, 14, 66
homelessness, 71
homes, 3, 73, 110
homework, 70
homicide, 13, 14, 49, 50, 82, 83, 84, 85, 86, 87, 88, 89, 90, 91, 136, 138
homicide rates, 50, 87, 136
hormones, 104, 105
hostilit(ies), 69, 93
hot spots, 7, 9, 11, 12, 13, 15, 50, 74, 92, 93, 139
housing, 71, 91
HPA axis, 115, 117
human, 17, 32, 58, 59, 60, 61, 71, 72, 74, 77, 104, 112
human behavior, 32, 60, 61, 112
human body, 104
human brain, 104
human capital, 17
human motivation, 32

Human Resource Management, 40, 41
human right(s), 59, 72, 77

I

ideal(s), vii, 45, 57, 62
identification, 11, 17, 112
identifying suspects, 83
identity, 62
ideology, 72
illegal aliens, 136
image(s), 4, 48, 52, 53, 66
immigrants, 70
immigration, 7
impairments, 103, 105
imprisonment, 7
improvements, 15, 51
impulsive, 106
impulsivity, 106
incarceration, 3, 14, 73, 99
independence, 64, 74, 80
individual character, 28
individual characteristics, 28
individual development, 34, 37
individuals, 6, 14, 27, 28, 30, 32, 33, 34, 35, 37, 45, 46, 50, 61, 71, 72, 73, 74, 76, 78, 87, 90, 91, 93, 94, 104, 106, 107, 108, 109, 111, 112, 127, 140
industry, 14, 42, 132, 142
inefficiency, 3
inequality, 72
information sharing, 1
infrastructure, 92
initiation, 87
injure, 72
injur(ies), 50, 107, 118, 137
innocence, 115
institutions, 52, 71, 73
integrity, 53, 120, 121, 122, 137, 140, 141, 142, 145
intellect, 60
intelligence, 58, 122, 128, 133, 136
interface, 115
interpersonal interactions, 53
interrogations, 130
intervention, 26, 49, 64, 66, 73, 104, 107, 110, 113, 114, 115, 122, 135, 140
intervention strategies, 66
intimidation, 121, 136
introspection, 66
intrusions, 72
investment(s), 30, 145
irony, 126
isolation, 49
issues, 4, 6, 27, 28, 29, 31, 37, 51, 62, 69, 70, 74, 76, 77, 82, 92, 95, 106, 108, 109, 110, 111, 112, 122, 133, 142, 143, 144, 145
iteration, 12

J

Jay, John, 96
journalists, 7, 131
justification, 10
juvenile delinquents, 117
juvenile justice, 114

L

Latinos, 70
law enforcement, vii, 9, 10, 13, 17, 27, 32, 33, 37, 39, 44, 46, 48, 49, 50, 54, 58, 59, 61, 62, 70, 72, 74, 93, 112, 128, 130
law enforcement organizations, 27
laws, 47, 50, 53, 58, 73, 74
lawyers, 131
leadership, vii, 18, 27, 28, 29, 30, 31, 32, 33, 34, 35, 36, 37, 38, 39, 40, 41, 42, 60, 61, 99, 124
leadership development, 30, 31, 33, 35, 37, 38, 39, 40, 41, 42
learners, 32
learning, vii, 28, 29, 30, 31, 33, 34, 35, 36, 37, 38, 39, 40, 41, 51, 105, 116, 131
learning culture, 37
learning environment, 39
LEED, 59, 64
legality, 43, 47, 134, 135
legislation, 50, 51
lens, 46
liberty, 45, 72
life course, 71
lifetime, 116
light, 14, 142
Lincoln, Abraham, 66
local community, 10, 18
local youth, 84
longitudinal study, 39, 65

M

magnitude, 26, 104
mainstream society, 84, 92
major depressive disorder, 115
majority, 12, 32, 63, 70, 78, 81, 84, 85, 90, 93, 103
maltreatment, 117, 118

management, 17, 28, 29, 31, 32, 33, 36, 39, 41, 125, 126, 132, 133, 134, 135, 138, 140, 142, 144, 150
manipulation, 120, 136, 137, 138, 140, 141, 142, 148
manslaughter, 99
mass, 14
materials, 7, 120
matrix, 26
matter, 3, 5, 8, 13, 47, 76, 123, 126, 129, 143, 145
measurement(s), 41, 119, 122, 126, 127, 129, 145
media, 4, 43, 66, 75, 82, 83, 99, 134
medical, 108, 110, 128
medical care, 108
membership, 75, 87
memory, 105, 115
mental disorder, 109
mental health, 103, 104, 106, 107, 110, 112, 113, 117
mental health professionals, 112
mental illness, 6, 64
mentoring, 32
messages, 52, 70
meta-analysis, 10, 11, 13, 49
microcosms, 77
militarization, 66, 68
military, 3, 59, 60, 65, 66
Minneapolis, 12
minorities, 2, 4, 77, 78, 81, 93, 94
minority groups, 70
miscarriages, 82
misconceptions, 82
mission(s), 5, 49, 57, 61, 64, 77, 119, 120, 123, 127, 128, 133, 136, 143, 144, 145
misunderstanding, 84, 109
models, 28, 58
modifications, 143
monopoly, 36
moral standards, 84, 92
morale, 62, 121, 125
morality, 47, 61, 71
motivation, 59, 135
MRI, 117
multivariate analysis, 87
murder, 90, 99, 101, 102, 148
music, 5
mutilation, 114

N

narcotics, 31
narratives, 53
National Child Traumatic Stress Network, 114
National Incident-Based Reporting System (NIBRS), 85
National Research Council, 8, 54
Native Americans, 84
negative effects, 13
neglect, 103, 110, 114
neighborhood characteristics, 26, 87
Netherlands, 26
neurobiology, 116
neuroscience, 65
New South Wales, 135, 138
New Zealand, 29, 35, 37
NHS, 40
NIJ, 6, 119, 129
nobility, 64
nodes, 90
nonprofit organizations, 77
NRC, 8, 10, 11, 12
null, 12

O

Obama, President Barack, 43
observable behavior, 105
obstacles, 36, 51, 95
offenders, 1, 2, 6, 8, 9, 13, 16, 44, 46, 49, 50, 72, 81, 85, 88, 89, 91, 92, 93, 129, 140, 143
officials, 7, 44, 75, 78, 83, 92
operations, 3, 51, 93, 109, 134, 135, 137
opioids, 117
opportunities, 6, 9, 27, 31, 33, 35, 37, 59, 78, 81, 91, 144
organizational behavior, 121
organizational culture, 31, 59, 140, 145
organizational development, 32
organizational learning, 31, 34, 36, 38, 39
organize, vii, 9, 71, 122
outreach, 3
outreach programs, 3
overlap, 9, 107
oversight, 75
ownership, 37

P

pain, 106, 112, 139
parental support, 102, 103
parenting, 104, 106
parents, 103, 128
participants, 1, 2, 14, 29, 37, 59, 124
pathway, 115
patriotism, 65
peace, 62, 64
peacekeeping, 64

penalties, 49
performance indicator, 123, 124, 145
performance measurement, 119, 120, 125, 131, 139, 143, 147
performers, 67, 121
permit, 38
perpetrators, 83, 103, 111
personal communication, 29
personal contact, 73
persuasion, 50
Philadelphia, 21, 45, 96
physical abuse, 103
physical environment, 15, 63, 71
physiology, 105
placebo, 115
Plato, 57, 62
PLS, 37
police, vii, 1, 2, 3, 4, 5, 6, 7, 8, 9, 10, 11, 12, 13, 14, 15, 16, 17, 18, 26, 27, 28, 29, 30, 31, 32, 33, 35, 36, 38, 39, 40, 41, 42, 43, 44, 45, 46, 47, 48, 49, 50, 51, 52, 53, 54, 55, 57, 58, 59, 60, 61, 62, 64, 66, 67, 68, 69, 70, 71, 72, 73, 74, 75, 76, 77, 78, 79, 81, 82, 83, 84, 90, 91, 92, 93, 94, 95, 102, 103, 106, 109, 110, 111, 112, 113, 114, 115, 119, 120, 121, 122, 123, 124, 125, 126, 127, 128, 129, 130, 132, 133, 134, 135, 136, 137, 138, 139, 140, 143, 144, 145, 146, 148
policy, 1, 8, 13, 54, 71, 74, 141
policymakers, 9, 13
politics, 71, 72
pollution, 121
poor performance, 125
population, 83, 84, 85, 87, 90, 99, 114
portability, 37
portfolio, 13
positive interactions, 59
positive relationship, 52
posttraumatic stress, 105, 114, 115, 118
post-traumatic stress disorder (PTSD), 105, 108, 114, 115, 116, 117, 118
poverty, 26, 71, 72, 82, 103
practical knowledge, vii, 1
precedent, 58
predation, 46
prefrontal cortex, 105, 116, 117
pregnancy, 71
prejudice, 78
preschool, 116
preschoolers, 116
President, 2, 4, 23, 43, 82
press conferences, 92
prevention, vii, 1, 2, 3, 5, 6, 7, 8, 9, 10, 11, 12, 13, 14, 15, 16, 17, 18, 51, 70, 71, 74, 93, 110
primate, 116
principles, 15, 16, 32, 34, 59, 64, 67, 73, 74
prisons, 129
private schools, 53
probability, 3, 90
problem-solving, 1, 2, 6, 10, 11, 13, 15, 16, 17, 18, 38, 52, 67, 136, 144
procedural fairness, 47
procedural justice, vii, 44, 47, 49, 50, 51, 52, 58, 59, 64, 67, 74, 75
production targets, 131
professionalism, 30, 45, 54, 74, 131, 133
professionals, 62, 112
profit, 129, 131
project, 4, 13, 36, 37, 119, 126, 133, 134
proposition, 6, 10
protection, 59, 77, 94, 102, 103, 104, 108, 113, 122
psychiatric disorder(s), 104, 116
psychiatric patients, 116
psychobiology, 118
psychologist, 138
psychotherapy, 116
public concern(s), 82
public goods, 82
public health, 137, 143
public housing, 54, 90
public interest, 124, 126, 135, 142
public officials, 6, 46, 92
public opinion, 72, 74
public policy, 9, 13, 72
public safety, 10, 27, 28, 29, 38, 44, 57, 58, 71, 72, 75, 93, 94
public schools, 53
public sector, 124, 138
public service, 71
punishment, 44, 47, 50, 53, 60, 61, 63

Q

quality of life, 5, 122
quality of service, 145
Queensland, 49, 50, 54
questioning, 112
quotas, 134, 135, 136, 140, 141, 142

R

race, vii, 26, 48, 69, 70, 71, 72, 73, 76, 77, 78, 79, 81, 86, 87, 88, 91, 94, 110, 112
racial issue, 82
racial minorities, 75
racism, 72, 82

radio, 3, 141
rape, 99, 120, 138, 148
reactions, 106, 109
reactivity, 115
reading, 130
reality, 4, 46, 60, 65, 73, 82, 83
reasoning, 60, 70
recession, 8, 14
recognition, 30, 116
recommendations, 73
reconciliation, 52
reconstruction, 72
recreation, 71
recreational, 116
rectification, 59
reform(s), 3, 67, 72, 74, 75, 76, 92, 98
regulations, 44, 77
rehabilitation, 2
reinforcement, 116
reinforcement learning, 116
relevance, 28, 67, 132, 134, 135
relief, 64, 82
religion, 58
remorse, 101
reputation, 4
requirements, 64
researchers, 2, 3, 4, 9, 17, 47, 50, 51, 64
resilience, 53, 115
resistance, 59, 62
resource allocation, 132
resources, 6, 10, 14, 35, 44, 71, 74, 76, 82, 83, 94, 112, 133, 136, 145
response, 3, 10, 11, 13, 14, 18, 31, 40, 43, 76, 81, 94, 104, 105, 106, 109, 120, 121, 124, 126, 135, 140
response time, 3, 94, 120, 121
rewards, 50, 72
rhetoric, 76
rights, 45, 52, 53, 57, 130
risk(s), 5, 9, 13, 14, 15, 17, 32, 36, 45, 60, 66, 67, 70, 71, 72, 76, 78, 88, 90, 91, 93, 103, 107, 108, 109, 110, 112, 113, 114, 115, 119, 121, 122, 127, 128, 132, 133, 134, 136, 139, 141, 142, 145, 147
risk-taking, 139
robberies, 81, 141
root(s), 5, 6, 41, 72
routines, 122
rubrics, 53
rule of law, 72
rules, 5, 47, 51, 59, 60, 61, 62
rural areas, 87

S

safety, 6, 46, 52, 57, 60, 61, 64, 70, 72, 75, 78, 82, 106, 110, 111, 112, 121, 129, 147
sanctions, 13, 75, 142
SARA, 76, 126
scholarship, 46, 72, 94, 101
school(ing), 3, 6, 33, 35, 53, 58, 72, 91, 101, 102, 111, 114, 120, 150
science, 32, 47, 51, 60, 61, 64, 149
scope, 14, 102, 108, 133
security, 52, 57, 73, 112, 119, 121, 127, 128, 129
segregation, 71
self-control, 87
sensitivity, 77, 78, 102
September 11, 128
services, 2, 10, 16, 40, 50, 52, 71, 92, 110, 112, 117, 128, 129
sex, 88, 106
sexual abuse, 103, 108, 114, 116
sexual assaults, 120, 136
shame, 128
shape, 52, 57, 72, 73, 79
shoots, 78
showing, 74, 120
side effects, 121, 134, 135, 142
signals, 5, 46, 53, 124, 125
signs, 52, 93, 122, 142
skilled workers, 131
skills training, 63
social capital, 30, 34, 50
social change, 138
social context, 51, 139
social contract, 53
social control, 1, 15, 59
social ills, 28
social indicator, 138
social institutions, 6
social interaction, 64
social network, 17, 34, 88, 90
social order, 59
social organization, 73
social problems, 28, 39, 92
social services, 6, 14, 112
social standing, 74
social support, 116
socialization, 87
society, 4, 5, 44, 45, 57, 70, 74, 78, 134
socioeconomic status, 87
Socrates, 57, 66
software, 58, 66, 123
solution, 4, 29, 134, 140
span of control, 60

specialists, 51
speech, 127
spelling, 58
St. Petersburg, 145
stability, 26
staff members, 30
staffing, 8, 39
stakeholders, 27, 29, 30, 128, 131, 132
stars, 29
state(s), 9, 36, 44, 45, 50, 53, 58, 62, 75, 99, 116, 131, 138
state authorities, 44
statistics, 44, 52, 60, 62, 91, 108, 118, 120, 122, 128, 129, 136, 137, 138, 140, 141, 142, 145, 148
stereotypes, 72, 82
stimulation, 104
strategic management, 3
strategic position, 39
street gang, 71, 90
stress, 65, 102, 104, 105, 106, 109, 114, 116, 117, 121, 142
stress response, 102, 105, 109
stretching, 34
structural changes, 71
structure, 3, 32, 34, 36, 37, 61, 62, 78, 104, 105, 147
style(s), 40, 50, 60, 61, 93, 124, 139, 140, 143, 144
substance abuse, 103, 106, 107, 109
substance use, 117
substrates, 115
suicidal behavior, 106
suicide, 90
Sun, 28
supervision, 3, 60, 61, 87, 90
supervisor(s), 29, 60, 61, 67, 76, 77, 141
suppression, 59, 120, 137, 141, 142
surveillance, 5, 46, 94
survival, 63
survivors, 116
symptoms, 103, 104, 105, 106, 107, 108, 109, 110, 112, 113, 115, 116
syndrome, 116
synthesis, 41

T

tactics, 1, 4, 6, 7, 13, 15, 16, 17, 49, 52, 58, 60, 61, 63, 65, 93, 94, 115, 125, 129, 130, 133, 143, 144
target, 3, 34, 49, 76, 78, 124, 125, 135
Task Force, 23
tax evasion, 121
teachers, 53
teams, 4, 18, 34, 124, 131, 144
techniques, 3, 64, 147
technological change, 32
technology(s), 27, 58, 118, 136
telephone, 55
tensions, 34, 77, 78, 92, 130, 147
tenure, 36
territory, 138
terrorism, 74, 121
terrorist attack(s), 128
testing, 50, 64
textbooks, 53
texture, 126
theft, 84, 148
threats, 14, 27, 28, 50, 58, 63, 78, 103, 105, 109, 122, 133, 145
time frame, 34
time periods, 121, 132
top-down, 29, 60, 61
trade, 30, 63, 64
traditions, 144
trafficking, 74
trainees, 124
training, 7, 31, 32, 33, 37, 51, 58, 59, 60, 61, 62, 63, 64, 65, 67, 75, 109, 112, 123, 124, 131, 132, 140, 147
training programs, 61
traits, 116
transactions, 132, 135, 142
transcripts, 140
transformation, 62
transparency, 77, 145
transport, 71
transportation, 71
trauma, vii, 101, 102, 103, 104, 105, 106, 107, 108, 109, 110, 111, 112, 113, 114, 115, 116, 117, 118
traumatic brain injury, 64
traumatic events, 101, 102, 103, 107, 109, 113
traumatic experiences, 102, 105, 109
treatment, 44, 47, 50, 51, 52, 53, 59, 74, 76, 77, 78, 92, 93, 104, 106, 107, 108, 112, 116, 117
trial, 50, 51

U

United Kingdom, 7, 10, 14, 42, 51, 138
United Nations, 75
United States (USA), 6, 7, 17, 26, 32, 33, 49, 52, 53, 64, 65, 66, 72, 73, 96, 114, 118
urban, vii, 6, 7, 9, 11, 48, 58, 81, 83, 87, 88, 92, 93, 94, 95, 114, 128
urban areas, 7, 11
Urban Institute, 80
urban life, 128
urban population, 87

V

vacuum, 83
valence, 51, 52
validation, 41
variables, 8
variations, 87, 88, 143
vehicles, 127
Vice President, 66
victimization, 2, 4, 14, 15, 83, 84, 85, 87, 88, 90, 91, 99, 103, 120, 121, 129, 137, 143, 145, 146
victims, 4, 6, 16, 70, 81, 82, 83, 85, 86, 88, 89, 90, 91, 93, 108, 109, 110, 112, 117, 127, 135, 136, 138, 139, 143
Vietnam, 4
violence, vii, 5, 6, 13, 14, 16, 26, 49, 50, 52, 75, 81, 82, 83, 84, 87, 88, 90, 91, 92, 93, 94, 95, 101, 102, 103, 105, 108, 109, 110, 111, 112, 114, 115, 116, 117, 118
violent behavior, 14
violent crime, 5, 7, 9, 26, 31, 70, 81, 83, 84, 87, 95, 99, 110, 120
vision(s), 10, 31, 57, 72, 81
Vitter, 21
vocabulary, 32, 132
voice mail, 142
voting, 52
vulnerability, 115

W

Wales, 138
walking, 101
war, vii, 57, 61, 76
Washington, 18, 19, 20, 21, 22, 23, 24, 25, 26, 41, 62, 66, 67, 72, 79, 80, 95, 96, 97, 98, 116, 117, 138, 146, 147, 149
weakness, 46
wealth, 74
weapons, 8, 60, 61, 106
wear, 61
weather patterns, 121
welfare, 71, 72, 73
well-being, 111, 112
windows, 5, 12, 13, 52, 71
Wisconsin, 10
witnesses, 4, 92, 103, 109, 112
workers, 131
working memory, 60
workplace, 32, 34, 35, 37
World War I, 3
worldwide, 33, 73

Y

Yale University, 58, 112
yield, 52
young adults, 60, 109, 112
young people, 83